UNITY 3 BLUEPRINTS
A Practical Guide to Indie Games Development

by
CRAIG STEVENSON & SIMON QUIG

Published in 2011 by Deep Pixel Publishing

Copyright © Deep Pixel Publishing 2011

ISBN: 978-0-9568887-0-9

All Rights Reserved. No part of this publication may be reproduced, stored in a retrieval system, or transmitted in any form or by any means, electronic, mechanical, photocopying, recording or otherwise, without the prior permission of the publisher.

This book is sold subject to the condition that it shall not, by way of trade or otherwise, be lent, re-sold, hired out or otherwise circulated without the publisher's prior consent in any form of binding or cover other than that it which it is published and without a similar condition including this condition being imposed on the subsequent purchaser.

Deep Pixel has endeavoured to provide trademark information about all the companies and products mentioned in this book by the appropriate use of capitals. However, Deep Pixel cannot guarantee the accuracy of this information.

Published by: Deep Pixel Publishing
39 Towerhill Avenue
Kilmaurs
Kilmarnock
KA3 2TS

www.deeppixel.com

Acknowledgements

Simon and I would like to give a big shout out to a number of people who made this book possible. To our reviewers Brian and David, a huge thank you. Without your keen eyes and expert knowledge this book would be rife with my spelling mistakes. David I apologize to you for the word Let's!

We would also like to give a shout out to our intern Alex. This guy did a fantastic job during his 2 week stint at Deep Pixel Towers and managed to create all the initial game packages that you will be enjoying soon!

Author Biographies

Craig Stevenson

Craig is co-founder and Managing Director of the indie game development company Deep Pixel, specializing in small rapid development games on the iPhone, iPad and web.

A designer by practice, he fell upon Unity by chance and attended one of the very first Unite conferences where he became hooked on the potential of the engine. From this he carved out a niche as a scripter/programmer, creating his first iPhone game for a marketing company.

Craig likes nothing more than experimenting with the fundamentals of games while making time for the odd game of 5 aside football.

"This book would not have been possible were it not for the love and support I received from my family and friends during the writing of this book. A special thanks goes to my Mum and Dad who gave me all the support I could have asked for and more. To my darling Laura I thank you for putting up with my late nights and later mornings, I couldn't have done this without you by my side. I would also like to thank the most fantastic group of people I know: Romana Khan, Gianna Cassidy, Brian McDonald, David Farrell and Dr Jonathan Sykes who taught me to always listen to him, because he is always right! You guys are the greatest! A big shout out goes to Brian, David and Alex who comprised our crack reviewing team, your dedication and hard work was instrumental in the release of the book. I must also thank Mr Andrew Gair for the various physical training activities that kept my mind and body alert and alive for this challenge. (And Mr Gray and Addison for FIFA nights).

And a final shout goes to my partner in crime Simon, a tremendously talented artist, "The Craig and Simon Show", 24 years and still going strong!"

Simon Quig

Simon is co-founder and Creative Director of the indie game development company Deep Pixel. After acquiring an Honours Degree in Computer Arts from The University of Abertay Dundee, Simon became lead artist at a small games studio startup in Edinburgh. This was to be a short-lived experience however, and after a brief stint in freelancing, he moved to Newcastle to take up an art position at a digital media company. For two years he worked on a variety of projects, gaining experience across the games and post-production arena. Seeking greater creative freedom, he set up Deep Pixel in the summer of 2010 with his life-long friend. They now annoy each other frequently.

"Principally, it would not have been possible to have worked on the production of this book without the support of my parents. There were some rather strained moments of uncertainty in between, but ultimately they have helped me in every way possible and I am indebted to them for their faith. Thanks also go to our two reviewers: Brian and David. They are exceptionally talented software engineers and educators, but moreover they are our friends; friends who have given their spare time willingly to our cause - the true spirit of indie. And finally, I would congratulate my partner in pixels, Craig. It has been a ramshackle road paved with doubt, setbacks and more than a few of the awkward trappings that go with mixing business and pleasure. We have come through it with a greater understanding of one another; quite the achievement after 20 odd years of acquaintance. To your good self and to the many others who have nudged me along the path in their little ways, I say thank you one and all."

Reviewer Biographies

Brian McDonald

Brian is a Lecturer in Games Programming at Glasgow Caledonian University. He has been in the position for six years and has taught several topics related to Games Programming including Games Graphics with Direct3D, Mobile Development using iOS, and an Introduction to Games Programming using Unity3D. His research interests include: Video Game Graphics, Pedagogy of Programming, and Augmented Reality in Video Games. In his spare time he develops applications and games for iOS and other numerous platforms.

David Farrell

David is a game designer, programmer and academic, currently teaching and studying for a PhD at Glasgow Caledonian University. Craig, Simon and David have worked together on a couple of Global Game Jam games (including the Scottish Game Jam winner 2010) and the team won the Dare to be Digital games competition in 2005. David was designer, producer and coder on the e-Bug games (http://www.e-bug.eu) and worked on a bunch of other cool projects and games. You can find his stuff at http://www.gameologist.com.

Alex Olsen

Alex (wunderkind programmer) enjoyed a 2 week placement with Deep Pixel while going through the review process of the book. He took each game and created each of the project files that make up the resources for each chapter of the book. A fantastic young gentleman with a great career ahead of him in the games industry.

Table of Contents

Preface

Chapter 1 - Setting up our Development Environment   1

Chapter 2 - Heiro Match – Part 1   15

Chapter 3 - Heiro Match – Part 2   41

Chapter 4 - Ace Invaders – Part 1   61

Chapter 5 - Ace Invaders – Part 2   81

Chapter 6 - Temple Defense – Part 1   105

Chapter 7 - Temple Defense – Part 2   129

Chapter 8 - Furry Hurry – Part 1   155

Chapter 9 - Furry Hurry – Part 2   171

Chapter 10 - Go forth and create Unity   195

Index   199

Visit us at Deep Pixel

For access to all our great content head on over to www.deeppixel.com. Over at the website you will find everything related to our work on Unity3D and more. Simon and I frequently post up our musings on our different disciplines.

You won't just find some really nice posts about Unity scripts and artwork you will find all our thoughts on game design and the industry in general. We will be updating the site daily as we start to move into creating our own IP and releasing games on the iPhone and iPad. Keep up to date with us on our indie game development journey!!

Oh and remember, please feel free to get in contact with us any time for help, advice or just a chat, we will be more than happy to get back to you.

enquiries@deeppixel.com

Preface

Welcome to Game Development, the Unity way. Unity 3 is a revolutionary 3D game engine that has opened the door to multi-platform game development for Indie developers.

Never in the history of game development has there been this degree of unencumbered access to such a wide range of platforms for non-industry developers. Unity 3 has taken its mission statement of 'Author once, Deploy anywhere' and carved out a niche as *the* Indie developer's engine of choice. With access to the web, iPhone, iPad and Wii already available and with the addition of Android, Xbox and PlayStation, Unity 3 is a tool that no aspiring game developer can afford to omit from their personal arsenal.

Budding game developers have always been hindered by the heavy investment of time involved in learning a game programming language. C++ is the industry standard, utilized in the creation of all the major game engines, from Unreal, to the CryEngine, and the physics engine Havok. These engines generally command substantial licensing fees which leave independents priced out of the market. The dependence on these expensive platforms, along with the astronomical cost involved in creating triple A titles has resulted in studios preferring sequels to new IP. The catalogue of truly enjoyable and innovative games on any platform has become limited at best. Enter the Indie game development scene.

Indie development has gone through something of a renaissance over recent years. While there has always been an Indie scene, it has not enjoyed a more prominent, successful or lucrative time in the games world, as can be seen today. With the advent of Unity 3, Flash, and improved web technologies, confidence has once again arisen in the realm of the bedroom coder. The success of 'Indies' such as Jonathan Blow (Braid), and Kyle Gabler (World of Goo) is a testament to the possibility of developing successful and critically acclaimed games outside the traditional development model. The time has come for the independent developer to stand shoulder to shoulder with the professionals, and this book aims to help you get there.

This book takes you through the development of four popular Indie games and allows you to customize and experiment with them to make them your own. *Experimentation* is a concept that is paramount to Unity and also to this book. Throughout our journey together we will look at the fundamental principles that underpin game development such as the invaluable game loop, scripting, physics, artificial intelligence, particle effects and much more. At the end of this book you will have created 4 of your own games, to do with as you please. Our hope is that with the help of this book, the next Kyle Gabler is *YOU*.

Unity 3

Unity is now in its 3rd version, and has once again broken through the barriers of expectation. Unity 3 boasts an impressive array of industry standard additions that really take development to the next level. Here are some of the additions:

- Beast lightmapping – is an industry standard light mapping technology that is generally licensed to top studios for upwards of $90,000. Unity has integrated this at no extra cost to the user.
- Lens Effects – have been improved to bring that professional look to your games with new, high-quality depth of field, internal lens reflections, and light plumes.
- Occlusion Culling – Unity has really upped their performance with this addition; they have integrated the #1 occlusion culling system into Unity. Again this would generally cost above $50,000 but has been added at no extra charge.

About Deep Pixel

Our company was born out of personal frustrations with the mass-market games industry and personal passions for games design. As its founders, we are dedicated to focusing on what we believe matters most in the creation of an engrossing play experience - the core mechanics. We stand for delivering a depth of interaction with elegant rules in a cohesive game world, so that instant accessibility goes hand in hand with the longevity of the player's engagement. We want the device to disappear and the player to get lost in the feel of the game. We want you to fall into the Deep Pixel and bask in its depths for countless hours. Hopefully, we will take you there one day.

What this book covers

The aim of this book is to cover the development of four Indie game blueprints in an easy-to-follow tutorial style. We will explore many different game concepts and mechanics that are prevalent in Indie game development, and will encourage you to innovate and experiment with the blueprints to make them your own. While we will provide all the materials and assets required to create the games, we encourage you to change them and use your own assets where possible, in order to give your own personal touch to the games. The Deep Pixel website offers the project files for the first chapters of each game, just in case anyone struggles or doesn't end up with a functioning game. The files should allow people to see where they went wrong and allow them to move on to the next chapter without hindrance.

Here is a chapter-by-chapter breakdown of what will be covered:

Chapter 1 – Setting Up Our Development Environment

This is where we kick-start the engine. In this first chapter we will cover the steps needed for setting up the Unity development environment. We will briefly run through the "layout of the editor" and spend time outlining the principles and concepts that underpin the process of creating games in Unity.

Chapter 2 – Heiro Match – Part 1

The first game on our travels will lay down the foundations of game development techniques and practices in Unity. We will look into the game loop and its importance to the games we will be creating throughout the book.

Chapter 3 – Heiro Match – Part 2

With the bare bones of the first game complete, we shall move onto implementing some of the crucial elements that make a game. The scoring system will keep track of the player's progress during the game. A count-down timer will bring another challenging element to the game with a sense of panic to identify as many pairs as possible in the allotted time. Finally some polish shall be added with Unity's particle effect system.

Chapter 4 – Ace Invaders – Part 1

The top down shooter is a classic game not only in Indie development but in the mainstream market as well. In this chapter we will look at a fundamental technique in 2D game development called: "Parallax Scrolling". "This allows us to create the illusion of depth in our game environment."

Chapter 5 – Ace Invaders – Part 2

In this chapter we will expand our top down shooter with a variety of different elements. We will create two different enemy types and make them move across the screen and attack the player. We will also look at the implementation of a scoring system.

Chapter 6 – Temple Defense – Part 1

The Tower Defense game has become a staple of the Indie game community with many unique and innovative versions developed over the years, such as the excellent Pixel Monsters by Pixel Junk. In this chapter we will look at the building blocks of this game: mouse interaction, scripted level creation and path finding using waypoints.

Chapter 7 – Temple Defense – Part 2

With our tower defense game coming together we will look to implement the mechanics that will make the game fun to play. These include, turret control to allow your guns to train their sights on the enemy, along with collision detection which will identify when an enemy has been hit by your turrets. We will also look at implementing some polish in the form of particle effects.

Chapter 8 – Furry Hurry – Part 1

Our final game takes us into the 3D realm with marble madness. In this game you navigate precarious levels with a small marble, avoiding obstacles and pitfalls along the way. This chapter will see us utilizing the different 3D capabilities that exist in Unity. Specifically we will be looking at camera controls and 3D world movement. Additionally, we will create a basic 3D level using Unity's native 3D models.

Chapter 9 – Furry Hurry – Part II

To extend the game we will look into some new game mechanics that we can add into the game using Unity's physic material creator. This allows different physical properties to be added to a 3D model to change its behaviour in the game.

Chapter 10 – Moving to the next level

In this chapter we will outline suggestions of how to take some of these games to the next level. We will challenge you to take your own innovations and apply them to the games and create something new and exciting.

What you need for this book

- A working copy of the most recent Unity3D (as of this book 3.3) – a free trial version is available from Unity3D.com.
- In order to download the supplied game materials and assets you will require an internet connection.

Who this book is for

Throughout my career, I have spent hours trawling the internet for forums and tutorial pages, searching for that one site that will teach me what I need to know. In my experience, game development books offer little in the way of diversity, dealing with a narrow project scope and often only helping the reader develop one game. With this book we hope to address this issue by bringing together 4 interesting projects under one roof to give you the necessary skills to start your own adventure into independent game development.

This book will assume no prior knowledge of Unity. Some scripting experience would be advantageous, but we will be taking a quick review of the coding practices that will be required for this book, so if you are a beginner don't worry we have you covered.

Conventions

Throughout this book you will notice a number of different styles of text that are used to identify various types of information. Below is an outline of these styles.

Code blocks are identified as follows:

```
if(Physics.Raycast (ray, hit, Mathf.Infinity) &&
   lastUpdateWasAHit != true)
{
    lastHit = hit;
lastUpdateWasAHit = true;
}
```

Words from code that appear in normal text are shown as: "We shall utilize `physics.RayCast` in order to cast a ray into our world."

To improve readability, and draw attention to an important word, menu item, or term - a **bold** font will be used to highlight the word.

You may also notice that in some cases the page is not wide enough to show a long line of code like this:

```
for ( var i=0; i < numberOfTiles; i++){
   Instantiate (tileObject, tileLocations[i],
       Quaternion.identity);
}
```

Here you can see the full line:

```
Instantiate (tileObject,tileLocations[i],Quaternion.identity);
```

If you see a line like this please, for the sake of the readability and cleanliness of your own code, make it one full line and do not copy the indented style shown above.

chapter 1

Setting up our Development Environment

Let's think of the Unity development environment as our playground, within which exist tools that give us the freedom to play, experiment and create. It is this playground that we must first familiarize ourselves with, and understand, before we dig into our practical efforts later in the book.

At its heart, Unity is a game development tool, designed to simplify the process of developing video games from start to finish. But the real beauty lies in its ability to empower you with tools and techniques which can be used to create games that would rival many of the independent professional developers out there.

The Fundamentals

When you set out to discover and learn something new there are always fundamental lessons and skills that need to be gathered together before you can dive head first into what you might call 'the good stuff'.

Unity's core system is based around the manipulation of objects, specifically **Game Objects**. Think of these objects as Building Blocks. These building blocks are the key to Unity and allow you to piece together your game in a structured and manageable way.

These Game Objects work as containers that you fill with various **Components**. By adding these components we begin to build up the properties that our Game Object will have and create interesting interactions within our game world. Below we will look at the different features that make up the Unity3D game engine.

Assets

Assets are everything! Assets are Unity speak for everything that makes up your game. Each unity project you create has a folder called **assets** created automatically by Unity in your designated folder structure. In this folder resides all your 3D models, images, sounds, etc. that come together to build up an asset library for your game.

Setting up our Development Environment

Scenes

A Unity **Scene** is the container of all your Game Objects, components and assets in the editor. Each can be thought of as a distinct scene in a play. When the scene changes so do the Game Objects such as the environment, the effects and actors. By building your game up in scenes you can apply a logical process to development, allowing you to easily design and build the game in segments or levels.

Game Objects

Let's expand upon our definition of Game Objects. Game Objects can be thought of as a kind of box within which the different properties and functionality of any desired object are placed. Every Game Object in Unity is created with a transform component by default. This gives the object a position, a rotation and scale in the 3D world.

Unity provides a number of template Game Objects that allow you to quickly create objects that are commonly required throughout the game making process. These include:

- Lights - light sources that allow you to create lighting effects in a scene.
- 3D objects – 3D objects created inside Unity or using an intermediate package.
- Particles – used to create particle systems to recreate effects like explosions.
- Cameras – can be placed in the scene to give different angles and effects.

There is also an option to create an 'empty' Game Object; this object is blank apart from its transform component, you can then add scripts and other components to create a desired effect.

Components

Components form the basis of every possible interaction and behaviour in the Unity world. In Unity you attach components to an object thus providing it with a new piece of functionality.

Every object created in Unity has a transform component by default. On top of this, new components can be added such as colliders that allow for the detection of collisions between Game Objects in your scene, a very important component that we will utilize throughout the book. We can expand the functionality of objects further by attaching scripts to objects; scripts are identified as components in Unity and are used primarily to give you the power to give objects your own customized functionality.

Scripts

Scripts are used to define the behaviour of components. Where every Game Object is built from components, scripts contain the code that allows you to control these components. Unity offers the choice of 3 distinct languages with which to develop scripts. These are:

- JavaScript.
- C#.
- Boo.

To create our scripts we will be using JavaScript, a dynamic scripting language that allows for varying degrees of flexibility within the Unity environment that other languages do not necessarily provide.

JavaScript is generally described as a *'weakly typed'* or *'dynamically typed'* language in that it does not require explicit type conversion. Effectively what this means is that when you declare variables at the start of a script they don't necessarily require a type to be assigned. For example, you could have a variable called `score`, where we would assume this is a number and probably a whole number so its type would be an integer (`int`). In JavaScript you don't need to specifically say it is an integer, you could just give it a value of 0 and JavaScript would infer that it is an integer. C# on the other hand requires strict typing where each variable is given a type. The type of variable declarations you do can have a direct impact on the performance of your scripts so have a look into JavaScript and its traits.

Unity itself is packaged with an application that allows you to write these scripts. On a PC it is called **Uniscite**, and on a Mac it is called **Unitron**. The application is launched any time you edit a script in the Unity editor, and saving the script updates the engine in real time allowing for changes to be made on the fly without the need for long compile times. For the purposes of this book we will be referring to *both* of the script-writing programs as Unitron.

Prefabs

One of my all-time favourite aspects of Unity is **Prefabs**. A prefab is like a blueprint of a Game Object where a reusable version of it is made with all the components and behaviours of the original.

Adding a prefab to a scene means it has been 'instantiated', creating an instance of itself, which is just a fancy way of saying a copy of itself. A prefab can be instantiated into any number of scenes and can be used many times in the same scene. You can think of an instance as a clone of the original.

If you have 5 prefab instances in a scene and you apply changes to the original, the changes will be mirrored across all instances of the prefabs in the scene. In this way you can create template objects

Setting up our Development Environment

that cannot only be placed around the scene but can *also* be instantiated from code at any point during the game. This is an incredibly powerful tool and one that we will be utilizing heavily throughout the book.

The Unity Environment

The Unity environment is arranged in a similar fashion to most popular 3D modelling packages. The interface is arranged into **views,** which are customizable and allow you to set up your development environment in a manner that best suits your work flow. Unity also comes with several predefined view setups that allow you to change the composition of the views with the click of a button.

The image above shows our preferred layout. Being able to see both the game view and the scene view while the game is running can be very advantageous when playing about with your 3D environment. This layout also gives you nice big vertical spaces for your other views which allow you to keep track of all the different assets and scripts.

In Unity there are several views in the Unity editor, each with a specific purpose. These are:
- Scene view – where the magic happens.
- Hierarchy – which contains every Game Object in the scene.
- Inspector – displays detailed information about assets and objects.
- Game view – a representative interactive view of your game.
- Project view – allows access to all the assets you store for the game.

The Scene View and Hierarchy

The scene view allows us to interact directly with the objects that make up our game in 3D space. To visually activate an object in the scene we use the project view to click and drag the asset onto the scene view. The hierarchy view then updates to reflect this addition to your scene.

The hierarchy view provides us with a place to store all our 'in game' assets. The easy click and drag functionality simplifies the process of building a game out of 3D objects by hand. This, however, is not the only way we shall interact with objects.

Up in the right hand corner of the scene view you will see the **Scene Gizmo**. This tool allows you to alter the scene camera's orientation.

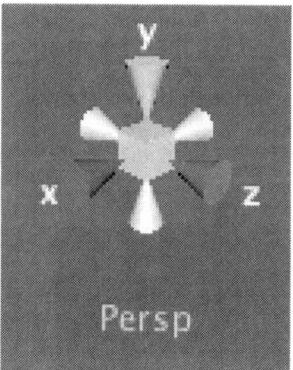

You can quickly snap to front, back, left, right, top and bottom views of your world with a click making this a very useful tool.

Setting up our Development Environment

To position Game Objects in the scene view we utilize the **Transform Gizmo** in the toolbar at the top of the editor.

These 'gizmos' can be used with the *Q, W, E, and R,* hot-keys on the keyboard, these relate to the following operations:

- Hand Tool [*Q*]: this tool provides you with the navigational functionality to pan around the scene view. The tool has 2 sub tools; the first is the orbit tool, which is activated by holding the *Alt* key then clicking and dragging. The second is zoom which is activated by holding down the *Command* Key (Mac) or *Ctrl* key (PC).
- Translate Tool [*W*]: this tool allows you to interact with the objects in a scene. Upon selecting an object the translate gizmo appears over the object giving you visible handles with which to manipulate the object in 3D space.
- Rotate Tool [*E*]: this is the same as the Translate tool where a rotation gizmo is used to rotate your object.
- Scale Tool [*R*]: same as above, only this tool is used to increase or decrease the size of a selected object.

Below you can see the visible handles for each of the gizmos. The Hand Tool is the only gizmo without a handle.

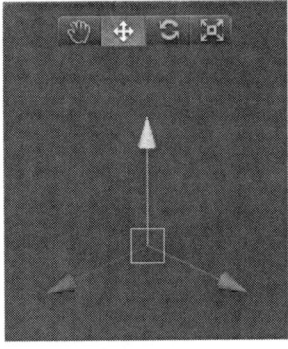 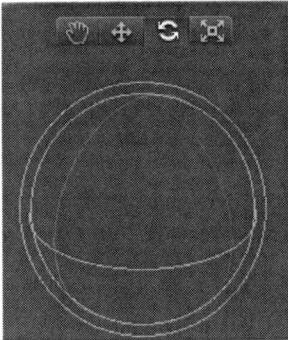 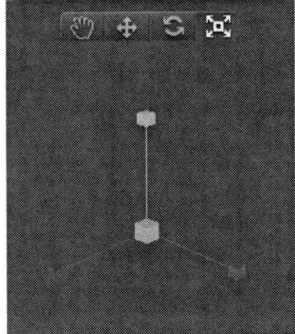

> Unity also provides a great function for quickly zooming in on a selected object by pressing the *F* key.

The Project View

The **project** view allows you direct control over the assets that make up your game. When a new Unity project is created a set of standard folders are created, one of which is the assets folder already mentioned. This folder is represented effectively as the project view. Dragging objects from your OS into the assets folder will automatically import them into Unity.

You can also drag your assets directly onto the project view. One of the very neat features of Unity is its ability to update files that have been changed by a 3rd party application such as illustrator or Photoshop. Any changes that are made to the file in the assets folder are reflected in the project view. At the top left of the project view is a **Create** drop down menu that allows for the creation of standard Unity assets such as material, scripts and prefabs.

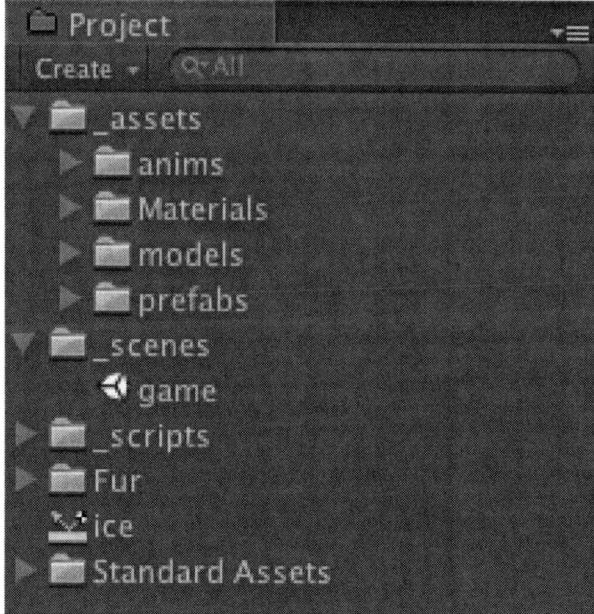

Setting up our Development Environment

The Inspector

The **inspector** gives access to the nuts and bolts of the assets in the Unity editor. It allows you to see into every aspect of any Game Object or asset that has been created in your project. The contents of the inspector are made up of the components that are attached to your assets during the development of your game.

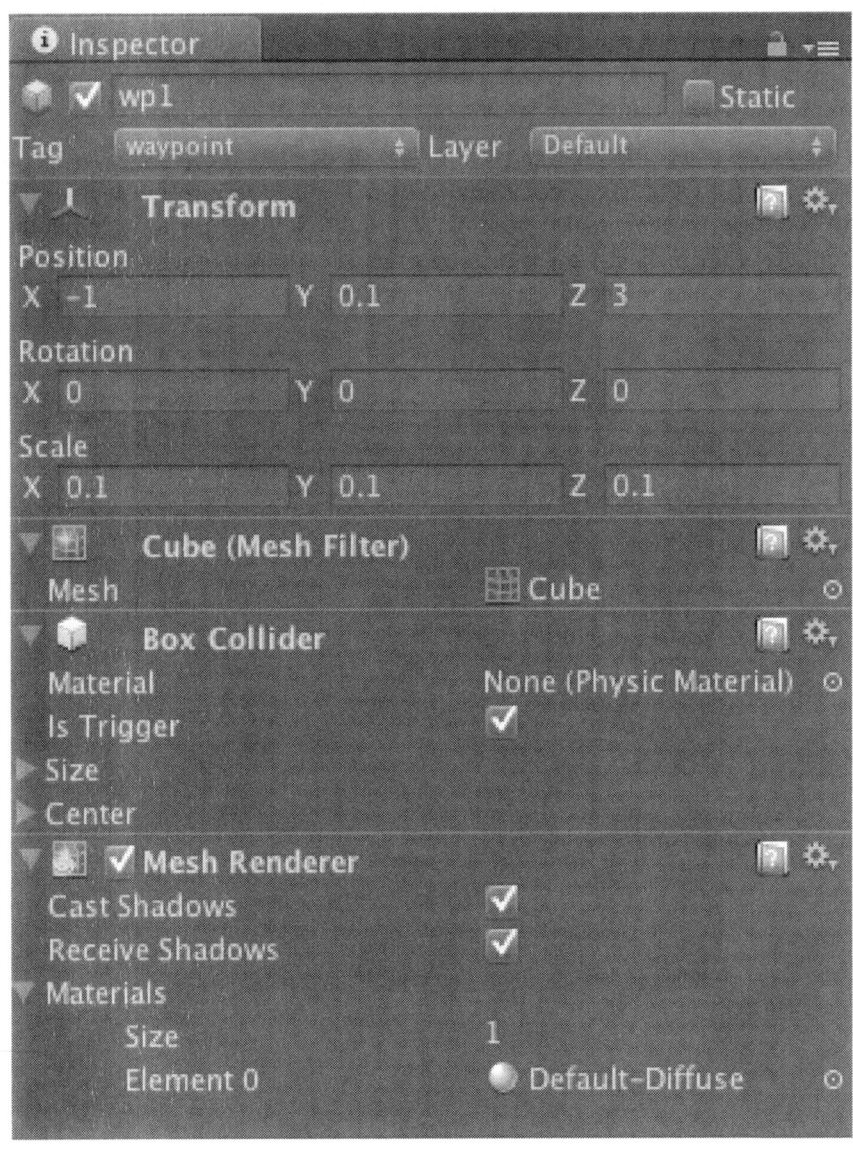

Chapter 1

The inspector's primary function is to allow for the editing of these components. In the example above we can see a **Box Collider** component which draws a collision box around an object. The inspector shows the properties that can be manipulated to create the desired effect upon the object. In this case the size of the objects collider can be altered along with several other variables.

The Game View

The **Game** view is your window into how the game will look upon publishing it to your chosen platform.

To control the game view we use the [Play/Pause/Step] buttons (shown above). The view also comes with controls to customize the screen ratio size which is particularly useful when there are constraints that affect the screen size - such as deploying to the web.

Setting up our Development Environment

> Important - When you press the play button any changes you make while in 'play mode' will *not* be saved upon returning to the development environment.

JavaScript 101

Our scripting weapon of choice will be the excellent JavaScript language. A language traditionally used in the creation of interactive web content. Unity integrated JavaScript for its ability to interoperate with other languages and its speed of compilation. Unity performs a really neat trick by allowing you to program in relatively simple JavaScript and then at run time compiles your code to native code which 'runs nearly as fast as C++'. The compilation to native code has given Unity JavaScript access to .NET libraries, networking, XML and databases, and incredibly cool programming stuff that although out of the scope of this book, I would highly recommend you look into!

Variables

Variables are names or symbols that represent a value. Every variable has a name and a data type. The data type indicates the type of value that the variable represents. Below are some JavaScript examples of variables:

```
var goSpeed : float;
var count : int;
```

The word `var` indicates that you are declaring a variable. The name can be any name you can think of, however it is best to use something that relates to the value you will be utilizing. The two variables above have been given 'types' to reflect what kind of variables they are. There are lots of different types that a variable can be; these are just two that I have selected for this example.

The `goSpeed` variable has been given a `float` type which means that the variable can be a floating point number. The `count` variable is given an `int` type which is short for integer. This means that the variable can be given whole numbers. If you were to try to put a float number in an integer type variable it would cause an error.

Arrays

An **array** is a special kind of variable that holds multiple values of the same type. Using this kind of variable we can reference any elements in the array using a single reference.

Think of an array as a number of boxes and into those boxes we put data. We can then access this data by referring to the number of the box. Below is an example of an array:

```
var myArray : Array(10);
```

```
myArray[0] = 4;
```

Here we set `myArray` to have a type of `Array` with a size of `10`. Now arrays have a quirky element to them in that the numbers start at `0` and not at `1`. So to reference the very first element in the array we would call the element `0` by using the square brackets as we have done above. We can then use an 'equals' expression to set the value of the element to an integer, or any other data type that an array can accept.

Conditions

Conditions are features of programming that perform a certain action or function whenever a user-specified condition has been evaluated to a conclusion. There are several types of conditions that can be used in programming - we shall look at the ones that will be most useful to us.

IF Statement

An `if` statement is one of the most widely used conditions in programming. It is made up of a predicate, a consequent and an alternative. Below is an example of how an `if` is constructed:

```
if (predicate) Then
    (consequent)
else
    (alternative)
end if
```

This reads as: '`If` the predicate has been satisfied `Then` perform the consequent `else` (otherwise) if the predicate has not been satisfied perform the `alternative`'. An example in JavaScript could be:

```
if (x == 10)
{
    x=0;
}else{
    x=5
}
```

Here if x is equal to `10`, then x is set to `0`, otherwise it is set to `5`.

For Loop

A `For Loop` allows for the repetition of a piece of code until a user-specified condition has been met. For example:

Setting up our Development Environment

```
for (i=0; i >=5; i++)
{
    var gmObj = gameObject.Find(i);
}
```

Here we have 3 controls separated by semicolons. They represent the initial value, the end value, and the incremental value. This loop functions by initializing the variable `i` to 0, and the end value to being greater than 5. When the loop is triggered we enter the `for` loop with a value of 0 in the variable `i`. In the case above, the variable `i` is used to find a Game Object with the name 0. Once this has been done the loop starts again but this time `i` is incremented to equal 1. This process is repeated until the end value is met which is when `i` is greater than or equal to 5.

Functions

A **function** is a piece of code that is directly 'callable' during run time, and which performs whatever the programmer has designed it to. In Unity one of the most important functions is the `Update()` function. This acts as a piece of code that is checked every frame throughout the run time of the game. In here we place code that we need checked and acted upon on (in every frame) according to our own predefined conditions. In JavaScript we can also create our own functions which allow us to build up our scripts in a modular way - keeping our code neat and tidy!

```
function fireCannon()
{
    //Fire Cannon Code
}
```

The example above shows how you would write a function for say firing a cannon. This function could then be called with this line of code in order to fire the cannon:

```
fireCannon();
```

Unity Scripting Reference

One of the best aspects of the scripting experience in Unity is the fantastic scripting reference documents. These easily searchable materials provide easy to follow examples with almost each scripting entry. Throughout the book, whenever I find myself reaching for the docs - I will be highlighting them in all their scripting glory.

Project Files
Each game will have 2 Unity3D project files that can be downloaded from the Deep Pixel website.

www.deeppixel.com/book-resources-2/

The first file will include a project folder completed up to the end of the first chapter of the game. So if you find that you have struggled with the chapter or something isn't quite right you can download these files and move onto the next chapter unhindered. We will also provide you with the completed project file again for the same reason just in case something goes wrong. Simon and I also did a fair amount of polish work on the games before they were to be released onto the website, these project files will also be available to download.

Errata
If you come across any errors or mistakes in the book or code, please drop us a line at Deep Pixel so that we can add your findings to the errata book page. Feel free to drop us an email if you have any questions as well.

Summary
You are now armed and ready for the challenges that lie ahead! In this chapter we have highlighted the main principles and concepts behind Unity and scripting practices in general. This however should not be the end of your quest for knowledge, there are many excellent Unity resources out there in web land that are just ripe for the picking.

The next chapter is where it all begins. We will look at our first Unity project, a nice card matching game that will give us some of the foundations we can then build upon throughout the course of the book. We will take our time to get comfortable with how Unity operates and take our first tentative steps into proper JavaScripting. Time to rock and roll!

Chapter 2

Heiro Match – Part 1

Match the Pairs, that classic game of mental sharpness and visual acuity! Sixteen tiles, eight pairs of doubles, randomized and then laid out in a 4 x 4 grid, the goal being to match each pair in the grid to complete the game.

This is an excellent game to begin our journey with. It allows us to highlight many of the fundamental principles that will be with us throughout the book. Let's wet your proverbial whistle with a look at what the final outcome will be over the next two chapters:

Heiro Match – Part 1

In this chapter we will go over the creation of your first Unity project, specifically using a setup that I myself have found incredibly useful when developing my games. We shall also be looking at:

- The game loop.
- Unity prefabs.
- Lighting.
- Arrays.
- User input.
- Ray casting.

Start your game engine

Let's begin with firing up Unity, if this is the first time you have opened Unity 3 you will be presented with an example project called *BootCamp*. This demo highlights the potential of Unity with a spectacular 3D 3rd person shooter scene. Feel free to play about before we begin!

To begin with we want to create a new project, so go to **File > New Project**. A dialog window titled **Project Wizard** will appear, offering you the choice of opening a previous project or starting a fresh one.

In the **Project Directory** field, you can either type in a project path, or you can set one using the **Set** button. I have named my project directory **matchGame**; use this or give yours a relevant name to your filing system. Once you are happy click the **Create Project** button.

Development setup

Throughout my time using Unity, I have seen several different approaches to setting up the Project View. Some Developers start with a blank template and fill-in the folder structure as they go along. I have a preference for setting up some general folders before I start creating anything. This ensures that all my files and assets are always in a logical place within the project. So, in the project view click the **Create** drop down menu (or right click in the project view) and select **Folder**. This will create a **New Folder** in the view. Click the **folder** once to select it, then again to change the folder name. Using this method create the folder structure shown next.

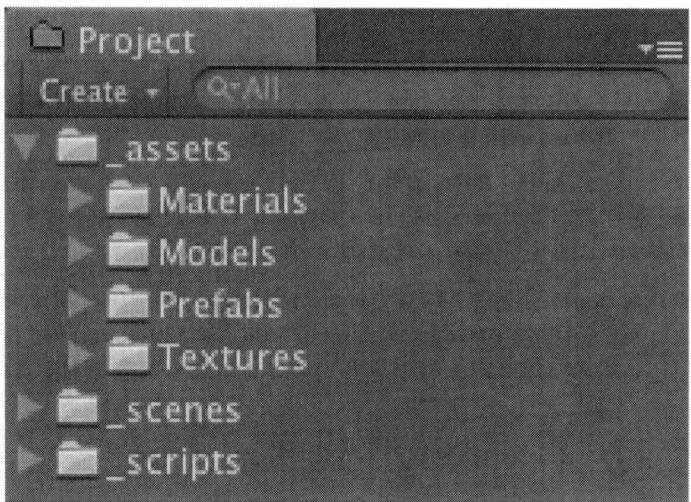

At this point we will save our scene. Choose **File > Save Scene As** and save the file into the _scenes folder in your project. Name the scene **game**. If you expand the _scenes folder in your project view you should see your saved scene.

Our first Prefab

With the folder structure setup, the next step is to get some assets created for us to start using in the game. From the toolbar menu at the top of your screen select **Game Object > Create Other > Cube**. Notice that this has created a cube object in the **scene** view but also in the hierarchy. If you can't see your cube, remember that pressing *F* focuses the camera on a selected object. For the purposes of our game we will be utilizing the default size of the cube. Unity has a scale of *1 unit =1 meter*.

Now we could duplicate this object 16 times to get all the tiles we need for the game, and spend time positioning them but that would be incredibly inefficient. The beauty of prefabs is that we can take this cube, drop it into a prefab and call it as many times as we want through our script. So, in the **Project** view, right click on the **Prefabs** folder and select **Create > Prefab.** Name the resulting prefab **tile**.

With our new prefab created we click and hold the **Cube** object in the hierarchy view and drag it onto our new prefab. If everything has gone to plan the small cube at the side of the prefab name should turn a light blue color. Voila! Our first prefab! We can now delete the object **Cube** from the hierarchy (and scene) by right clicking on it and selecting **Delete**.

Our first Script

Now we get to the good stuff, our first script. Let's dive right in, create a new JavaScript file in your **_scripts** folder by right clicking and selecting **Create** > **JavaScript**. A new file will be created called **NewBehaviourScript.** Rename this as **TileGenerator** by clicking twice on the name, or clicking once on the file and hitting the *enter* key.

You will notice that we use a capital letter at the start of the name **TileGenerator**, this is a programming/scripting protocol that tells us that the name **TileGenerator** is a class and not a variable. Therefore every script we make will start with a capital letter.

To start editing the script, double-click on the file in the **Project** view and the script will automatically launch either Unitron on Mac, or Uniscite on PC. Open up your new JavaScript file and you will see the `Update()` function declared by default; this acts as the 'game loop'.

The Game Loop

The game loop is a function that is called at every frame of the game, it is used to constantly check the game's state and react accordingly to any changes in the game. A video game is different to most software as it is constantly doing something, whether the user is interacting with it or not. For example if a user is walking around a 3D world and then takes their hands off the controls and stops, the world must still remain active. This is where the game loop comes in. It ensures that every aspect of the 3D world is kept in motion regardless of whether the user is active or not.

Activating the script

Let's jump back to the editor. To allow our script to become active in our scene we need to create a **Game Object** to hold it. Select **Game Object** > **Create Empty** from the menu toolbar, this will put an empty object named **GameObject** in your hierarchy and show you a transform gizmo in your scene view. Rename this object **tileGenerator**, and click and drag the script named **TileGenerator** onto the game object in your hierarchy. Click on the object and you can see in the inspector view we now have a script attached to an object:

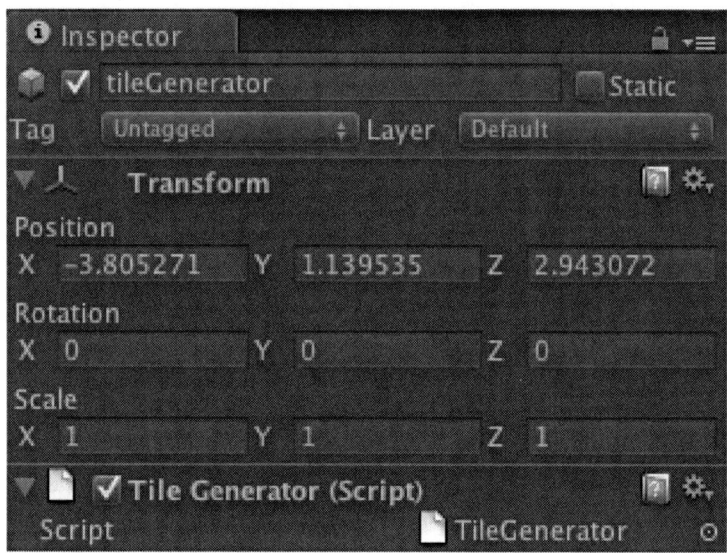

Now, let's get our first script up and running. As I said before, rather than spending time placing *each* tile block for our game, we will look at a method of creating them on the fly and placing them through scripting.

Our first code

We have 16 tiles; each of these tiles is a game object instantiated using the prefab we created earlier. So let's begin. Add these variables to the very top of your script:

```
var numberOfTiles = 16;
var tileObject : GameObject;
```

We have created a variable called `numberOfTiles` which is set as an integer type by making it equal to the numeric value 16. Next we set up a variable with a `GameObject` type. This is an excellent opportunity to highlight how you can access variables from the Unity environment. Click back to Unity, and click on the object named **TileGenerator** in the hierarchy view. In the inspector you should be able to see the name of your script and underneath the two variables you just declared. Similar to this:

Heiro Match – Part 1

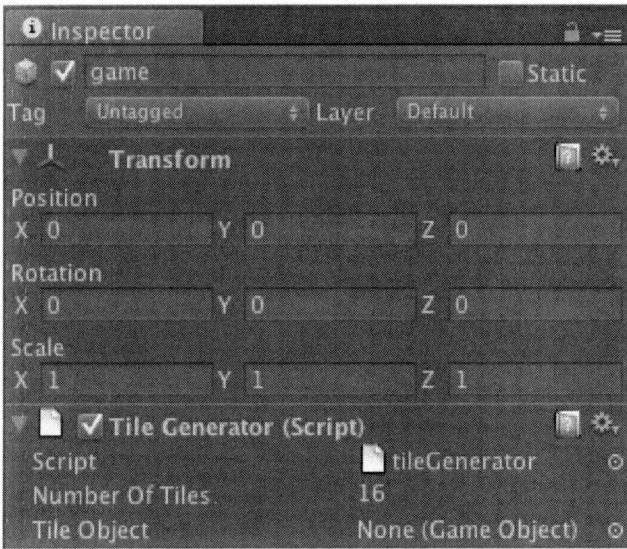

At this point our `tileObject` variable doesn't have an object attached to it. Click the small circle to activate a drop down menu; this will show you all the available Game Objects that can be used. Find and select the object named `tile`. We now have a variable with our tile object attached. We'll use this variable to bring the object onto the screen.

Next we need a grid that is equally spaced, and we need to know the coordinates of the places where we will place each tile. As stated before, Unity defaults to 1 unit = 1 meter, so from the origin, which is (0,0,0), we can create 16 coordinates that equally space each tile, like so:

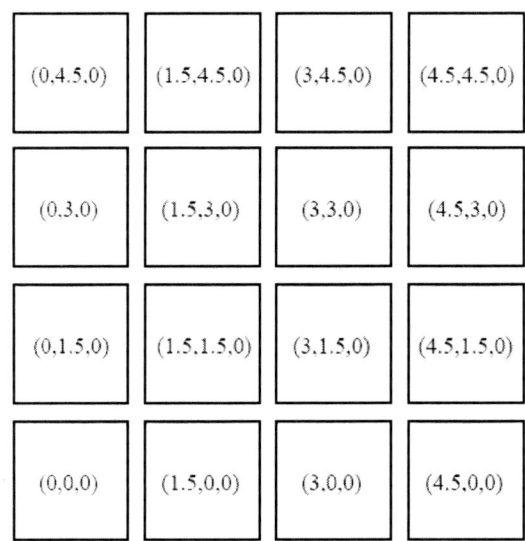

To store these values we must create an array.

Arrays

If you remember from the first chapter, an array is like a number of boxes, each of which can hold values that can be accessed at any time. Let's look at how we define an array. Take the following code and put it beneath the first variable we declared:

```
var tileLocations =   new Array
(
   Vector3 (0, 0, 0),    Vector3(1.5, 0, 0),
   Vector3(3, 0, 0),     Vector3(4.5, 0, 0),
   Vector3 (0, 1.5, 0), Vector3(1.5, 1.5, 0),
   Vector3(3, 1.5, 0),  Vector3(4.5, 1.5, 0),
   Vector3 (0, 3, 0),    Vector3(1.5, 3, 0),
   Vector3(3, 3, 0),     Vector3(4.5, 3, 0),
   Vector3 (0, 4.5, 0), Vector3(1.5, 4.5, 0),
   Vector3(3, 4.5, 0),  Vector3(4.5, 4.5, 0)
);
```

We start by giving the variable a unique and meaningful name (`tileLocations`). We then declare this variable as an `Array`. We can then fill it with the positions of our tiles. As you can see the positions are something called `Vector3`, a vector is used to declare a position in 3D space, using X, Y and Z coordinates. The values above will yield positions that form a 4 x 4 grid starting from the origin and moving right positively along the X and upwards positively in the Y axis. Next we will look at placing objects at these coordinates by instantiating our tile prefab.

Instantiate this!

The ability to instantiate objects in Unity is incredibly powerful. When an object is instantiated it is cloned from the original prefab that was created. The beauty of instantiating objects rather than creating them from scratch is that they can be instantiated with one line of code. The `instantiate()` command looks as follows:

```
Instantiate(object to instantiate, position, rotation);
```

Let's look at the parameters that are required to instantiate an object:

- Object to instantiate: The prefab game object we want to create.
- Position in 3D space: A Vector3 component that defines the object position in 3D space with X, Y and Z coordinates.

Heiro Match – Part 1

- Rotation in 3D space: Here a Quaternion function is used to declare the objects rotation coordinates in 3D space. The most commonly used is the `Quaternion.identity`. Quaternions are funky Unity rotation things that are tough to explain but relatively simple to use!

Start() Function

Now that we have our initial variables all set up and ready to go, we want to make the script set up our game world at the start of our game. Unity gives us a lovely predefined function called `Start()` that is executed before any of the `Update()` methods are called in the script. This allows our scene to be set up before the game loop begins.

Put this code between your variables and the `Update()` function.

```
function Start () {
    Camera.main.transform.position = Vector3(2.25,2.25,-8);
    for ( var i=0; i < numberOfTiles; i++) {
        Instantiate (tileObject, tileLocations[i],
            Quaternion.identity);
    }
}
```

Let's break down the code inside our `Start()` function. The first line of code deals with setting up the Main Camera in the scene:

```
Camera.main.transform.position = Vector3(2.25,2.25,-8);
```

This line takes a `Vector 3` position in 3D space and applies it to the transform component of our Main Camera. However, this is not the only way to position a camera and with Unity 3 a cool new **Camera Preview** window has been included to allow you to see what the camera will see without constantly having to change the position and checking by playing the scene.

Chapter 2

To alter the position of the main camera in our scene we need to access it using an **Inherited variable** of the camera object. Unity provides an excellent resource in their **Scripting Reference** that provides numerous examples of code that will help you get the most out of your game.

Scripting Reference

Select **Help > Scripting Reference**. This opens an html page in your web browser with the Unity documents. Type "Camera" into the search text box and hit *enter* to bring up the results of the search. Select the first result and scroll down to Inherited members.

Here is a list of variables related to the Camera that can be accessed. We want the transform variable, click on it to open up a description and example of the transform variable.

If we then click on transform again we are taken to the details of the Transform class. The variables that we can access are at the top of the page under Variables. Specifically we are looking to manipulate position. Clicking on position shows us the details of this variable. We can see that it is a Vector3 and requires an X, Y and Z value to identify the position in space.

So in other words, when we write `Camera.main.transform.position = Vector3(0,0,0);`, what we are doing is creating a Vector in 3D space at those coordinates. We are then telling the camera to move its position to that point in space.

The next 3 lines of code are the most important as this is where we instantiate the 16 tiles that will make up our game grid. To do this we use a `for` loop.

```
for ( var i=0; i < numberOfTiles; i++){
    Instantiate (tileObject, tileLocations[i],
        Quaternion.identity);
}
```

For our end value we want the loop to run until 16 tiles are displayed on the screen, so we use the `numberOfTiles` variable that we declared above. The next line of code is where an object is **instantiated**, using a `Vector3`. In this case we use the `tileLocations` array and access it using the number contained in the variable `i`. Finally, a `Quaternion.Identity` is used to give the object no rotational value.

Now all this code should look like this:

```
var numberOfTiles = 16;
var tileObject : GameObject;
var tileLocations =   new Array
(
```

Heiro Match – Part 1

```
        Vector3 (0, 0, 0),    Vector3(1.5, 0, 0),
        Vector3(3, 0, 0),     Vector3(4.5, 0, 0),
        Vector3 (0, 1.5, 0),  Vector3(1.5, 1.5, 0),
        Vector3(3, 1.5, 0),   Vector3(4.5, 1.5, 0),
        Vector3 (0, 3, 0),    Vector3(1.5, 3, 0),
        Vector3(3, 3, 0),     Vector3(4.5, 3, 0),
        Vector3 (0, 4.5, 0),  Vector3(1.5, 4.5, 0),
        Vector3(3, 4.5, 0),   Vector3(4.5, 4.5, 0)
    );

    function Start (){
        Camera.main.transform.position = Vector3(2.25,2.25,-8);
        for ( var i=0; i < numberOfTiles; i++){
            Instantiate (tileObject, tileLocations[i],
                Quaternion.identity);
        }
    }
```

Hit the play button at the top of your screen and you should *fingers crossed* be confronted with a screen like this:

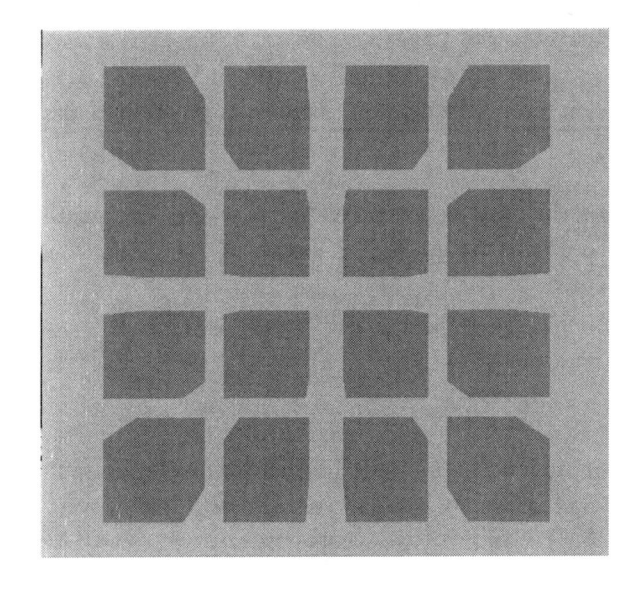

Now if this was up on a wall in an art museum it may be hailed as art nouveau, however this will not do for our game, we need to be able to see the detail on our tiles. Next we will turn on the lights.

You've got the light stuff (rather than go for the cheesy heading of 'let there be light'!)

Here we will look at setting up our scene with a light to illuminate our tiles. There are 3 main types of light that can be created in a Unity scene, these are:

- Directional light: a light source that emanates evenly in a single direction, used primarily to recreate the effect of the sun.
- Point light: shines from a single point over your 3D scene, usually utilized for producing ambient light and fires.
- Spot light: Does exactly what it says on the tin. The spot light creates a single direction light that has a radius variable that can be changed to increase or decrease the size of the spot.

So, let's create our own light. From the toolbar select **GameObject > Create Other > Point Light**. You now have your first light in your scene. The light has to touch each block evenly so in the **inspector** change the values of the light's position to the following:

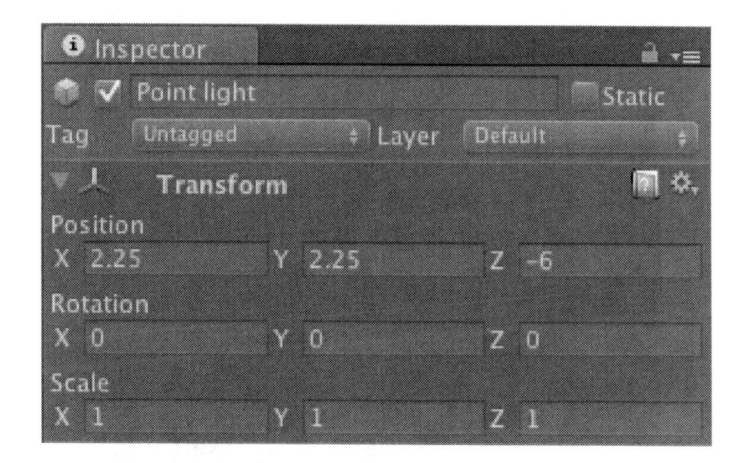

```
Inspector
☑ Point light                          ☐ Static
Tag  Untagged          Layer  Default

▼ ⬩  Transform
Position
X  2.25        Y  2.25        Z  -6
Rotation
X  0           Y  0           Z  0
Scale
X  1           Y  1           Z  1
```

These values position the light in the same X, Y and Z coordinates as the main camera in the scene. Next change the light components properties to match these:

Heiro Match – Part 1

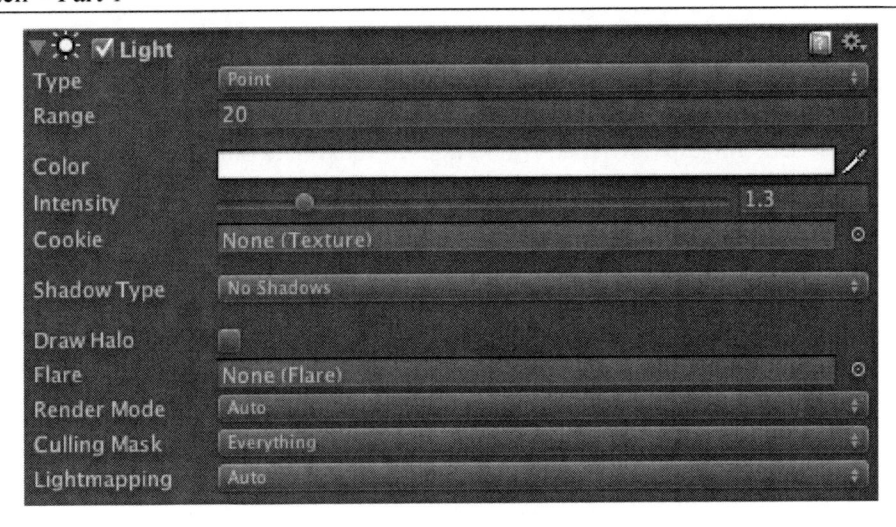

Now hit the Play button to see your scene lit up:

With the grid laid out, the camera in place and light illuminating our scene we are ready to start putting in the art assets to bring the game to life.

Walk like an Egyptian

With the layout of our game in place our next port of call is to get some assets with the appropriate textures into the game. We have provided you with all the models you will require for the exercises in this book. Go to:

> www.deeppixel.com/UnityBookPackages/match/tileModel.unitypackage

An automatic download should begin. Go back to Unity and go to **Assets > Import Package**, then choose **custom package** and navigate to the downloaded package.

All tick boxes should remain ticked. Click on the **Import** button to have Unity import the package into your game. All the models and textures should place themselves in the appropriate folders in your project view, if this doesn't happen place them in their appropriate folders manually. Now we have imported a new base model called **tileModel**, but before we can use it we need to look at its FBX Importer Settings.

FBX Importer settings

Unity3D requires 3D models to be imported in the **FBX file format.** It uses a built-in FBX importer to bring your model into the game and set up its various settings. You can adjust values such as:

- Scale Factor: Unity has a scaling system that is set to 1 unit = 1 meter in the game world. This number is usually set to 1, however it can be altered at any time before you utilize your imported model in your scene.

- Generate Colliders: activating this checkbox generates collider meshes for every part of your imported model. This allows you to perform collision checks later on your model to identify if a collision has occurred.

- Calculate Normals: a normal is the surface of the mesh that faces outwards and is therefore rendered. This setting sets up each normal for every surface of your model and allows Unity to render the object properly.

- Smoothing Angle: the smoothing angle is a value that indicates to Unity how detailed an edge has to be in order to be deemed a hard edge.

- Split Tangents: this is used when the Bump Map lighting is imported incorrectly.

- Swap UVs: should an error occur during the importing of the model and the light shaders are incorrect, this can swap the primary and secondary uv channel.

Heiro Match – Part 1

- Materials: this controls how the materials that are imported with the model are interpreted. There are three settings; the first turns the effect off so no materials are generated. The second allows materials to be used through different scenes, and the final setting generates the materials per scene so only the current scene can use them.

> It is a good idea to get into the habit of checking the **FBX Importer** settings for your imported game object. Specifically the **Scale Factor** as sometimes 3D packages can have different scaling units to that of Unity. Most of the stuff above isn't needed for what we are doing so don't worry too much about understanding it all.

Click on the **tileModel** and navigate to the FBX importer. We will need each tile to have a Mesh Collider to let us identify when one has been clicked, so at this point ensure that **Generate Colliders** is checked. Finally ensure that the scale factor is at 1 and click **apply**.

Out with the old...

Now that we have our nice new models imported, the next step is to replace the place holder prefabs we have at the moment with our nice new Egyptian sand blocks. Before we begin we will do some housekeeping on our **Project** view:

- Create a new prefab in the **Prefabs** folder

- Hit the ⌘+D (Mac) or ctrl+D (PC) to duplicate the prefab, do this 15 more times until you have 16 prefabs

- Open up the **Textures** folder and rename each prefab using the name of the texture, like the image below.

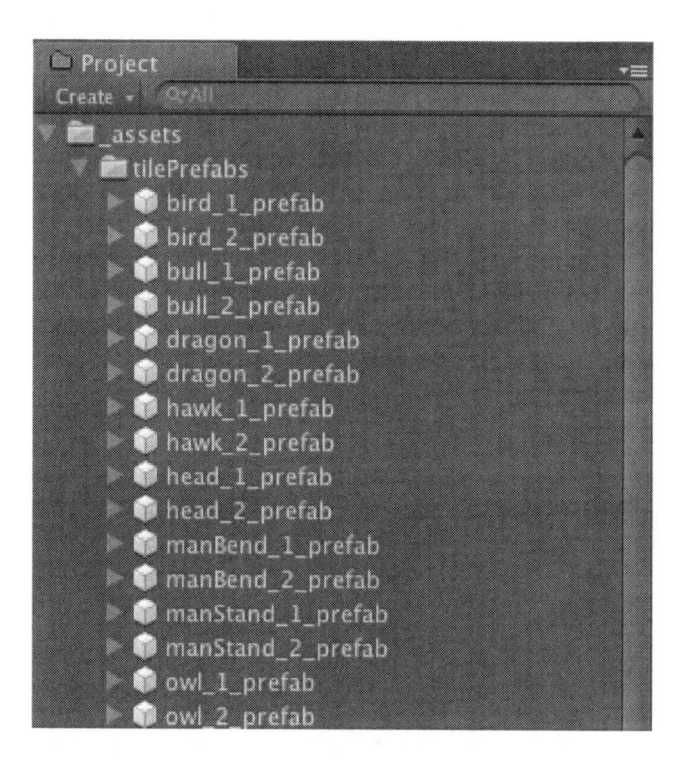

With everything set up we now want to attach our imported model to our newly created prefabs and match them to the materials. Click and drag the **tileModel** prefab down onto each of the new prefabs we created earlier. When you click on each prefab the inspector should update to show the details of the prefab (turn the name blue).

Each block has a small arrow that can be expanded to get access to the model. A default material is attached called **hiero_hawk**. Underneath **Mesh Renderer > Materials** in the inspector, expand the materials property and change the **Element 0** material to correspond with the prefab that is currently selected. For example the **Element 0** value of the **bird_1_prefab** should be **bird_material**.

> At this point, check to ensure that a **Mesh Collider** component is visible in the Inspector for each prefab. This is crucial for the latter stages of the chapter. If a mesh collider is not attached you can attach one by selecting **Component > Physics > Mesh Collider** from the toolbar.

Our next step is to add some code to the **TileGenerator** script that will allow us to utilize our new prefabs. We no longer require access to a single game object so we can remove the `tileObject` variable. Since we now have a number of different objects we want to access the most appropriate

Heiro Match – Part 1

way for doing this – which is by using another array. Put this line of code beneath the `tileLocations` variable:

```
var tileObjects : GameObject[];
```

This sets up a static array that can be altered through the Inspector in Unity. Click on the **TileGenerator** object in the hierarchy to bring up the variables that are exposed in our script. Expanding the Tile Objects property will reveal a **Size** variable, set this to **16**. Sixteen elements will appear beneath the variable in the inspector and each will require a **GameObject** type. In here we will place the sixteen tiles that make up the interactive elements of our game. Using an array allows us to manually set up how the grid will appear. So, go through each element and randomly place two of each prefab, bearing in mind that the order here will reflect the placement of the objects in the game. Here is an example of my layout:

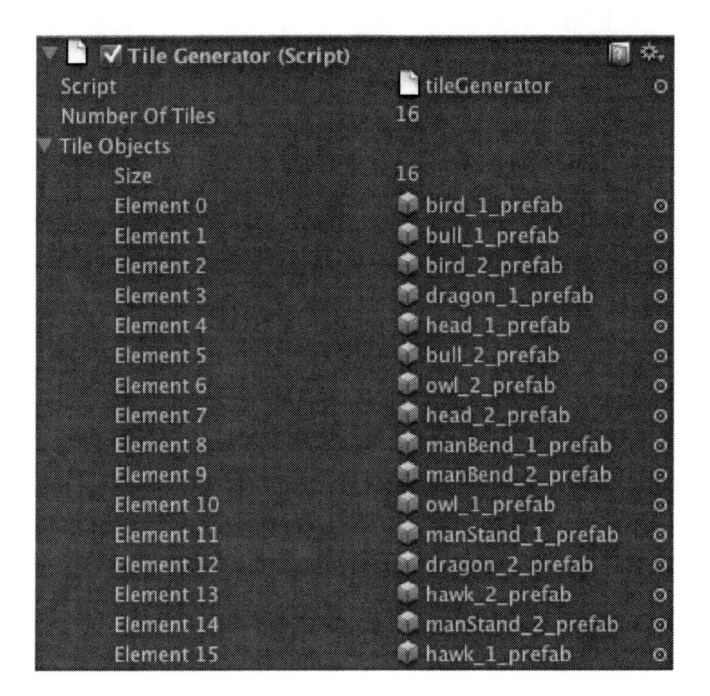

Tile Generator (Script)	
Script	tileGenerator
Number Of Tiles	16
▼ Tile Objects	
Size	16
Element 0	bird_1_prefab
Element 1	bull_1_prefab
Element 2	bird_2_prefab
Element 3	dragon_1_prefab
Element 4	head_1_prefab
Element 5	bull_2_prefab
Element 6	owl_2_prefab
Element 7	head_2_prefab
Element 8	manBend_1_prefab
Element 9	manBend_2_prefab
Element 10	owl_1_prefab
Element 11	manStand_1_prefab
Element 12	dragon_2_prefab
Element 13	hawk_2_prefab
Element 14	manStand_2_prefab
Element 15	hawk_1_prefab

Press play and you should be confronted with your new tiles:

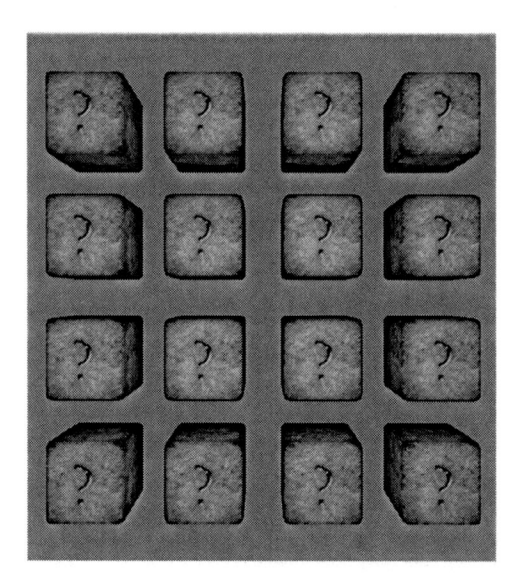

The scene is starting to take shape. We now have all the elements we require to start putting in the core mechanics of the game play. Next we will look at adding some interactive functionality along with a journey into Unity's excellent animation editor.

Player Interaction

This is where we start to make our game sing. The interaction is obviously the most crucial part of the game as it forms the basis of how the player will play with our game. Unity provides us with a class that defines the interface to the input system. If you open up the **Unity Scripting Reference** again from the help menu and type in 'input' you will see a list of the variables and functions that can be utilized in this class. We are interested in identifying when the player has clicked a button, specifically the mouse button. The function used to find this out is the `GetButtonDown()` function. Let's look at a piece of sample code:

```
function Update () {
   if(Input.GetButtonDown("Fire1")){
      print ("The mouse button has been clicked!");
   }
}
```

The function is commonly used as an `if` statement where if the button that is declared is found to be active, then action is taken, in this case, a message is printed to the screen. Having it in the `Update()` function allows the game to always be checking for a button press, that way as soon as it happens the game can react instantly with no delay.

Heiro Match – Part 1

In this example "Fire 1" is given as the button name, however this isn't the only button that can be checked. Unity automatically sets up a list of input **Axes** and **Buttons** that link to key presses, mouse clicks and even joy pad clicks. To access these, select **Edit > Project Settings > Input**. This reveals the **Input Manager** in the inspector. Here you can see all the types that have been declared.

Expand the one called Fire 1 and we can see that there are many settings that can be applied. The crucial setting to look for is **Alt Positive Button**, here the left mouse button is declared as mouse 0, Unity has a list of names and examples in the documents under **Input Manager** in the **Input** class screen.

Let's get some interactivity into our game; in your script put this code in the Update() function:

```
function Update () {
    if (Input.GetButtonDown("Fire1")){
       print ("Mouse clicked");
    }
}
```

Now hit the play button and look at the bottom of the screen. All things going well you should see the words 'Mouse clicked'. If you click on this bar at the bottom of the editor a pop up box will appear. This is your **Console** (you may have seen this already if you have had any errors). The console allows you to output information from the game processes to the console view, just as we have done here. This can be invaluable when attempting to identify errors in your code by using comments like the one above to step through line by line to highlight the problem.

We can now identify when the player has clicked the mouse. The next step is to find out when the player has clicked on a tile. To do this we will look at a technique called **Ray Casting**. The principle of ray casting is relatively simple, a ray is cast from a point, and anything that intersects with the ray is recorded. For our purposes we want to cast a ray from the mouse pointer, out into our scene, and if it collides with one of the tiles we want to be informed with some sort of feedback. Declare this variable at the top of the script:

```
var hit : RaycastHit;
```

Put this code inside the if with the GetButtonDown() function:

```
var ray1 = Camera.main.ScreenPointToRay
    (Input.mousePosition);

if (Physics.Raycast (ray1, hit, Mathf.Infinity)){
   print ("Help my bob i've hit something");
}
```

Here we set up two variables. The first, hit is declared as a global variable structure called RaycastHit, which used to get data back from a raycast. The second is a function that sets up our ray that will go from the main camera through a point in the screen that we identify. The position of the screen point is a Vector, which in this case has been declared as the position of the mouse. The final portion of the code creates a case where if the mouse is clicked, a ray is cast into the scene, and if the ray collides with an object (**the object MUST have a physics collider attached**) then a message is returned. Run the scene and click on one of the tiles to see the message displayed in the console.

It's all about tiles

The game can now identify when a player has clicked on a tile, what we need to do now is:

- Identify the name of the tile.
- Rotate the tile to reveal the other side.
- Allow the user to only select two tiles at a time.
- Check if the two tiles match.
- Remove the tiles if they match, otherwise rotate them to their original position.

In order to keep our code structured in a coherent manner, we will be breaking down the actions associated with selecting one tile and then another into two separate functions. Let's begin by setting a global variable at the top of the script:

```
var matchOne : GameObject;
```

Next change the `Raycast` to match the code below:

```
if (Physics.Raycast (ray, hit, Mathf.Infinity)){
    //print ("Help my bob i've hit something");
    if (!matchOne)
    {
        revealCardOne();
    }
    else{
        revealCardTwo();
    }
}
```

and finally create two new functions:

```
function revealCardOne()
{
}

function revealCardTwo()
```

Heiro Match – Part 1

```
    {
    }
```

That was quite a lot of code so let's take a moment to go through what we have just put into our script. The two variables as you will see are `GameObjects` that will be used to store instances of our two tiles. The new `Raycast` code has an `if` statement which states that if the game object variable `matchOne` is **null** (has no value assigned), then the function `revealCardOne()` is called. If `matchOne` is not null then `revealCardTwo()` is called.

We find ourselves with the `matchOne` variable at null at the start of our game, and it is in need of some game object loving. Whenever we click on a tile, our fancy `Raycast` brings back all kinds of information in our `hit` variable. The most important for us being the identification of the game object that it has collided with. Put the following code in the `revealCardOne()` function:

```
matchOne = hit.transform.gameObject;
if (matchOne == null)
{
    print("No object found!");
}
else
{
}
```

The first line, takes the `matchOne` variable and applies the `gameObject` that the Raycast has collided with to it. Next we set up an `if` condition to ensure that we account for a null reference being passed to the function, which means if the program manages to force its way through to this point without a game object attached to the `matchOne` variable we will know about it!

Let's now use the game object variable to find out the name of our tile we have just clicked on, put the variable up at the top, and the next line before the `if` statement:

```
var tileName1 : String;

tileName1 = matchOne.transform.parent.name;
```

This line allows us to access the `name` variable of the `parent` of our prefab object. The parent is the top level of the prefab and in order to compare the names of the tiles we need to get this name. If you put a print statement (`print(tileName1);`) underneath and hit play and click on a tile - the name of that tile should be displayed in the console. You will see from the names of the prefabs that we split up the words with underscores (_). This was a deliberate trick of the trade, since we have two tiles that are identical, we needed them to be treated as separate objects, so we gave them different names, but now we want to use those names to see if the two tiles that are selected match. For this we will use a function in JavaScript call `Split()`.

The `Split()` function allows a string be split into an array of substrings, with the array being the value that is returned. For example, here we have a variable with a string:

Chapter 2

```
var myString = "hello*world";
```

If we wanted to split the string by the * character we would create an array variable, and use the following line of code:

```
var myArray : Array;
myArray = myString.Split("*"[0]);
```

We specify the * as the separator value, the result of this line of code will be two entries into the array which, when accessed, will look like this:

```
myArray[0] - contains "hello"
myArray[1] - contains "world"
```

So now in our script we want to declare a global variable for an array (remember that means at the top of the script):

```
var tName1 : Array;
```

Then put our split code into the else, using our tileName1 variable as the String and underscore _ as the separator:

```
tName1 = tileName1.Split("_"[0]);
```

Our revealCardOne() function should now look like this:

```
function revealCardOne()
{
    matchOne = hit.transform.gameObject;
    tileName1 = matchOne.transform.parent.name;

    if (matchOne == null)
    {
        print("No object found!");
    }
    else
    {
        tName1 = tileName1.Split("_"[0]);
    }
}
```

Put a print statement underneath the split line of code and print out tName[0] to see the name of the object you are clicking on.

35

Heiro Match – Part 1

We are looking good now, let's keep this pace up and put in the code that lets us see what tile we have picked. At the moment we are going to do a really lo-fi hack of revealing our tile. We will end up replacing this with some nice animation later on. For the moment though, put this line of code after the split code.

```
matchOne.transform.Rotate(Vector3(0,180,0));
```

Hit play and click on a tile and it should magically show you the other side of the tile with our nice little Egyptian symbol on it! Like this:

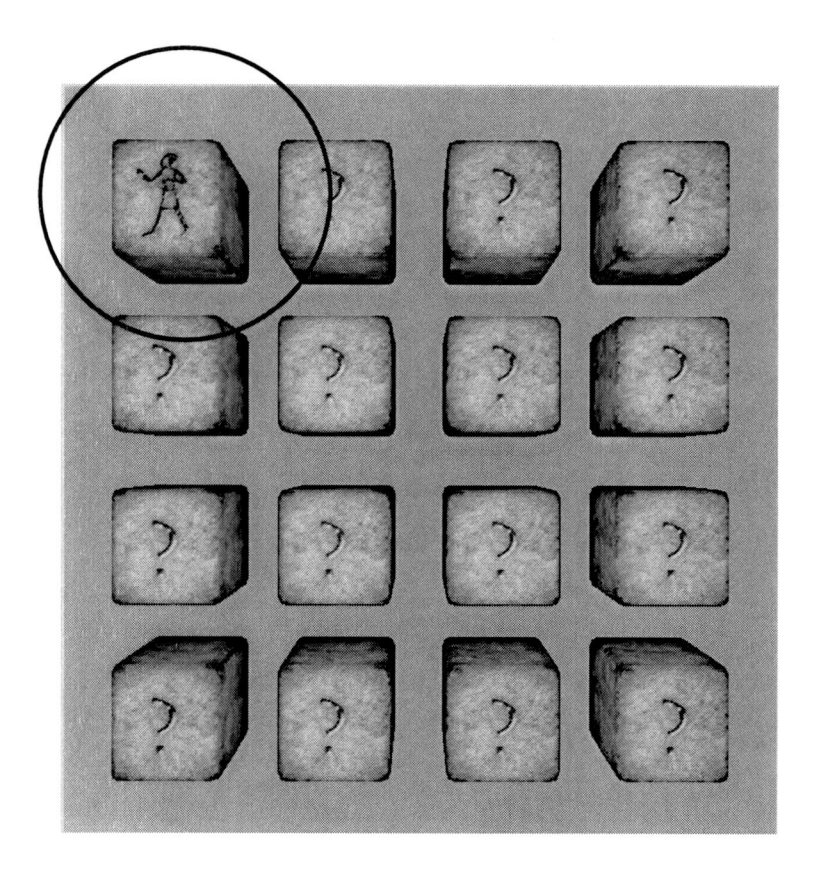

Add in these global variables:
```
var matchTwo : GameObject;
var tileName2 : String;
var tName2 : Array;
```

Now take the code inside of the `RevealCardOne()` function and copy it into the `RevealCardTwo()` function. Alter the code to match this:

```
matchTwo = hit.transform.gameObject;
tileName2 = matchTwo.transform.parent.name;

print (tileName2);

if (matchTwo == null)
{
   print("No object found!");
}
else
{
   tName2 = tileName2.Split("_"[0]);
   print (tName2[0]);
   matchTwo.transform.Rotate(Vector3(0,180,0));
}
```

Hit the play button and you should now be able to reveal two of the tiles!

This is us on the home streak now ladies and gents - our last piece of the puzzle is to check whether the tiles we just clicked matched, and if they did, remove them. If they did not match, we need to turn them back over. Copy this portion of code into the `RevealCardTwo()` function beneath the first `if` statement:

```
if (tName1[0]  == tName2[0] )
{
   yield new WaitForSeconds (2);
   Destroy (matchOne);
   Destroy (matchTwo);
   numberOfTiles = numberOfTiles-2;
   if (numberOfTiles == 0)
   {
      print ("End game");
   }
}
else
{
   yield new WaitForSeconds (2);
   matchOne.transform.Rotate(Vector3(0,-180,0));
```

Heiro Match – Part 1

```
        matchTwo.transform.Rotate(Vector3(0,-180,0));
    }
    matchOne = null;
    matchTwo = null;
```

We use another `if` statement to check if the values in both name arrays match, if they do, then we use the `WaitForSeconds()` function. This function pauses the running of the game by a set number of seconds, in our case 2. We then use `Destroy()` to remove our selected Game Objects from the scene. We decrement the number of tiles by 2 and use this number as an `end` clause, checking that when it reaches zero, and there are no tiles left of the screen, the game is over. If the tiles don't match, then we wait for two seconds, and rotate each tile object back to its original position. Upon exiting the `if` we set the two game object variables to null; this basically empties the variables and ensures that we avoid any conflicts between selected objects. Run the scene and click on two tiles and view the results.

> One of the crucial elements to developing games that I want to highlight at this point is that regardless of what you think your users will do with your game, they will end up doing the exact opposite! I once gave a game I developed on the iphone to the mother of a friend of mine, quite similar to this one, it had a grid of squares and you had to remove them to see the image underneath. I handed her the iPhone and she said "what do I do?".
>
> I wanted to see how she interacted with the game without my input, so I said: "I can't tell you. Just do whatever you think is right".
>
> For 5 minutes she stared at the iPhone, and in the end became quite frustrated so I had to ask her: "well what do you do with an iPhone?"
>
> She replied: "You touch it".
>
> Bingo, after 10 minutes of looking at this game she managed to start playing. Functionally it told me I needed better instruction screens, for my 'experience bank' it told me - *always expect the worst from your potential players!*

Now what could easily happen here in our game is that players start clicking anywhere and everywhere. Try that now, click as many tiles as you want, eventually you will get an error in the console. So we have to put a check in that says that the player can't click when both tiles are turned over. Create a new global boolean variable:

```
    var canClick = true;
```

Then in the `Update()` function, put another `if` statement around the existing `GetButtonDown()` code, like this:

```
    if (canClick == true){
        if (Input.GetButtonDown("Fire1")){
            var ray = Camera.main.ScreenPointToRay
                (Input.mousePosition);
            if (Physics.Raycast (ray, hit, Mathf.Infinity)){
                //print ("Help my bob i've hit something");
                if (!matchOne)
                {
                    revealCardOne();
                }
                else
                {
                    revealCardTwo();
                }
            }
        }
    }
```

We can use this `canClick` variable to turn the button functionality on and off. Make these changes to the `RevealCardTwo()` function, in the name checking if:

```
    if (tName1[0]  == tName2[0])
    {
        canClick = false;
        yield new WaitForSeconds (2);
        Destroy (matchOne);
        Destroy (matchTwo);
        canClick = true;
        numberOfTiles = numberOfTiles-2;

        if (numberOfTiles == 0)
        {
            print ("End game");
        }
    }
    else
    {
        canClick = false;
        yield new WaitForSeconds (2);
        matchOne.transform.Rotate(Vector3(0,-180,0));
        matchTwo.transform.Rotate(Vector3(0,-180,0));
        canClick = true;
    }

    matchOne = null;
    matchTwo = null;
}
```

Heiro Match – Part 1

Our code now waits for the tiles to be removed or moved back to their original position. Hit the play button and play about with the game.

Finally we want to put in a bit more error catching, specifically player error catching. Try clicking on the same tile twice, you will notice that our code basically reads this as another tile and removes the tile you have clicked because both names match. To counter this put this `if` statement after we set the `tileName2` variable and have it end after the final line of the `revealCardTwo` function.

```
if (tileName1 != tileName2){

}
```

This checks to see if the first tile's name matches the second tile. Since we haven't done our string split the tiles should only match if they have been clicked twice. Voila we have a stable Match the Pairs game.

Summary

How are you feeling? The good news is that we have just completed the core functionality for our first game. Sit back and relax for a bit. We have gone through a crash course in some really nice scripting techniques using JavaScript. In particular our work with accessing Game Objects and their properties will stand you in good stead for the rest of the book. What can we take from this chapter?

- Arrays are incredibly useful tools for creating games. You now know how to create an array and a static array, the latter of which you can use the inspector to populate with a specific type of object.

- Player input is a fundamental aspect that we have touched upon here. We have looked into mouse input, however there are many more input methods available to us such as keyboards and game pads.

- Ray casting allows us to perform a multitude of tasks; we have used it to cast a ray from a position from the mouse, but it can also be used to cast rays from objects to identify collisions during gameplay. We will utilize Ray casting more in later chapters.

We've had the good news, now for the excellent news. The next chapter is where all the bright shiny stuff comes in. We will be filling out our scene with some rather wonderful Egyptian artwork. Looking into giving our game a more professional feel with some nice animations using Unity's own built in animation editor. We will be creating some amazing effects with particles, and finally adding in those crucial elements like time and score. Go now, get yourself a beverage, possibly a snack, and get ready to finish off your first Unity game.

Chapter 3

Heiro Match – Part 2

During my earlier years developing video games, at the start of any project the development of the game would be split 80/20%. The 80% would correspond to getting all the functionality in: the main art assets, and basically getting the game to a functional point. The last 20% was for "polish", things that I deemed less important for the main portion of development, along with some "if there is time" features. So you fight hard, get that 80% done, and the game looks good and plays the way it should, just 20% left, that'll be nothing! As I soon found out, when you come to that last 20% you find that there is 80% of the work in there! To me, the 'polish' stage of game development is where the real work gets done. This is where you can raise your game from being good to great. The time spent here will be noticed by your players, reviewers and critics.

We have just done our 80% to get the core functionality and basic artwork into our Match Game. Now we come to the last 20%, this is where we make it shine. We will look at:

- Unity Animation Editor
- Particles
- Scoring
- Timers
- Scene Management

All things being well at the end of this chapter you will have completed your first Unity game, ready to be uploaded and shared with the world.

Animation Station

As of Unity version 2.6, a fully integrated **Animation View** was included to allow users to create and modify animations inside Unity.

Heiro Match – Part 2

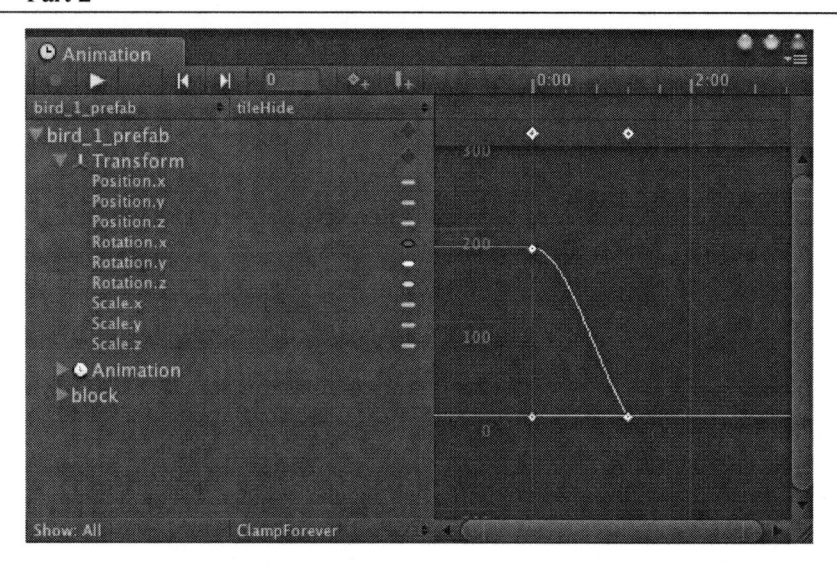

The animation editor works in a similar way to the **Hierarchy View** and the **Inspector,** if an object is selected, the animation view will display the properties of that object in the left hand panel of the editor. This panel is ordered in the exact same way as the inspector with **Components** and **Materials**. Expanding a component will reveal any editable properties that are attached.

Let's get started by first opening the animation view. Above the **Stats** button in the **Game View** you will see an expandable menu, click on this, choose **Add Tab > Animation** and you should see a new animation view appear over the game view. Click on the animations view's tab and drag it to somewhere else on your screen to 'unmount' it from Unity. Place it in a convenient place where you can see both the editor and the animation view.

With the animation editor ready, we need to have a think about what we would like to animate. For the purposes of our game we will require 2 animations, a **reveal** animation that is played when the user clicks on a tile, and a **hide** animation that is played when two tiles need to return to their original positions after an incorrect match. We will keep our first animation nice and simple and rotate the block 180 degrees positively in the y axis, outlined in the image below:

Creating our first Animation Clip

Let's dive right in and get cracking with the first animation. Select the **bird_1** prefab from the **Project View** and drag it onto the **Hierarchy View** or onto your scene. Clicking on the prefab will naturally bring up the properties of this object in our animation editor. To create our animation we need to select **[Create New Clip]** from the right hand drop down menu on the left pane in the animation view. This will then prompt you to save the animation somewhere in the assets folder. For the purpose of our project I have created a new folder under **_assets** and called it **Animations**, so create this folder and save your animation as **tileReveal** here. When a clip is created an **Animation Component** is added to the selected object, our prefab however already has an animation component attached to the parent object.

It's Alive

To start animating make sure that the **Animation Mode Button (red circle)** in the top left hand corner of the editor is activated. With this on, any changes that we make to the animation will be recorded in our newly created animation clip.

We now want to add in a curve to our **Transform** component, specifically the `Rotation.y` property. Click on the drop down menu at the side and select **Add Curves** as shown below:

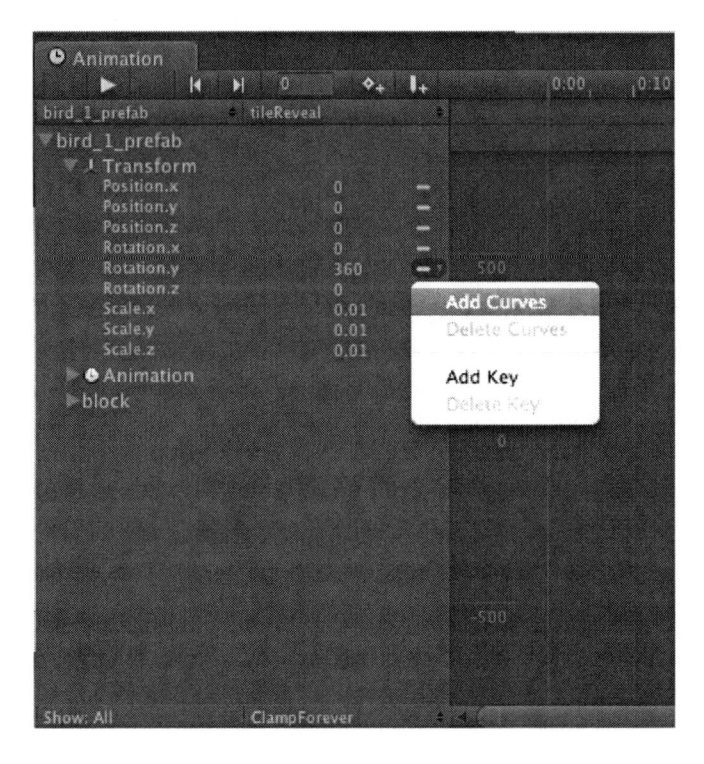

Heiro Match – Part 2

A red vertical line will appear that identifies which frame of the animation clip is currently being previewed. By clicking on the **Time Line** at the top of the editor you can preview and modify any frame in the animation clip.

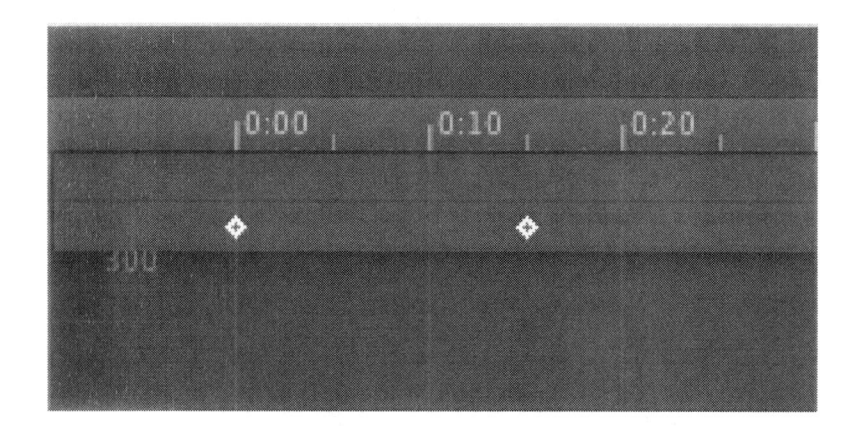

You will notice a small white diamond shape called a **Keyframe** on the animation time line. If you can't see the keyframe, click the **Rotation.y** property in the right panel and hit the *F* key to focus on the property's keyframes.

A keyframe stores information about a particular property at a particular point in the time line. So, in the image above, the first keyframe is at time 0:00, and has a rotational value around the Y axis of 0.

On the **Time Line** click on 0:15, this will move the red time indicator (There is also a small text field above the right hand drop down menu where you can type in the desired frame). Locate the `Rotation.y` property in the left hand panel and change the value to `180`. You will see the line in the animation editor update, if it goes off the viewing area hit *F* again to focus it. In the **Scene View** locate your prefab using the *F* short cut key, and hit the play button in the animation editor. The result should be the tile rotating in a loop around its y-axis.

Excellent, we now have our animation that will reveal our tile when it is clicked. Next we need to create an animation to hide the tile if the selection is incorrect. Create a new animation clip and call it `tileHide`. Now we want this animation to be the exact opposite of the animation we just created for revealing the tile. Add a **curve** like before and move along to 0:15 in the time line and create a keyframe using the **Add Keyframe** Button (The button with the diamond and plus sign).

Now move the red line back to `0:00`, and change the value in the `Rotation.y` to `180`. Play the animation and the result should be the tile rotating continuously in the opposite direction.

With our two animations created, we need to apply them to the prefab, whenever you have made alterations to a prefab, the changes *must be applied manually*, so select the prefab go to **Game Object** in the tool bar and select **Apply Changes To Prefab**.

Chapter 3

Before we put the code in to play our animations, check in the **Inspector** that our prefabs animation component is not set to **Play Automatically** as we want the animation to play when a click happens; turn it off and apply the changes to the prefab again. Now you can delete the prefab.

Our next step is to get these animations on each of our prefabs, repeat these steps for each of the remaining prefabs:

- Select the prefab in the Project View.
- Expand the Animations property in the Animation component.
- Increase the size to 2.
- Select the `tileHide` animation for element 0.
- Select the `tileReveal` animation for element 1.
- Ensure that Play Automatically is unchecked.

With our prefabs all set up, the next step is to put in a couple of lines of code that will play these animations when the tiles are clicked. In your script replace this piece of code:

```
matchOne.transform.Rotate(Vector3(0,180,0));
```

with:

```
matchOne.transform.parent.animation.Play ("tileReveal");
```

Then replace this one:

```
matchTwo.transform.Rotate(Vector3(0,180,0));
```

with:

```
matchTwo.transform.parent.animation.Play ("tileReveal");
```

Here we are accessing the Game Objects stored in the variables `matchOne` and `matchTwo`, and then accessing the parent's animation component attached to each of these; we play the animation called `tileReveal`.

The final step is to replace the code that rotates the objects to their original positions:

```
matchOne.transform.Rotate(Vector3(0,-180,0));
matchTwo.transform.Rotate(Vector3(0,-180,0));
```

with these lines:

Heiro Match – Part 2

```
matchOne.transform.parent.animation.Play ("tileHide");
matchTwo.transform.parent.animation.Play ("tileHide");
```

Run your scene and click on the tiles, you should be greeted with a very nice smooth animation. Excellent, we now have a basic grasp of the animation editor, I would encourage you to experiment with all the different properties that you can manipulate with the editor and even try and make a snazzier animation than the one we have here.

IMPORTANT Having written this chapter in full I was sure that I was all ready to move onto the next game, all I had to do was clean up the code a little bit and build a version of the game to put up on the Deep Pixel website. So I built a version and played it on the web and for some strange reason the animations that worked so well now seemed to stop short of the last few frames in the animation, basically never reaching 180 or 0.

I spent a good few hours one Sunday afternoon with James Bond's Octopussy on the TV in the background while I desperately tried to find the problem. It turns out that I was using the default **Wrap Mode** setting in the animations that is quite inaccurate. To fix the problem all that was required was to change the wrap mode to **ClampForever**. You can do this by clicking on the animation file in the project view and selecting **ClampForever**. This setting allowed the animation to reach 180 and 0 respectively and after that the game was mine! :)

Score & Time

Score and time are two of the most fundamental mechanics used in video games. Both have been used throughout the history of games to create exciting game play experiences and encourage re-playability. Our use for these mechanics is along the more traditional route, we will utilize the score element to count the number of correct matches the player gets. The time element, on the other hand, will be used as a countdown clock to add that classic feeling of arcade timer pressure into our game.

To create both the time and score elements let's look into Unity's built in Graphical User Interface (GUI) class and function. Unity provides us with a function called OnGUI(), this function is similar to the Update() function in that it is executed on every frame. The difference being that this is where all of your GUI code will go. Let's take a look at an example:

Chapter 3

```
function OnGUI(){
    if(GUILayout.Button ("Instructions")){
        //Do something
    }
}
```

In this example a button is placed on the screen with the text "Instructions" inside. The button is enclosed in an `if` conditional statement which upon the button being pressed executes the code inside the brackets. Let's begin by putting our own `OnGUI()` function between the `Update()` and the `revealCardOne()` functions:

```
function OnGUI()
{
    GUI.Label (Rect (10, 10, 100, 20), "Hello World");
}
```

Hit the play button and you will see the text "Hello World" in the top right hand corner of your game view. At the moment it is quite small but we will add some polish later on. This piece of code creates a GUI label on the screen using the following parameters, a `Rect` which is a 2D rectangle defined by **x** and **y** positions and **width** and **height**, and a **String** for the text that is displayed in the label.

The label also takes in several other parameters; these can be found in the **Unity Script Reference** docs. Our label based on these values is placed 10 pixels from the side and top of the screen, and has a size of 100x20 pixels.

So we want to use this label as the display for the players score. Our label needs a couple of variables to be able to get the players score from the game; declare these variables:

```
var scoreInt = 0;
var scoreTxt : String;
```

These variables will store two versions of the score. The first is an integer which will hold the actual number of the player's score, the second is a String which will be used to display a text version of the score. Locate the `revealCardTwo()` function and add this line to the `if` condition that checks if the tiles match:

```
scoreInt++;
```

This line of code increments the `scoreInt` variable (which has been set to 0) by 1 every time the player gets two matching tiles. We now have a score for our player. However we need to be able to display this score on screen. Since the GUI label only takes in Strings we need to convert our `scoreInt` variable to a string; replace the code in the `OnGUI()` function with the code below:

Heiro Match – Part 2

```
scoreTxt = scoreInt.ToString();
GUI.Label (Rect (10, 10, 100, 20), scoreTxt);
```

Here we use a JavaScript function called `ToString()` to change our `scoreInt` variable into a String and store it in our `scoreTxt` variable. We can then use this in our GUI label as our text parameter. Hit the play button and match some tiles to see the score increment. Now that we have our score counter in, we can leave it alone for the moment and move on to the timer, we will come back at the end and add some polish.

Timer

Time is the classic game mechanic, it has been used throughout game development in so many different and innovative ways. We are going to go the traditional route and use it as a countdown timer to add some pressure to our game. So let's start by declaring some variables:

```
private var startTime;
private var Seconds : int;
private var roundedSeconds : int;
private var txtSeconds : int;
private var txtMinutes : int;
var countSeconds : int;
private var stopTimer = false;
```

Here we have declared some of our variables as `private`, this takes away the ability to alter them in the Unity editor. So without the word 'private' before the `var` our variable is public, thus making it editable. We are going to use another of Unity's build in functions called `Awake()`.

```
function Awake(){
    startTime = 5;
}
```

This function is called whenever the instance of the script has been called by the game. So rather than setting the `startTime` at the start of the game, we set it when the script is called. So you would use `Awake()` when setting up components and references that need to be set up before any `Start()` functions are called. Now let's get to the meat of the timer code. Place the following into the `OnGUI()` function underneath the existing lines:

```
if (stopTimer == false){
    var guiTime = Time.time - startTime;
    Seconds = countSeconds - (guiTime);
}

if (Seconds == 0){
    print ("The time is over");
    stopTimer = true;
}
```

```
//Display timer
roundedSeconds = Mathf.CeilToInt(Seconds);
txtSeconds = roundedSeconds % 60;
txtMinutes = roundedSeconds / 60;

text = String.Format("{0:00}:{1:00}", txtMinutes, txtSeconds);
GUI.Label(Rect(10,30,100,30), text);
```

The first `if` sets up a condition where **if** the timer is not to be stopped then the time from the system is retrieved using `Time.time`. We then work out the number of seconds by taking our `countSeconds` variable and taking off the newly worked out `guiTime`. We then utilize the maths function `Mathf.CeilToInt` to round the number to the nearest full integer. We then take a division and percentage of 60 for our rounded seconds to give us the correct integers to display.

The final two lines of code set up the way our timer will look. The function `String.Format` is used to create a format that integers can be placed in. The first 0 in `{0:00}`, represents the first element in the array, and the 00 displays single digit values with a leading 0, which gives 01, 02, 03.

Since we have minutes and seconds we have a second array, set up with the same values as the previous one. We then declare our two Strings which are the minutes and the seconds. Hit the play button to see the results. As you will see the `startTime` variable is set to 5 so the timer counts down from 5 seconds, change this to 60 to give the player a minute to complete the game.

Setting the scene

Now that we have all our game functionality in place, the next step is to add in some art assets that will add some polish and shine to our game. Go to:

www.deeppixel.com/UnityBookPackages/match/envModel.unitypackage

Download the package. Return to Unity and import this package into your project view. As before ensure that in the FBX Exporter of the imported model, the Scale Factor is set to 1, and that the **Generate Colliders** property is checked. Click and drag the model onto the Hierarchy View to add it to the scene. Hit play and the tiles **should** appear similar to the picture below:

Heiro Match – Part 2

If it doesn't, leave the scene playing and re-position the background environment based on the tiles and note down the X, Y and Z values as these won't be saved when you click off play mode. Shut off play mode and enter in these new positional coordinates for the background.

Now you may have a couple of things that aren't sitting right. The camera may be sitting too near to the tiles and not showing enough of the background; find this line of code in your script and play around with the Z value to get an effect similar to the next image:

```
Camera.main.transform.position = Vector3(2.25,2.25,-8);
```

The tiles are slightly overlapping at the top with some of the scene, so a really easy fix here is to go into your **scene view** and use the transform gizmos to move the whole environment up slightly on the y-axis; I landed on 0.3 as a nice number.

Particle Systems

With our lovely Egyptian scene set up, we can now add some of those little touches that make really interesting dynamic looking games. Particle effects are a fantastic way to bring a scene to life and give it a more vibrant feel. A Particle System consists of a cluster of 2D images that are rendered in our 3D world with specific properties that affect the system's behaviour. Particle Systems are generally used in games to simulate flames, explosions, blood and other visual effects. For our purposes we want to have a fire like particle system. Unity's particle system is comprised of three components: the **Particle Emitter**, **Particle Animator**, and **Particle Renderer**.

Heiro Match – Part 2

Particle Emitter

The Particle Emitter is the main component that is used to define the properties of the particle system. The most important of these properties are the spawning properties, specifically the:

- Size – size of an individual particle.
- Energy – the lifetime of each particle in seconds.
- Emission – the number of particles spawned every second.
- Velocity – speed of particles in world space.

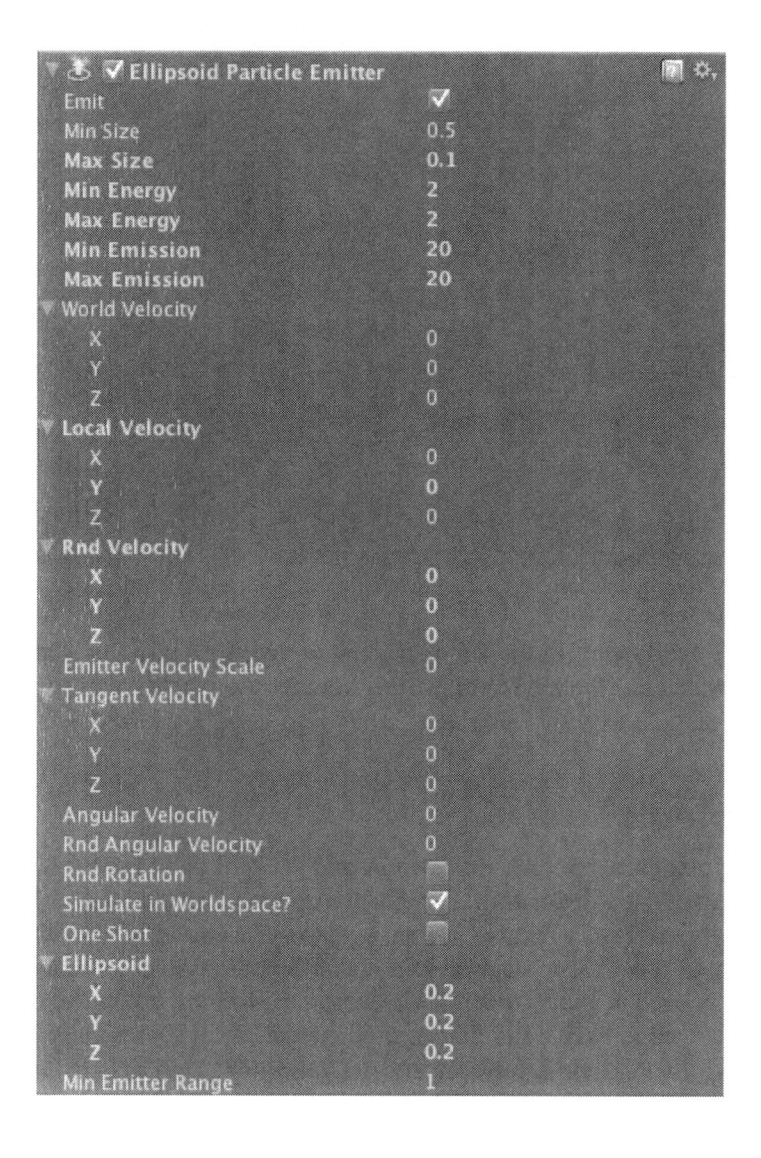

Ellipsoid Particle Emitter	
Emit	✓
Min Size	0.5
Max Size	0.1
Min Energy	2
Max Energy	2
Min Emission	20
Max Emission	20
World Velocity	
X	0
Y	0
Z	0
Local Velocity	
X	0
Y	0
Z	0
Rnd Velocity	
X	0
Y	0
Z	0
Emitter Velocity Scale	0
Tangent Velocity	
X	0
Y	0
Z	0
Angular Velocity	0
Rnd Angular Velocity	0
Rnd Rotation	
Simulate in Worldspace?	✓
One Shot	
Ellipsoid	
X	0.2
Y	0.2
Z	0.2
Min Emitter Range	1

Particle Animator

This component is used to set how each particle will move over time. This allows you to make your particles react to certain elemental forces like wind and drag. Specifically for our uses we will look to the **force** property to make our flames move towards the sky.

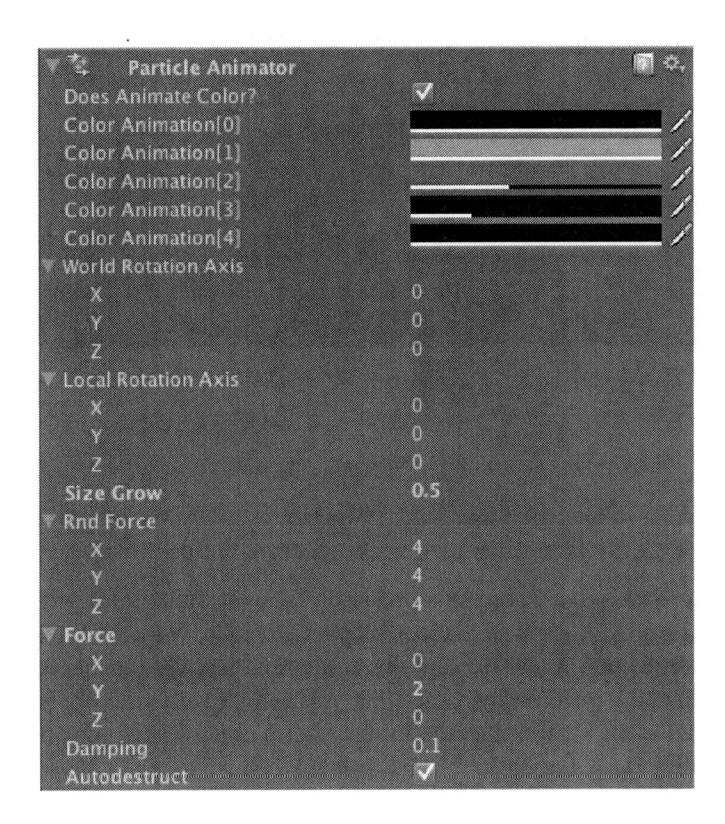

Particle Renderer

The particle renderer renders the particle system in our 3D world. The particles that we create each have a **Particle Texture** that we set with a 2D image of our particle. Altering values here affects the way in which the particles are rendered. Typically particles are rendered using a technique called **billboarding**, which gives the effect of the particles always facing the camera. Unity provides a number of other settings but generally billboarding will be sufficient for most needs.

Heiro Match – Part 2

```
▼ ✓ Particle Renderer
    Cast Shadows              ✓
    Receive Shadows           ✓
  ▼ Materials
        Size                  1
        Element 0             ● fire smoke
    Camera Velocity Scale     0
    Stretch Particles         Billboard
    Length Scale              2
    Velocity Scale            0
    Max Particle Size         0.25
  ▶ UV Animation
```

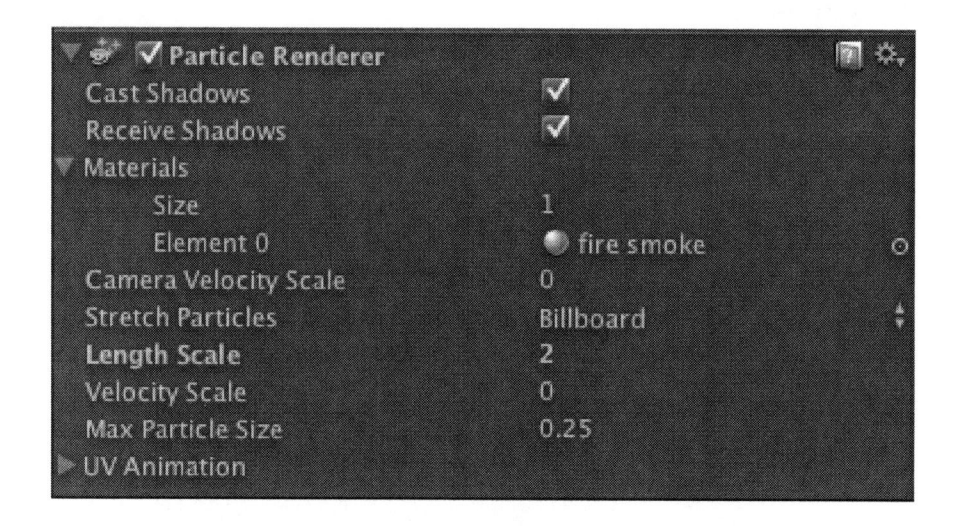

Our Scene

In our scene we have two statues on either side of the central tiles. We are going to use Unity's particle system to create a fire like effect that emanates from these statues.

Unity in all its genius wisdom has given us a preset prefab with flame like particles already set up. If you right click on the project view and select **Import Package > Particles** the view will update with a **Standard Assets** folder, if you expand this folder and navigate inside the resulting folder structures you will see many different particles that you can play about with. Now the flame particle that is included in the standard assets folder is a bit complicated for our needs so we have provided you with a nice simple one:

www.deeppixel.com/UnityBookPackages/match/flame.unitypackage

Once you have imported the model click and drag it onto the hierarchy view to activate it on your scene. Locate the particles in the scene and move them into the scene as follows:

With a nice flame effect created, place it into one of the bowls and then duplicate the prefab to create a new version, moving it across to the other bowl like this:

Heiro Match – Part 2

Our scene is really starting to come together. Next we will look at the last bits of polish that are needed to finish our game.

Little bits of polish

We are nearing the end of our first journey. We have some final additions to make to the game before we can call it complete. We will look at:

- Making the score and timer GUI labels more in keeping with the theme.
- Add a well done screen and a time up screen.
- Finally, a 'play again' button.

At the moment the text on our GUI is a bit out of context for our Egyptian scene. Unity provides a way in which you can customize your GUI using **GUI Skins**. These are basically a collection of **GUIStyles** that are applied to your GUI. Right click on the **project view** and select **create/GUISkin**, click on the resulting object to see the inspector.

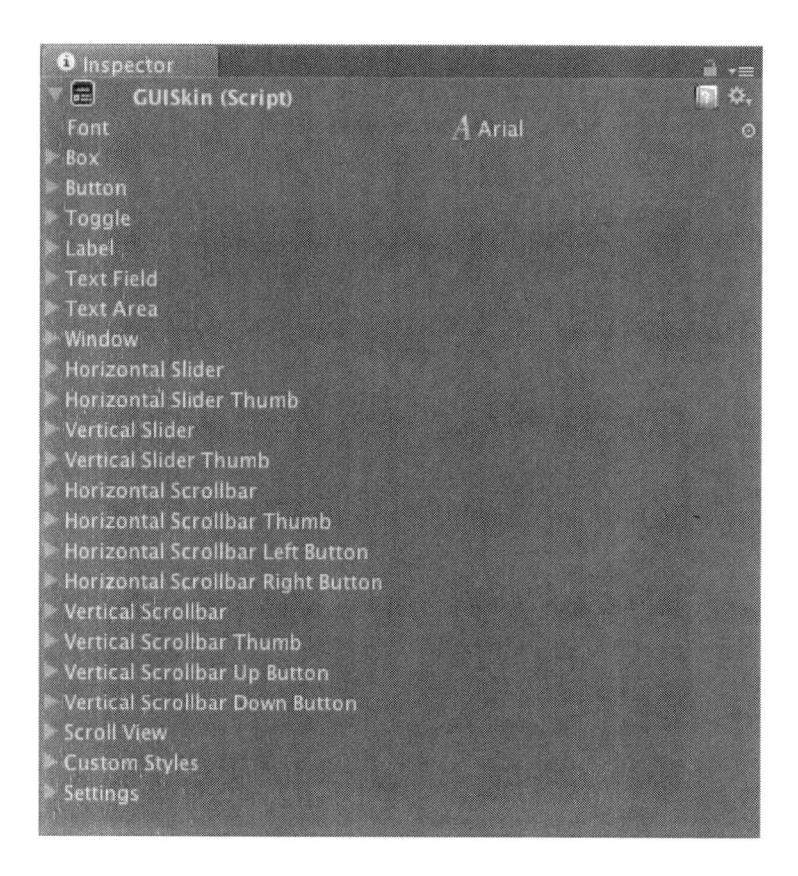

Chapter 3

There are a number of different properties that can be explored using the GUISkin, but specifically we want to look at the **Label** property as our two GUI elements are labels. Expanding this node shows all the different sub properties that can be set to alter the appearance and functionality of the labels. For the purposes of our game we want to change the font type to something that is a bit more in keeping with our Egyptian theme.

We have a nice font already picked out for you, so go to:

www.deeppixel.com/UnityBookPackages/match/egyptianFont.unitypackage

Download and import the package into Unity. The font will be in a folder called **Skins & Fonts** and be shown in the project view with a blue 'A' next to it. Clicking on the font will bring up some details in the inspector. (At this point for cleanliness you will probably want to put the GUISkin object into the same folder as the font).

Now in the font sub property of the **Label** property we can select our new font to be used. Also while we are here, expand the **Normal** sub property of the GUISkin and change the text colour to a nice bright yellow colour, that will stand out from the dark sandstone texture we have on the level. With our GUIskin and font set up let's look at the code to get this into the game:

Create a new variable with the `GUISkin` identifier –

```
var egyptSkin : GUISkin;
```

In the `OnGUI()` function put -

```
GUI.skin = egyptSkin;
```

Finally, we need to alter the positions of the labels. This is probably a good place to tell you about one of the limitations to Unity's GUI. When using labels, buttons, etc., when you place them in the **game view** and then hit **Maximize on Play** you will find that the positions of the labels don't match up.

To make sure your labels match up to the correct positions click the drop down menu with **Free Aspect** shown, then choose **Web (1024x768)**; this standard setting will ensure that when you build your game for this resolution the correct positions of all your GUI elements will be saved.

Congratulate the player

We will now put in a couple of UI elements that will indicate to the player that either the time has run out, or in the event of the player completing the game, that they are finished. On both occasions they will be given the choice to play again with a button. Download and import the **egyptian_ui_package.unitypackage** from:

57

Heiro Match – Part 2

www.deeppixel.com/UnityBookPackages/match/egyptianUi.unitypackage

Expand the resulting **uiElements** folder in the **Textures** folder to reveal two textures named **UI_finished** and **UI_timeUp**.

So in our code we want to declare the following variables:

```
var finishedTxture : Texture2D;
var timeUpTxture : Texture2D;
var finished = false;
var timeUp = false;
```

Now this is the first time that we have declared a **Texture2D** variable. Essentially this allows us to expose these two variables in the inspector to allow us to select 2 textures that we want to use. Textures in Unity are handled using the power of 2 principle. Therefore when you are creating textures Unity prefers them to be in power of 2 so that they can be compressed into smaller files upon run time, which makes all the difference when you have a lot of textures in the game. Power of 2 values start at 64, and get multiplied by two. You will see in the inspector, if you click on the textures, that they are 1024x512.

So let's choose our textures now. Click on the Game Object in the hierarchy to bring up the `tileGenerator` script in the inspector, look for `finishTxture` and `timeUpTxture`, use the drop down menus to apply the textures that you just downloaded.

The next step is to identify the conditions that have to be met that will trigger the textures to be displayed. For the purposes of our game we want to reveal the `finishTxture` if the player has removed all the tiles successfully, and the `timeUpTxture` when the time runs out. In the code above we declared two boolean variables called `finished` and `timeUp`, and set them to `false`. Now we want the textures to be displayed whenever these are true so let's go ahead and put in two `if` statements in the `OnGUI()` function that will handle these variables.

```
if (finished == true){
}

if (timeUp == true){
}
```

Now, we have placed the `if` statements in the `OnGUI()` function because we want to use a GUI element to display the textures, specifically a label. Put this piece of code in the first `if`:

```
GUI.Label (Rect (270, 305, 512, 256), finishedTxture);
```

Here we set up a GUI label, we set the correct X and Y coordinates, and set the size of our label to be power of 2 values but half of the original values. This will scale our image by half without losing any quality. We then declare the texture to be used in the label, in this case the `finishTxture`. Copy this line and put it into the other `if` statement and change the `finishTxture` to `timeUpTxture`.

Excellent, now we want these `if`s to fire when certain events occur. We actually already have these events set up. Find this `if` statement and add in the finish variable:

```
if (numberOfTiles <= 0)
{
    stopTimer = true;
    finished = true;
}
```

Finally, locate the if statement in the `OnGUI ()` function where we end the game and place the `timeUp` variable:

```
if (Seconds == 0) {
    stopTimer = true;
    timeUp = true;
}
```

To run a quick test to see if this code works, change the `startTime` variable in the `Awake ()` function to a small number and play the game, let it count down and the "Time Up" texture should be displayed.

Summary

That's it, boom(!), your first game. Go show your friends, family, co-workers, and be proud. This is a great start in our journey. We have covered a lot of excellent techniques and principles over the course of the last two chapters. We have scratched the surface of the very powerful animation tool, and looked into a rather deep and complicated method in RayCasting. You now have the fundamental skills that will form the basis of your Unity knowledge. We encourage you now to take this game and spend some time experimenting with it. Throughout my career one of my favourite past times has been taking a piece of code and changing the behaviour of the game, trying new game mechanics and testing new game play ideas.

Try putting in:

- An energy bar system, where for every wrong match a piece of energy is lost.
- Speeding up the time whenever the user matches incorrectly.
- Exploding particles whenever tiles are removed.

Heiro Match – Part 2

> We really wanted to put in a cool effect where the tiles would look like they disintegrated into sand whenever they were removed from the game. If any of you manage something like this **send it over** - we would love to see it!

Chapter 4

Ace Invaders – Part 1

We are going to go a bit retro here and possibly a tad predictable by moving on to create a 2D scrolling shooter. This may seem like an obvious route to go down and you may think you would have liked something a bit more imaginative but the Unity forums and the web in general are filled with posts from beginners to intermediates asking how to create certain aspects of functionality that are fundamental components in a two dimensional shooter.

For the purposes of this chapter we are going to take inspiration from a really nice shooter called Ikargua. This game started life in the bustling Japanese arcades of 2001 and became an instant cult classic. It was released on the ill-fated Dreamcast console only in Japan, and then ported to the GameCube where it has been enjoyed by a worldwide audience. Its most recent incarnation has been on the Xbox Live Arcade and in my humble opinion is up there as one of the best releases on the platform.

Ikaruga has a core mechanic that revolves around changing the "polarity" of your ship to combat enemies. This gave Ikaruga a unique and enjoyable twist on its competitors and ensured that it was a critical success. For our purposes we won't be utilizing this particular mechanic but we will be looking at some of the central features to the game:

- Parallax Scrolling.
- Ship control.
- Enemy Attack.
- Scoring.

Basic setup

Let's dive straight in and create our new project and call it **spaceShooter** and include the **Particles** package. Set up your **Project View** in the same way as before with 3 folders:

- _assets
- _scenes
- _scripts

Ace Invaders – Part 1

In the **_assets** folder, add four additional folders called **Textures**, **Materials**, **Models** and **Prefabs**. With everything setup, **save** the project and save your scene into the **_scenes** folder calling it **game**.

Game Breakdown

When designing this game our thoughts almost instantly went straight for the tried and tested **Space** shooter – i.e. a starry background with some nice galaxies going by. We thought "excellent, that will do," (words that get you nowhere in life). Then Simon went off and started designing and modelling the ship. I expected a shiny silver little craft, but he ended up coming up with this really cool grimy Steam Punk-esque ship. We loved this little ship so much we decided to go all out with a cool 3D post-apocalyptic motif.

The clouds in the sky

Our first port of call is the creation of the environment that our ship will fly through. Two dimensional shooter environments generally fall into two categories, **vertical scrolling** and **horizontal scrolling**. Ikagura is an example of a vertical scroller, while Steel Saviour on the PC is an example of a horizontal scroller. Typically vertical scrollers are more popular in the 2D shooter genre so we will stick with that.

To create a scrolling background a technique called **Parallax Scrolling** is used. Parallax scrolling is a technique that creates the illusion of depth in a 2D environment by moving images at different speeds, specifically moving background images slower than foreground ones. The most popular method in this technique uses layers to create the effect. Take a look at the example below:

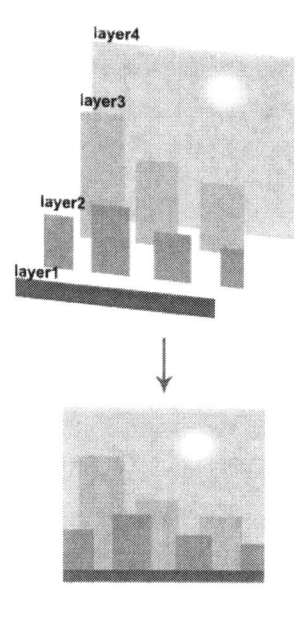

Chapter 4

Here we have four layers. If we had a character running through this environment (which is horizontally set) then the layers towards the front would move faster than the ones at the back. This creates a really rich and immersive effect that allows two dimensional games to simulate pseudo 3D environments. Let's get cracking and create our own vertical parallax scrolling environment!

Start by creating a plane object and naming it **background1**. Move to the inspector and make these changes to the transform component:

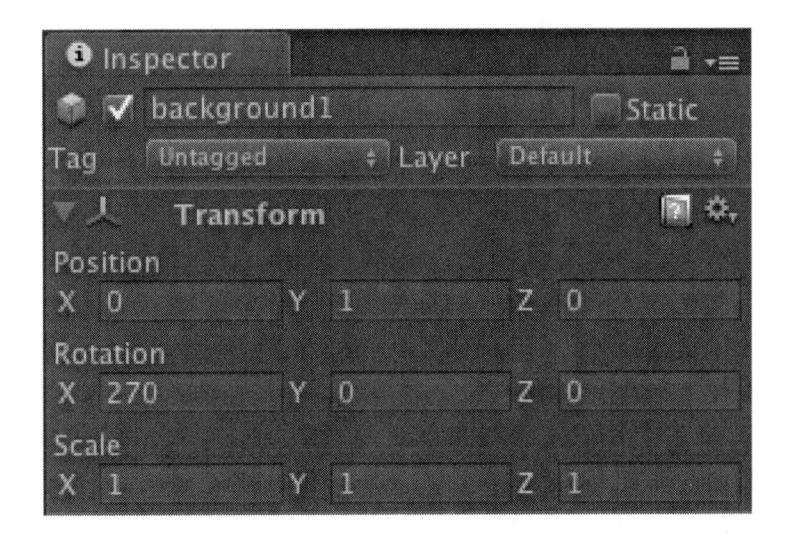

Next click on the camera and make these changes to its transform component:

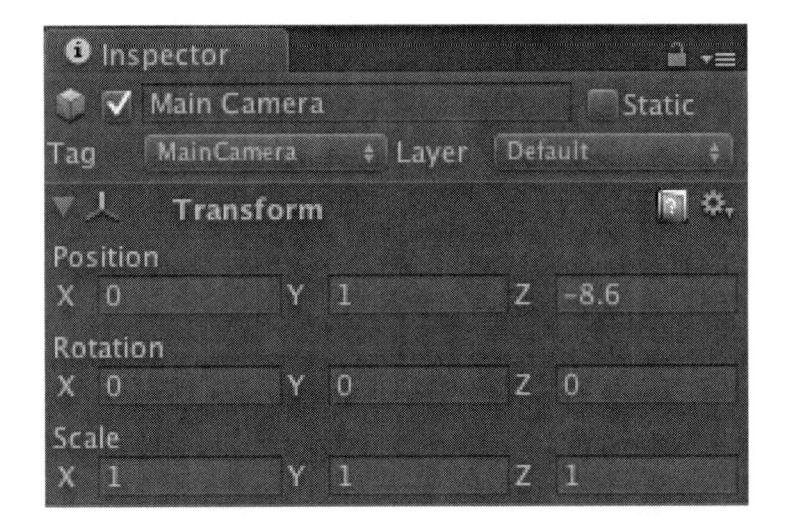

63

Ace Invaders – Part 1

Now if you have ever played a top down shooter before, the dimensions of the screen are similar to that of an iPhone, where the screen area takes a portrait shape rather than a landscape one. Let's change our work area to reflect this. Go to **Edit > Project Settings > Player**, expand **Resolution and Presentation** in the **web player** section as shown below, and enter the width and height values:

Chapter 4

Move to the Game view and change the dimensions of the screen to Web (512x768). Finally move back to the scene view and add a **Point Light** and position it so that the illuminates the plane. Your game screen should resemble the image below:

To complete our setup for the scrolling effect we need another plane, follow these instructions:

- Duplicate (ctrl + D, or cmd(⌘) + D) the plane object in the scene and name it **background2**.
- Change its Y axis position to 11, it should now be positioned directly above the other plane.

The plan now is to create a script that will be attached to each plane. The script will move both planes towards the bottom of the camera. When the first plane is no longer visible to the camera it will jump to the top of the other plane, this will happen continuously giving us our scrolling effect.

Ace Invaders – Part 1

Create a new script in the **scripts** folder and call it **parallaxScrolling**, open it up and enter in this code:

```
var speed : float;

function Update ()
{
   var move : float = speed * Time.deltaTime;

   transform.Translate(Vector3.down * move, Space.World);

   if (transform.position.y < -8.99)
   {
      transform.position = Vector3(transform.position.x, 11,
      transform.position.z);
   }
}
```

First off we create a variable called `speed` and declare it as a float. In the `Update()` function we create another float that will calculate the speed at which the planes will move. To do this we use the Unity variable `Time.deltaTime` that holds the time in seconds that it took to complete the last frame. We use this function for moving objects as it not only provides a nice incremental floating number to multiply our speed variable with, it also ensures that movement is consistent across all kinds of computers regardless of specification. The next line uses the `Translate` function of the transform component to move the transform in the direction and distance of the translation. Let's take this opportunity to look at the Unity Scripting Reference. **Remember it is under Help**. Type **Transform.Translate** in the search bar and click on the top result.

```
function Translate (translation : Vector3, relativeTo : Space
      = Space.Self) : void
```

The Translate function allows us to move a game object using two values, a translation value in the form of a Vector3, and a value that indicates how the transform is to be applied; we can see in the reference document that we can use either `Space.Self`, `Space.World` or in some cases `Camera.main.transform`.

If `Space.Self` is set then the movement of the object is applied relative to the transform's local axes. If `Space.World` is set then it is applied using the world axes, and finally if you use the camera transform - the object is moved relative to the camera's axes.

In our code we used `Vector3.down` which if you look to docs is shorthand for (0, -1.0, 0). We take this vector with a negative value in its Y component and multiply it by our `move` variable. The result is a value that increases negatively in the Y direction, thus moving our plane downwards. Finally, we want the object to move relative to the world axes so we use the appropriate value.

The final part of the script is where we create the looping effect for our scrolling background.

```
if (transform.position.y < -8.99)
{
   transform.position = Vector3(transform.position.x, 11,
      transform.position.z);
}
```

We want to do a check such that when the plane moves completely off the screen we move it to a position above the other plane. In the `if` we access the object's transform component and check its y axis to see if it is less than -8.99. Now if you are wondering, why -8.99 (?), move to your scene view and move the bottom plane using the transform tool until it is off the screen. Look at the plane's y axis value in the inspector and it should be around -8.99.

Undo this action so that the plane is back to its original position. The final line of code places the plane that has moved out of view back to the position of the top plane, and then starts moving again in unison with the other plane. So let's see this working.

Attach the script to both planes by clicking and dragging it onto the object in the scene or hierarchy. Go to the **Hierarchy** view and select each plane in turn, and in the inspector, under the scrolling script, change the speed to 3. Hit play and take a look at this in action in the Scene view. You may see something a bit like a blinky line across the screen, this is called Z fighting.

Z-fighting

This happens when 3D models are rendered and two or more of the models have similar values in the z-buffer. Essentially when two faces of a model occupy the same 3D space where neither face is at the front (or back) you get a *flickery* overlap effect. There is no real one stop fix for this effect, the best bet is to either tinker about with the values until the effect is lessened, or change the background colour of the camera so that if z fighting does occur the default blue background of Unity doesn't shine though.

A City That Never Sleeps

Now that we have our parallax scrolling scripts, we need to go a step further and get a start filling out our game world.

Please download the files from this link:

www.deeppixel.com/UnityBookPackages/Shooter/city.unitypackage

Import the package into Unity, you should have the following:

Ace Invaders – Part 1

1. clouds.png
2. citybaked.png
3. citybaked.mat
4. city model (FBX)

Click on the city model and check the usual culprits -

- Ensure the scale factor is set to **1**.
- Activate generate colliders.
- Make sure the textures are correctly selected in the material for the model.

Drag the model into the scene, this is going to be our very cool 3D post-apocalyptic city that we are going to be flying over during the game. We want the city to be underneath our current planes that exist in our 3D world, so make these changes to its position transform:

x = 0

y = 1

z = 7

Now at the moment we can't see through the planes, so create a new material called **clouds** and change its shader to **Transparent/Diffuse**, and select the clouds texture that we just imported. Then, apply the textures to the backgrounds and you should be able to just make out the city beneath.

To brighten the city up, change the light from a **Point Light** to a **Directional Light** and adjust the intensity to suit. You should now see something like this:

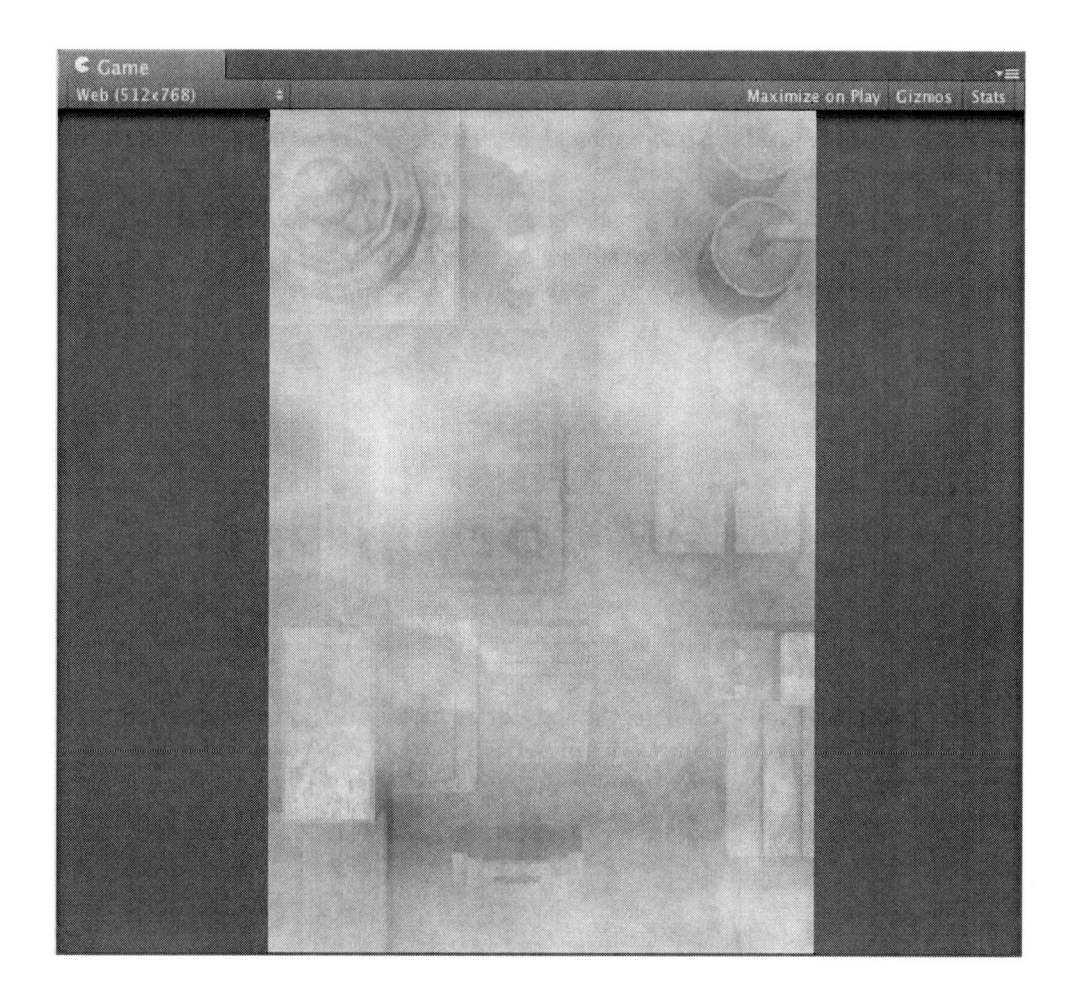

To give our post-apocalyptic world an even more dynamic feel to it we are going to reuse our parallax scrolling technique with the city model. Let's first **duplicate** the city and position it and position it on **top** of the first city similar to what we did with the two planes earlier (I hit a value of 19.153). Next duplicate the **parallaxScrolling** script and rename it to **cityScrolling**. The only changes that we will make to this script are to the two values, change the value in the if() to -17.1 and the value inside the if to 19.154 (*these values worked for me, you may have to change them about a bit*). Remember to set the speed value on both city object scripts to something other than zero.

For the finishing touch to our doomsday world, change the colour of the light in your scene to a rusty orange making the game seem like it is being played in the twilight. Change the speed values for the city models scrolling scripts and hit play to see the results.

Ace Invaders – Part 1

> Now the Z-fighting may or may not be an issue on your screen with the cloud planes. For us we could see it like a red hot poker burning our eyes! So, Simon the absolute genius that he is suggested that, rather than animating the planes to move, why don't we animate the texture? Absolute stellar idea!!
>
> As we only need one of the planes, deactivate or delete the plane that is not in the sight of the camera. Remove the **parallaxScrolling** script and create and attach a new script called **uvScrolling**. Put in the following code:
>
> ```
> var scrollSpeed : float = 1.0;
> function Update() {
>     var offset : float = Time.time * -scrollSpeed;
>     renderer.material.mainTextureOffset = Vector2 (0,
>         offset);
> }
> ```
>
> Hit the play button and you should get the same effect as before, however this time no silly Z-fighting. A rather excellent work around, thank you Simon - we will make a coder out of you yet! FYI, you may need to play about with the `scrollSpeed` to get it perfect.

Made It in Less than Twelve Parsecs

We come now to the main component of any shooter, the ship. Now this is no ordinary ship, twin blasters, small, fast and as you see by the heading, well you've heard of the Kessel Run haven't you? So let's get this baby downloaded and into our scene:

www.deeppixel.com/UnityBookPackages/Shooter/ship.unitypackage

As always check the necessary import settings for the model, and place it into your scene. Ensure that the ship is above the clouds, I have a value of around `-1.5` in the ship's Z axis. Now we need to set up our ship ready for flight. Add a **Rigidbody** component to the ship and deactivate the **Use Gravity** variable. Create a new script called **shipController**, attach it to the ship and open it up.

Here is an overview of some of the core functionality our ship requires:
- Movement.
- Attack.
- Shield.
- Spawning.
- Destruction.

Most of these are pretty self-explanatory; each one is required to make the ship functional and to give the player all the tools required to play our game.

Movement

A ship's movement in any form of shooter is generally constrained to the dimensions of the screen on which the game world is displayed. In the case of Space Invaders, the player was constrained to a horizontal line that ran along the bottom of the screen underneath four barriers. Modern arcade shooters give the player the space to roam to the edges of the screen, in all directions.

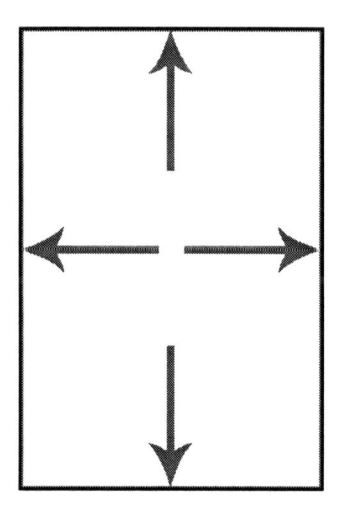

This greatly alters the games mechanics from the simplicity of Space Invaders. The game can vary how enemies enter and leave the screen, and also how they act while they are there. Enemies can swoop around the player from all directions and create really interesting gameplay.

To create the movement for our ship we are going to use a selection control technique called a **Switch Statement**. A switch statement allows a control variable to change how the program is

Ace Invaders – Part 1

being executed at any time. A switch statement is broken down into **cases**, each case holds a piece of code that is executed when the switch is turned on to that case. For example:

```
switch (e){
    case 1:
        print ("number 1");
        break;
    case 2:
        print ("number 2");
        break;
}
```

Here we have a `switch` statement with a control variable e. Each case has a number, so if e = 1 then "number 1" would be printed to the console. The premise for a switch statement is very simple, but has very useful applications. In general, programmers and scripters find the switch statement to be a better choice over using a sequence of `if-else` statements. The repetition of code is reduced and the code becomes easier to understand due to its encapsulation in case statements. Let's start now with our switch statement, add the following variables to the top of your script:

```
enum shipState {MOVINGUP,MOVINGDOWN,MOVINGLEFT,MOVINGRIGHT,
    SHOOT, IDLE};
var currentState : shipState;
var speed : float;
```

The first variable is a new one to us, this is an **enumerated** data type. An enumerated data type allows us to declare a set of named values called elements of the data type. So that basically means that `shipState` can be thought of as being able to be in any one of the 6 states that we have declared to the right of the variable. The second variable is called `currentState` and is given the type `shipState`. This means that the variable can hold the state of the ship based on one of the elements of the enumerated data type. The final variable will control the speed of the ship, but we won't use that until a bit later.

With our data type set up to track the state of our switch statement we can move on to utilizing it to set up the controls for the ship. For the purposes of this game we are going to use standard keyboard controls of UP, DOWN, LEFT and RIGHT. In the `Update()` function put the following:

```
function Update()
{
   if (Input.GetKey (KeyCode.UpArrow))
   {
      if(transform.position.y < 3.75){
         currentState = shipState.MOVINGUP;
      }
   }

   if (Input.GetKey (KeyCode.DownArrow))
    {
      if (transform.position.y > -3){
         currentState = shipState.MOVINGDOWN;
      }
    }

    if (Input.GetKey (KeyCode.LeftArrow))
    {
      if (transform.position.x > -2){
         currentState = shipState.MOVINGLEFT;
      }
    }

    if (Input.GetKey (KeyCode.RightArrow))
    {
      if (transform.position.x < 2){
         currentState = shipState.MOVINGRIGHT;
      }
    }
}
```

Here we create four conditional statements that check for key presses. We use `Input.GetKey` as this returns `true` while a user holds down an identified key, in our case the arrow keys. We then do a check on the ship's transform component to ensure that the ship has not moved beyond the boundaries of the game screen, if the ship is near the boundaries the keys become disabled. Finally we come to the line where we set what state our switch statement should be in. To see this in action, switch back to the editor and play the game, reveal the script in the inspector and use the arrow keys, the exposed variable `currentState` should change accordingly.

We come now to the most important part of the script where all the magic is going to happen, the switch statement! Put this function outside the `Update()`:

```
function ActionShip( state : shipState ) {
   switch (state) {
      case shipState.SHOOT:
         break;
      case shipState.MOVINGUP:
```

Ace Invaders – Part 1

```
            break;
        case shipState.MOVINGDOWN:
            break;
        case shipState.MOVINGLEFT:
            break;
        case shipState.MOVINGRIGHT:
            break;
    }
}
```

The switch statement is put inside a function called `ActionShip()` which takes in one argument of the data type `shipState` called `state`. The switch is then activated and a case is selected based on the contents of the `state` variable. To activate the switch statement we simply call the function with the `currentState` as the argument to pass. Make these amendments to the `Update()` function:

```
function Update()
{
    if (Input.GetKey (KeyCode.UpArrow))
    {
        if(transform.position.y < 3.75){
            currentState = shipState.MOVINGUP;
            ActionShip(currentState);
        }
    }

    if (Input.GetKey (KeyCode.DownArrow))
    {
        if (transform.position.y > -3){
            currentState = shipState.MOVINGDOWN;
            ActionShip(currentState);
        }
    }

    if (Input.GetKey (KeyCode.LeftArrow))
    {
        if (transform.position.x > -2){
            currentState = shipState.MOVINGLEFT;
            ActionShip(currentState);
        }
    }

    if (Input.GetKey (KeyCode.RightArrow))
    {
        if (transform.position.x < 2){
            currentState = shipState.MOVINGRIGHT;
            ActionShip(currentState);
        }
```

            }
        }

We are close to getting our ship up and running now. Let's keep the momentum going and make these changes to the switch statement:

```
function ActionShip( state : shipState ) {
    switch (state) {
        case shipState.SHOOT:
            break;
        case shipState.MOVINGUP:
            transform.Translate(0,speed*Time.deltaTime,0,
                Space.World);
            break;
        case shipState.MOVINGDOWN:
            transform.Translate(0,speed*-Time.deltaTime,0,
                Space.World);
            break;
        case shipState.MOVINGLEFT:
            transform.Translate(speed*-Time.deltaTime,0,0,
                Space.World);
            break;
        case shipState.MOVINGRIGHT:
            transform.Translate(speed*Time.deltaTime,0,0,
                Space.World);
            break;
    }
}
```

To move our ship we are using the `Translate` function of our ship's transform component. The `speed` variable is used with the `Time.deltaTime` to give us a value that will create a constant speed when the switch statement is activated, and we use positive and negative numbers to allow the ship to move in any direction in the screen. This is a great time to give it a try, go back to the editor, in the inspector change the `speed` variable from 0 to around 6 and hit play (Remember to use the arrow keys to move!!).

Pretty sweet huh? Next we move on to charging up the lasers, firing up the shields and kicking this bad boy into overdrive!!

Charge the weapons

Of course as you will be fully aware with your Intergalactic Space Driver's License that the ship is armed with two Class A Trident Torpedo Blasters. Our first port of call is to get these bad boys functional. Firstly navigate to the **Textures** folder under the hierarchy, find the **laser** texture and

Ace Invaders – Part 1

create a new material with it called **laser**, the texture should have transparency so be sure to create the material as a transparent diffuse material.

Create a new **plane** object and set its material to our newly created laser material. Now, as you will see, the plane is far too big and probably facing the wrong way. Rotate the plane around so that you can see it on the game screen and shrink it until it looks like a cool laser that fits the size of the ship. I ended up with `x = 0.013, y=0.05, z=0.05 0.013` for the scale and `270` for the X rotation.

Navigate to the Mesh Collider component in the inspector and remove it. Click on the **Component** menu at the top of the screen and select a new box collider. Expand the size property of the box collider and change the Y value to `0.5`, and make sure the **isTrigger** value is active. Add a **rigidbody** component to the object and deselect use gravity. Create a new prefab from this model called **laser** and delete the original from the scene.

Now we want our laser to shoot from the two ends of the ship. To do this we are going to create two empty game objects and position them in front of the ship just at the ends of the blasters. *Remember to make sure they are right at the ends of the blasters in all of the axes.*

Name the objects `shootSpwn1` and `shootSpwn2` and make them children of the ship. To make objects children of another object, select the objects you want to be children in the hierarchy view and drag them onto the object you want to be the parent. Finally rotate them 270 degrees in the X axis so that the blue arrow in the gizmo is pointing forward. This will make sure (later on) that the laser fires in the correct direction.

Open up the **shipController** script and let's put in some nice code to get these lasers firing. You will see from the script that our switch statement already has a case for the shooting functionality. We are going to stick with the tried and tested controls for shooters and make the **SPACE** bar the trigger for the lasers. Start by copy-pasting one of the `Input.GetKey if` statements and changing the `KeyCode` to `Space` like so:

```
if (Input.GetKey (KeyCode.Space)){
    currentState = shipState.SHOOT;
    ActionShip(currentState);
}
```

Excellent, now every time we press and hold the space bar the `SHOOT` case will be activated. Let's declare a couple of variables that we will use to get these lasers firing properly:

```
var laser : GameObject;
var shootSpwnPos1 : GameObject;
var shootSpwnPos2 : GameObject;
private var initialLaserSpeed = 10;
private var fireRate : float = 0.2;
private var nextFire = 0.0;
```

Now set the laser object prefab in the inspector, along with the `shootSpwnPos1` and `shootSpwnPos2` objects, these are found in the **scene** tab and not the **assets** tab of the game object select pop up.

Next, go to the SHOOT case and put in this code:

```
var cloneLaser1 : GameObject = Instantiate(laser,
    shootSpwnPos1.transform.position,
        shootSpwnPos1.transform.rotation) as GameObject;

cloneLaser1.rigidbody.velocity =transform.TransformDirection
    (Vector3.up*initialLaserSpeed);

var cloneLaser2 : GameObject = Instantiate(laser,
    shootSpwnPos2.transform.position,
        shootSpwnPos2.transform.rotation) as GameObject;

cloneLaser2.rigidbody.velocity = transform.TransformDirection
    (Vector3.up*initialLaserSpeed);
```

We use the `instantiate` function to create a laser object at the position of both spawn points. When the object has been created we access the velocity value of its `rigidbody` component with a direction, in this case `Vector3.up` and multiply it by `initialLaserSpeed`. Hit the play button and check out your lasers.

What you will probably notice is that there are a lot of lasers instantiated, in fact it's basically a string steady line of lasers when you hold down the space bar. This isn't particularly realistic, any ballistic system has a *rate of fire* that governs how fast the weapon shoots. Above, we declared two variables:

```
private var fireRate : float = 0.2;
private var nextFire = 0.0;
```

Use these variables to expand the SPACE bar code:

```
if (Input.GetKey (KeyCode.Space)&&Time.time > nextFire)
{
    nextFire = Time.time + fireRate;
    currentState = shipState.SHOOT;
    ActionShip(currentState);
}
```

The `if` now has an extra check to do each time space is pressed, where the variable `Time.time` is checked to see if it is greater than the `nextFire` variable. If it is, we set the value of the `nextFire` variable to equal the value in `Time.time` plus the `fireRate`. The next time the check is done `nextFire` will be greater than `Time.time` and the laser won't be fired.

`Time.time` is not under our control and keeps incrementing over time and when the next check is done it is back to being greater that the `nextFire` variable. In this way the laser is given a cyclic fire rate.

With our lasers firing at an optimum rate, the next task is to remove them from the scene. The lasers will be subject to two rules when they are created. The first is that if they hit an enemy they will be destroyed. The second is that after 4 seconds they will be destroyed and removed from the scene to ensure that we don't affect the game's performance by instantiating hundreds of lasers. Create a new script called **laserDestroy** and put in the following code:

```
function Start()
{
    run();
}

function run()
{
    yield WaitForSeconds(4);
    Destroy(this.gameObject);
}

function OnTriggerEnter(col : Collider)
{
    if (col.tag == "enemy")
    {
        Destroy(this.gameObject);
    }
}
```

When the object is instantiated the function `run()` is called once which starts a `yield` statement that waits for 4 seconds before destroying the object. Simple! The final function destroys the laser on collision with an enemy which we will utilize in the next chapter.

Summary

It's starting to look pretty good, even if I dare say so myself. This has been a great chapter to introduce you to two very good techniques for scrolling backgrounds in games. The first - **Parallax Scrolling** is an excellent technique for when you have built up a complicated 3D scene and want to repeat it over time.

The second method of **UV Scrolling** is used to animate the clouds is a perfect way to animate tileable textures on a plane that doesn't have a z dimension. Using this scrolling technique we managed to avoid that nasty Z-Fighting effect which can be seen when two meshes are close to each other.

We have also got a fair chunk of the interactive functionality working in the game with our ship. The utilization of the switch statement really makes the code that much tidier and easier to manage.

We have a clearly defined case system that allows us to easily switch between the different states that the ship can be in.

Our next port of call is with the antagonists of our game. We will take a look at the enemy ships, looking at their movements and in particular how to create wave patterns with different types of enemies to give the game a bit more of a dynamic feel. Grab yourself a soda, get refreshed and let's head on to the next chapter.

Chapter 5

Ace Invaders – Part 2

Our shooter is starting to look the business. The post-apocalyptic atmospheric world is in, flight navigation systems are functional, and of course we have our kick ass photon laser cannons. All we need now is something to shoot at!

Enemies in games like ours have come in all shapes and sizes over the years. But one thing that they have in common is that they appear to the player in "waves". These waves of enemies come in an almost infinite number of patterns and shapes, challenging the player to come up with strategies to defeat particular sets of waves. In Ikaruga a wave of enemies enters the screen in a circular pattern around the player which begins to shrink towards the player's ship. The player has to carve a hole in the circle of enemies and escape before they consume the ship. The fact that the player has to rely on some form of strategy to keep defeating the waves of enemies is why most games like Ikaruga are scripted and the generation of the enemies is designed and not randomized. This is where game designers make their money; a balance must be maintained between challenging play and allowing the user to progress once they have learned how to tackle specific waves. We will spend a little bit of time taking this into consideration.

Let's quickly take a look at the breakdown of this chapter and move straight on to the game:

- The design of and implementation of enemy waves.
- Collision detection.
- Player HUD (Heads Up Display).

Our choice in enemies!

Let's start by getting the enemy models downloaded from the website:

> www.deeppixel.com/UnityBookPackages/Shooter/enemies.unitypackage

Import them into Unity and check that the usual elements, scale factor, collisions are all in order. Also check the materials that have been included in the import, we have had times when Unity loses the connection to the textures from the materials. If some of the materials don't have a texture,

Ace Invaders – Part 2

select the appropriate one from the two enemy textures provided with the package. This import may also not put the materials in the correct folder, select them all and move them to keep your project nice and manageable.

Now, put both models into the scene and you should see two very snazzy alien enemies like the ones below:

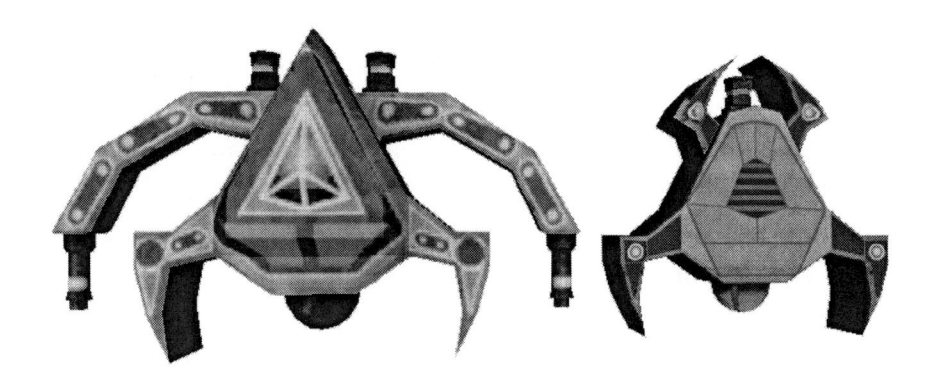

You will see two other models called **enemy1_Death** and **enemy2_Death**, we won't use them just now. You will notice the enemies are a tad on the small side, increase their X, Y and Z scale values to **0.014**. Click on the enemy and in the inspector you will see all the normal components, collider, material, but in order to get this guy active and moving we need a **rigidbody.**

We start by creating a new prefab called **enemy1**, under the Prefabs folder, and click and drag our **enemy1** model onto it. Next add the **rigidbody** component and remember to uncheck the **Use Gravity** variable. You will be prompted to lose the prefab, hit ok, and then apply the changes to your prefab. Repeat this process for the **enemy2** model.

Excellent, now what we need is a little script to attach to the enemy. Create one called **normalEnemy** and add it to the **enemy1** and **enemy2** prefabs (remember to apply changes to the prefabs). There are two functions that we want our enemy to be able to perform: shooting and dying! When an enemy enters the screen it should shoot, and when it is hit by the player's photon cannon it should be destroyed.

Fire() in the hole

Let's start by declaring some variables in the script:

```
private var startTime : float;
private var shootTimeLeft : float;
private var shootTimeSeconds = 1;
var enemylaser : GameObject;
private var laserSpeed = 0.8;
```

In the `Update()` function put the following code:

```
shootTimeLeft = Time.time - startTime;
if(shootTimeLeft >= shootTimeSeconds){
    Fire();
    startTime = Time.time;
    shootTimeLeft = 0.0;
}
```

Then after the `Update()` function, create a new function called `Fire()`:

```
function Fire(){

}
```

Before we move on, quickly duplicate the **laser** prefab we currently have and call it **enemyLaser**. We will need to differentiate the two later on.

In the `Update()` function we have used a similar method to our ship shooting mechanism that allows the enemy to shoot based on the variable `shootTimeSeconds`. We have a value of 1 in there so the enemy should shoot its cannon every 1 second. Let's get the code in to fire the cannon. Add these lines to the `Fire()` function:

```
var instLaser : GameObject = Instantiate (enemylaser,
    transform.position, transform.rotation);

instLaser.rigidbody.velocity =
    transform.TransformDirection(Vector3.up*-laserSpeed);
```

Now if you jump back to the Unity editor, click on the **enemy1** and **enemy2** objects and in the inspector select the **enemyLaser** prefab for the laser game object variable. Now hit play and you should be able to see the lasers being instantiated but they are facing the wrong direction. This is again similar to the ship where we need a spawn point for our laser that is facing in the right direction.

So, make an empty game object and place it in front of our **enemy1**. Give its rotational X axis a value of 270, make it a child of the **enemy1** and call it **shootSpwn**. Do the same for **enemy2**. Declare a new variable in the **normalEnemy(bold)** script:

```
private var shootSpwnT : Transform;
```

83

Ace Invaders – Part 2

Add in a start function like this:

```
function Start()
{
    shootSpwnT = this.transform.Find("shootSpwn");
}
```

Finally, alter the laser instantiation code to match this:

```
var instLaser : GameObject = Instantiate (enemylaser,
    shootSpwnT.transform.position,
    shootSpwnT.transform.rotation);
```

Hit play and you should have an enemy that fires! Now you may have noticed that rather than using `gameObject.Find`, we have used `transform.Find` to find our spawn object for the enemy laser. This method is used when you are looking to access a child of a game object. It also ensures that the script finds each enemy's unique `shootSpwn` object, rather than just finding one.

Feel free to play about with the speed and shoot time of the laser, we will be looking at these again when we come to create the waves. Next we will look at the enemy death animations.

What a way to go

The final piece of functionality we want our enemies to have is to be destroyed by the player. Click on both the **enemy1_Death** and **enemy2_Death** objects to ensure that their scale factors are set to 1 and **Generate Colliders** is active. Now if you scroll down to the bottom of the inspector in both of the objects you will see the animations section. In this section check to see that the values match the following:

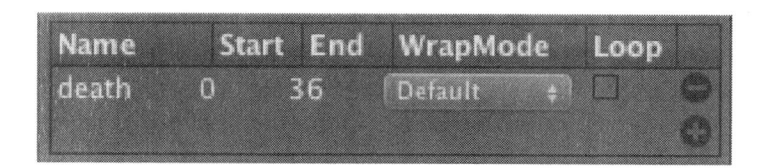

Name	Start	End	WrapMode	Loop
death	0	36	Default	☐

If not click the **add (+)** button and put in the values above. Place both death models in the scene and immediately you will see that they are smaller than their counterparts, increase the size of the **enemy1_Death** and **enemy2_Death** models to match the size of the other ones. Hit the play button to see the animations. As you will notice, the pieces remain after they have exploded, this will be where we remove them from the scene in the script. Delete the death models from the scene and move over to the **normalEnemy** script. Declare a game object variable for the death animation:

```
var enemyDeath : GameObject;
var deathAnim : GameObject;
```

Next create a new `OnTriggerEnter()` function:
```
function OnTriggerEnter(col : Collider)
{
   if (col.tag == "laser")
   {
      renderer.enabled = false;
      deathAnim = Instantiate(enemyDeath,
         transform.position, transform.rotation)as GameObject;
      deathAnim.animation["death"].speed = 2;
   }
}
```

Now, what you will notice here is that we have a condition that says that the death animation will only be played if the enemy object collides with an object that has the tag `laser`.

So, head back into Unity and in the project view, locate the laser prefab and add a tag to it called **laser**. To add a **tag**, click on the object to be tagged and locate the tag dropdown at the top left of the inspector.

Expand the menu and click **Add tag...**, this opens a new window in the inspector. At the top you will see the word Tags with an arrow to the left; clicking on the arrow will expand the menu. Click to the right of `Element 0` and type in the word "laser". Navigate back to the object and assign the new tag by clicking the drop down menu and selecting the appropriate tag. Voila your laser is tagged.

Next, assign the relevant enemy death animations to each enemy object; hit play, shoot at an enemy once and it should explode! Shoot it constantly and the death animation will play over and over, we will fix this after taking a look at the previous code snippet. If the animation isn't playing the chances are that your ship's lasers and the enemies aren't colliding. Make sure the ships and enemy's Z position is the same.

In the code above we are doing a nice little trick where we make the current model of the enemy disappear by disabling its renderer. We do this because if we destroyed it then the script would be destroyed as well and the script that is attached to the enemy is still controlling the animation. We then instantiate the death animation object and use the speed function of the animation component to increase the speed of the animation by a factor of 2. Let's move on and take a look at tidying up the animation. We need to be able to tell the script when the enemy has been hit and only play the animation once. So let's declare a nice boolean value to use:
```
var canBeHit = true;
```

With the `OnTriggerEnter()` function we will put an conditional statement in to check if the enemy can be hit:

Ace Invaders – Part 2

```
function OnTriggerEnter(col : Collider)
{
    if (canBeHit == true)
    {
        if (col.tag == "laser")
        {
            canBeHit = false;
            renderer.enabled = false;
            deathAnim = Instantiate(enemyDeath,
                transform.position, transform.rotation) as
            GameObject;
            deathAnim.animation["death"].speed = 2;
        }
    }
}
```

If you go back to the editor and play the scene, the animation now only plays once the enemy is shot. The final step in the creation of our enemy is to remove all trace of the enemy from the scene.

Put this code in the `Update()` function:

```
if (deathAnim != null){
    if (!deathAnim.animation.IsPlaying("death"))
    {
        Destroy(deathAnim);
        Destroy(this.gameObject);
    }
}
```

Here we do a check on every frame to see if the death animation has been instantiated. When this has happened, the code then checks to see when the animation has finished playing. When this happens, the animation and the original enemy game object are destroyed. Run the scene and you will be able to destroy the enemy completely. We now have our first fully functional enemies.

You don't want to catch these waves

With our enemy functionality sorted we can move onto sending the enemies to the player in challenging and interesting ways. As said at the start of the chapter, the most common term for how enemies appear in space ship shooters is **waves**. The design of these waves is generally left up to a game designer who must meticulously balance and test each wave to see how players strategize in order to overcome each wave.

The scope of this book will only allow us to scratch the surface of this design work but we will do our best to equip you with the techniques that will allow you to go off experimenting on your own. We will look at two ways of creating waves of enemies. The first is a very simple waypoint system, which allows the enemies to shoot across the screen firing at the player. The second is an augmentation of the first, where we utilize the waypoint system but use code to animate a wave pattern to make the shapes of the waves a bit more dynamic.

Wave 1

Wave 1 will be our bog standard attack wave. Enemies will enter from one side of the screen and move in a diagonal motion to the other side of the screen and leave. The diagram below outlines the general idea:

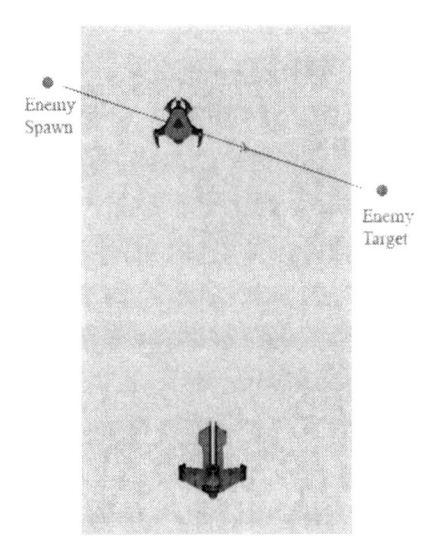

The **Enemy Spawn** point gives us positional information for where the enemy will be instantiated. The **Enemy Target** point gives the enemy a position to aim for during its flight across the screen. Let's dive in now and try this out.

First create an empty game object, and name it **enemySpwn1**. Move it to a position that is in the top left hand corner of the screen, out of the view of the player. The idea here is that the player doesn't see the enemy being instantiated. Create another empty game object and name it **enemyTarg1**. Place this just off the other side of the screen to create an imaginary diagonal line, just like the image above. As we did above, ensure that the Z position for each of these objects is the same as the ship. Excellent we have the nice path on which our enemies will travel across the screen. Next on the agenda is the script.

Game Manager

In the Match the Pairs game, we used only one script to control our game. As you will have noticed we have several scripts controlling this game, each with their own control over the object they are

Ace Invaders – Part 2

attached to. Now we could keep going, creating lots of scripts of each object on the screen, but this becomes a little bit counterproductive when trying to map out all of the different interactions over each script. So what we are going to do is create a script that will act as our **game manager**. The game manager will control things like:

- Creation of enemy waves.
- Score.
- GUI.
- Player re-spawning.

So let's create a new empty game object and name it **gameManager**, then create a script with the same name and attach it to our newly created empty object. Right, let's start on our script by declaring these variables:

```
var enemySpwn1 : Transform;
var enemyTarg1 : Transform;
var enemyPrefab : GameObject;
var targetDir : Vector3;
private var enemySpeed = 0.1;
```

These variables, I'm sure, are very straightforward for you to understand. We have two transform variables to hold the positional data for our two spawn points. A variable to hold the enemy prefab, the `targetDir` variable will be used to hold the direction in which the second spawn point is from the first, and `enemySpeed` gives us a nice float number that can be adjusted to get various speeds of enemy movement.

Next on the agenda is a little `Start()` function:

```
function Start()
{
    targetDir = enemyTarg1.position - enemySpwn1.transform.
        position;
    SendEnemy();
}
```

In the first line we work out the direction of the second spawn target from the first by subtracting the two vectors, this gives us a new vector which we can use as a value that (when multiplied by our speed variable) should move the enemy in the direction of the second spawn point. Finally we have a function call to `sendEnemy()`:

```
function SendEnemy()
{
```

```
    var instantiatedProjectile : GameObject = Instantiate
       (enemyPrefab, enemySpwn1.transform.position,
           this.transform.rotation);

    instantiatedProjectile.rigidbody.velocity =
       transform.TransformDirection(targetDir*enemySpeed);
}
```

This function is almost identical to that of the `Fire()` function that controls the firing of an enemy's photon cannon that we created earlier in this chapter. Again we instantiate the object which is our enemy, then using the object's rigidbody we access its `velocity` and use the `TransformDirection` function to work out where the object should move to using the variables we have at our disposal.

Go back to the editor. In the inspector, navigate to the **gameManager** script and select the appropriate objects for, `EnemySpwn1`, `EnemyTarg1` and `EnemyPrefab`. **Make sure you select the prefabs and not the original models.** Also ensure that all the correct objects are selected for both enemy prefabs variables. The result should be the enemy moving across the screen from left to right shooting at you!!

Wave 2

For our second wave we are going to spice things up a little bit and create one that is a bit more visually interesting and challenging for the player. The pattern we are going for this time will be similar to the one below. The enemies will rotate in a clockwise fashion while moving between the enemy spawn and target.

Ace Invaders – Part 2

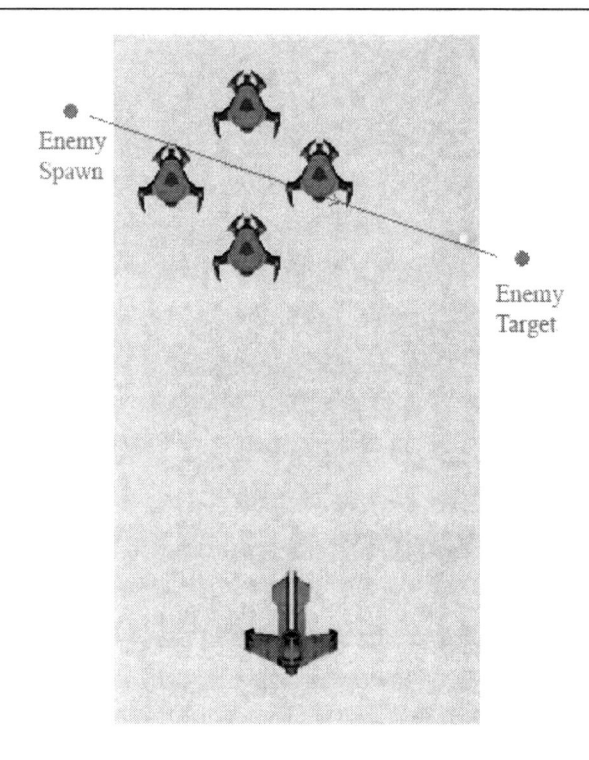

We will start by making the enemy wave, so create a new empty game object and name it **wave2**; add a **rigidbody** component, and turn off gravity. Drag four enemies onto the scene view and child them to the **wave2** object. Arrange the enemies around the parent object like so:

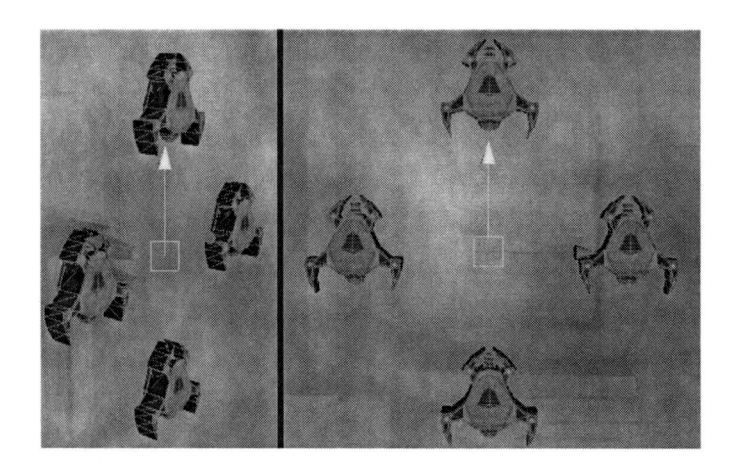

Remember to ensure that the parent object's Z axis is equal to 0 to ensure the enemies and the ship are on the same level.

Excellent, now for the purpose of this wave of enemies - we are going to have to make some alterations to the enemies themselves. On each enemy's **rigidbody**, activate **isKinematic**. By making the enemy objects kinematic we tell the engine not to allow physics to affect this object, therefore any forces that are applied will not affect their movement. Finally, make this group of objects into a prefab called **wave2**.

> When developing this second wave I had a problem where I was getting weird rotations around the parent of the enemies. It turns out (after some fresh eyes had a look) that having each object including the parent as rigidbodies was causing some grief. I removed the rigidbodies and thought to myself, excellent problem solved. Then I tried to shoot the enemies and obviously I couldn't because they had no rigidbody to collide with! I'm going to be very honest here, the solution was a complete fluke. I had a go at flicking some of the check boxes on and off in the inspector for the enemies. It turned out like discussed above. If **isKinematic** is set then the rotations are normal! Try turning off **isKinematic** and you will see what I mean :)

We will move on now to create the script and call it **wave2Script**. This is a small script so here it is:

```
var rotationDirection = Vector3(0, 0, 1);
var rotationSpeed = 50.0;
private var parentTransform : Transform;

function Update(){
    parentTransform=this.transform.parent;
}

function FixedUpdate() {
    if (parentTransform!=null) {
        transform.RotateAround(parentTransform.position,
            rotationDirection, rotationSpeed *
                Time.deltaTime);
        this.transform.rotation.z = 0;
    }
}
```

The variables are self-explanatory. In the `Update()` function we check on each frame what the position of the parent object is, and store it in the `parentTransform` variable. We then make use of the `FixedUpdate()` function to execute our code on every fixed framerate frame. This makes sure that our rotations have a consistent movement and are not affected by a frame rate that

Ace Invaders – Part 2

is either too fast or too slow depending on the performance of the system that is running the game. We utilize the `RotateAround` function to move the objects around the parent object.

If we take a look at the script reference the function looks like this:

```
function RotateAround (point : Vector3, axis : Vector3, angle : 
    float) : void
```

We use the position of the parent as the point, and use the `rotationDirection` variable to give us our axis, which in this case is Z. Finally we work out the angle using our `rotationSpeed` which is increased over time using our old friend `Time.deltaTime`.

Now attach this script to each of the enemies and hit play to see them rotate around! Be sure to **apply your changes to the prefab** from the **GameObject** menu.

Move over to the **gameManager** object and in the inspector change the enemy prefab to **wave2** to see the new wave spawn in game. Great, we now have our two waves that we will use in the game. The next step is to expand on the game manager to allow a number of waves to be sent to attack the player.

Wave Generator

To make our waves a bit more interesting we need another couple of spawn points. So duplicate two objects from the existing spawn points and set them up on the opposite side of the screen. So **enemySpwn2** should be on the right hand side, with **enemyTarg2** on the left. Now there are literally hundreds of ways we could implement our wave generator, such is the joy of programming! However for the scope of this book we are going to implement a relatively simple one where 5 waves of enemies are sent to the player over a period of time.

> **Challenge:** try implementing a wave generator system that sends waves based on how well the player is doing!!

Open the **gameManager** script and add in these variables, replacing all of the old ones:

```
var enemySpwn1 : Transform;
var enemyTarg1 : Transform;
var enemySpwn2 : Transform;
var enemyTarg2 : Transform;
var enemyPrefab1 : GameObject;
var enemyPrefab2 : GameObject;
var enemyPrefab3 : GameObject;
var enemySpeed = 0.1;
var enemySpeed2 = 0.2;
private var targetSpwnDir1 : Vector3;
private var targetSpwnDir2 : Vector3;
```

We need two directions for each of our enemy spawn paths so make these alterations to the `Start()` function:

```
function Start()
{
    targetSpwnDir1 = enemyTarg1.position - enemySpwn1.position;
    targetSpwnDir2 = enemyTarg2.position - enemySpwn2.position;
}
```

Now, as I said before, this solution is very lo-fi, but therein lies the challenge for you to come up with something more engaging. So we are going to use 5 functions to instantiate each one of our waves, so put these under the `Start()` function:

```
function SendWave1()
{
    for (var i = 0; i <= 3; i++)
    {
        var instantiatedProjectile : GameObject = Instantiate
            (enemyPrefab1, enemySpwn1.transform.position,
                this.transform.rotation);
        instantiatedProjectile.rigidbody.velocity =
            transform.TransformDirection(targetSpwnDir1*enemySpeed2);
            yield WaitForSeconds(1.0);
    }
}

function SendWave2()
{
    for (var i = 0; i <= 5; i++)
    {
        var instantiatedProjectile : GameObject = Instantiate
            (enemyPrefab2, enemySpwn2.transform.position,
                this.transform.rotation);
        instantiatedProjectile.rigidbody.velocity =
            transform.TransformDirection(targetSpwnDir2*enemySpeed);
        yield WaitForSeconds(1.0);
    }
}

function SendWave3()
{
    var instantiatedProjectile : GameObject = Instantiate
        (enemyPrefab3, enemySpwn1.transform.position,
            this.transform.rotation);
    instantiatedProjectile.rigidbody.velocity =
        transform.TransformDirection(targetSpwnDir1*enemySpeed2);
    yield WaitForSeconds(1.0);
}
```

Ace Invaders – Part 2

```
function SendWave4()
{
    for (var i = 0; i <= 7; i++)
    {
        var instantiatedProjectile : GameObject = Instantiate
            (enemyPrefab2, enemySpwn2.transform.position,
                this.transform.rotation);
        instantiatedProjectile.rigidbody.velocity =
            transform.TransformDirection(targetSpwnDir2*enemySpeed);
        yield WaitForSeconds(1.0);
    }
}

function SendWave5()
{
    var instantiatedProjectile : GameObject = Instantiate
        (enemyPrefab3, enemySpwn1.transform.position,
            this.transform.rotation);
    instantiatedProjectile.rigidbody.velocity =
        transform.TransformDirection(targetSpwnDir1*enemySpeed2);
    yield WaitForSeconds(1.0);
}
```

Each wave uses a `for` loop to instantiate a number of enemies at a particular spawn point with a particular speed. The circular wave is instantiated on its own without the use of a `for` loop. All we need now is to simply call these functions in the `Start()` function after the target direction has been calculated:

```
SendWave1();
yield WaitForSeconds(5);
SendWave2();
yield WaitForSeconds(5);
SendWave3();
yield WaitForSeconds(5);
SendWave4();
SendWave5();
```

Alter the **gameManager** script in the inspector to match this:

Game Manager (Script) inspector panel:

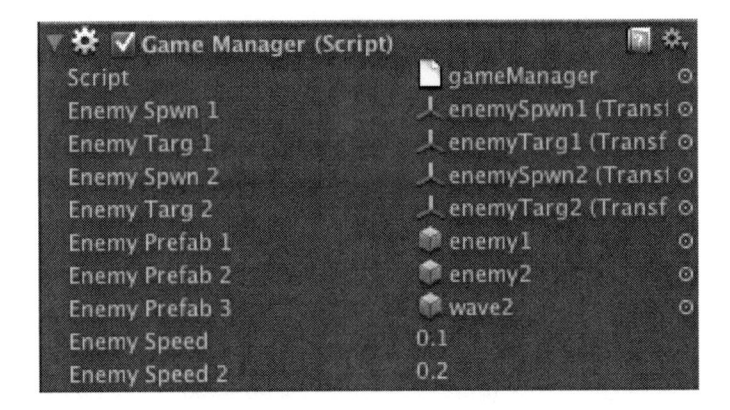

Script	gameManager
Enemy Spwn 1	enemySpwn1 (Transf)
Enemy Targ 1	enemyTarg1 (Transf)
Enemy Spwn 2	enemySpwn2 (Transf)
Enemy Targ 2	enemyTarg2 (Transf)
Enemy Prefab 1	enemy1
Enemy Prefab 2	enemy2
Enemy Prefab 3	wave2
Enemy Speed	0.1
Enemy Speed 2	0.2

After making these changes, hit play and you should see 5 waves of enemies hurtling down to destroy your ship!

Lives save lives

With our enemies swarming around us, photon cannons charged and a bloodthirsty look about them, it's time to make our ship vulnerable to attack. At the moment the enemy fire merely bounces off our hull; what we want to do is up the stakes a bit and make the enemy fire count. We are going to stick to the old space shooter adage of "one hit, one kill" just like we have for the enemies, so if the ship is hit it will be destroyed.

Open up the **shipController** script and add in these variables:

```
var playerInvincible = false;
var gameMgObj : GameObject;
```

Next add in an `OnTriggerEnter()` function:

```
function OnTriggerEnter(enemy : Collider)
{
    if (enemy.tag == "enemyLaser" || enemy.tag == "enemy"){
        Destroy(this.gameObject);
    }
}
```

If something collides with our player that is called `enemyLaser` or `enemy` then the ship is destroyed. If you play the game now and allow an enemy's laser to hit you it probably won't do anything. This is because the **enemyLaser** doesn't have a tag yet. We are also using the **laser** material for the enemies as well as our ship so let's quickly sort this. Download the texture from this url:

Ace Invaders – Part 2

www.deeppixel.com/UnityBookPackages/Shooter/enemyLaser.unitypackage

Create a new material called **redLaser** with a transparent/Diffuse shader on it and select the texture you just downloaded. Now change the **enemyLaser** prefabs name to **enemyLaser1** and apply the new material. Next, duplicate the **enemyLaser1** prefab and call it **enemyLaser2**. Duplicate the **redLaser** material and change its name to **blueLaser** and alter its colour using the **Main Color** picker in the inspector of the material. Apply this new material to the new **enemyLaser2** prefab.

You should now have two enemy lasers of differing colours. Last but not least, create a new tag called **enemyLaser** and apply it to both new enemy laser prefabs.

If you click on both **enemy1** and **enemy2** you will see they both have **enemyLaser1** as their primary laser. Change **enemy2**'s laser to the new blue one we created. Hit play and you will see the lasers, but they might look a bit squished. That is because the texture we have for both is square in dimension. Put both **enemyLaser1** and **enemyLaser2** prefabs onto the hierarchy view and change their X scale to match the Y and Z. This should give you a round looking photon.

With our lasers set up, hit play again and move into an oncoming laser to see the ship disappear. Now the ship is similar to the enemies in that it has a death animation. If you navigate to the **Models** folder you'll see **playerShip_Death**. Click on it and in the inspector ensure that all the import settings are correct. Check to see if the animation section has been set, with the name **death** and a Start of 0 and an End of 48. If not put these values in now.

To keep things a bit tidier and get some more practice with accessing other objects and scripts we will be controlling the ships death and re-spawn from the **gameManager** script, so open that up now. We will create two functions, called `destroyPlayer()` and `respawnPlayer()`.

Update the **gameManager**'s variables with these:

```
var playerObj : GameObject;
var playerSpwn : Transform;
var respawn = false;
var playerLives = 4;
var script1 : Component;
var player1 : GameObject;
var shield : GameObject;
var playerDeathObj : GameObject;
```

Next add in the `destroyPlayer()` function:

```
function destroyPlayer(dpos : Vector3)
{
   var player1 : GameObject = Instantiate(playerDeathObj,
      dpos, playerDeathObj.transform.rotation) as GameObject;
   player1.animation["death"].speed = 3.5;
   yield WaitForSeconds(0.5);
   Destroy (player1);
}
```

This function takes in a **Vector3** position that tells it what position the ship was at, when it was destroyed. With the ship model being destroyed in the **shipController** script, we can then instantiate the **playerShip_Death** model at the position received and control its animation to speed it up to an appropriate level. We then wait for a period of time before destroying the newly instantiated ship death game object.

Now this function won't work straight off the bat because we haven't yet called it from anywhere. Move back to the **shipController** and create the `Start()` function with this line of code:

```
gameMgObj = gameObject.Find("gameManager");
```

Then update the `OnTriggerEnter()` function with these lines of code inside the `if` statement:

```
var script1 = gameMgObj.transform.gameObject.GetComponent
    ("gameManager");
var pPosition = transform.position;
script1.destroyPlayer(pPosition);
script1.respawn = true;
script1.playerLives -=1;
```

Here we are finding an instance of the **gameManager** and accessing the script on the object called **gameManager**. We then take the final position of the ship and call the `destroyPlayer()` function, sending across the position we just got.

We now have the necessary code to let our ship be destroyed. Navigate back to the inspector and in the **GameManager** script select the **playerShip_Death** model for the `playerDeathObj` variable. Hit play and see the results:

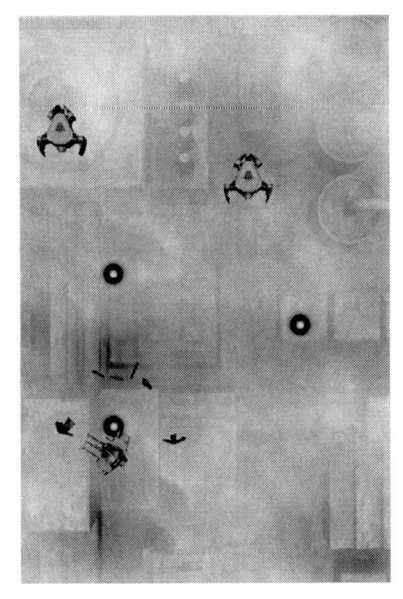

Ace Invaders – Part 2

Be kind, Respawn

We turn now to that mainstay of all games, the player respawn. When the ship is destroyed we want the player to be instantly respawned at the original start location of the ship and given a shield which makes it invincible to attack for a short period of time.

To identify what position we want for our respawn, create an empty game object and call it **playerSpwn**. Change the objects positional data to the following:

   x = 0

   y = -3.5

   z = -0.5

Next, open up the **gameManager** script and add in this function:

```
function respawnPlayer()
{
    player1 = Instantiate(playerObj,playerSpwn.transform.
        position,playerObj.transform.rotation) as GameObject;
    respawn = false;
}
```

Now if you quickly go back to the **shipController** script and look in the `OnTriggerEnter()` function, you will see where we set the variable **respawn** to `true`. We can use this boolean to call our `respawnPlayer()` function. Go back to the **gameManager** script and put in this check in the `Update()` function:

```
if (respawn == true && playerLives != 0)
{
    respawnPlayer();
}
```

This `if` condition is initialized when `respawn` is set to `true` and `playerLives` does not equal 0. When the respawn is called, a new player ship object is instantiated at the player's spawn position. Move back to the editor and, in the inspector of the **gameManager**, change the values to match these:

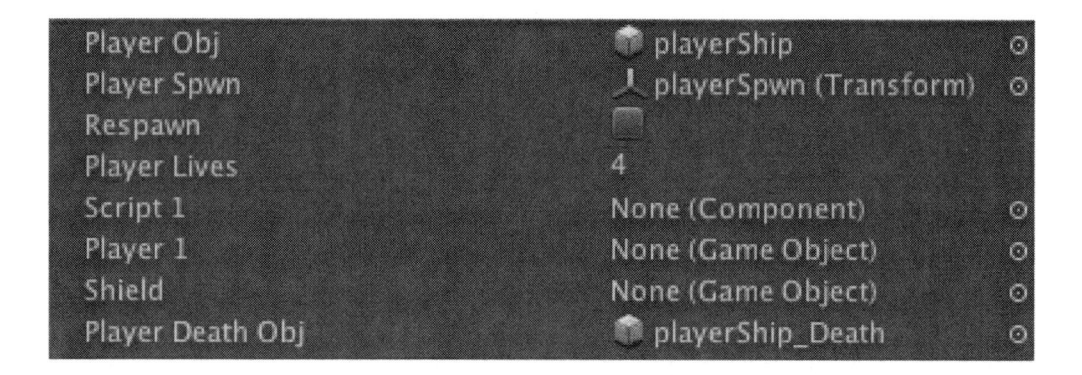

Player Obj	playerShip
Player Spwn	playerSpwn (Transform)
Respawn	
Player Lives	4
Script 1	None (Component)
Player 1	None (Game Object)
Shield	None (Game Object)
Player Death Obj	playerShip_Death

> If you haven't made the **playerShip** a prefab yet do so now and assign it to the `Player Obj` variable in the inspector.

Hit the play button and a new ship should be respawned when the old ship is destroyed. You'll notice that the ship is spawned right back into the thick of battle and chances are it may be respawned on an enemy laser which would destroy it through no fault of the player. This is where a period of invincibility is useful. Most games give players anywhere between 1 and 3 seconds to compose themselves before their ship or character comes under attack again. For our purposes we are going to create a shield that will surround the player for 2 seconds to allow them to quickly regain control of the situation.

Let's start with the shield itself. Go to this URL and download the package:

www.deeppixel.com/UnityBookPackages/Shooter/shield.unitypackage

The package contains a prefab for the ship's shield, including a texture and a material. Take this prefab and make it a child of the **playerShip** object in the scene. Be sure to apply the changes to the ship prefab by selecting **GameObject > Apply Changes To Prefab**.

Now in the **shipController** script, add in these variables:

```
var shield : GameObject;
var shieldOn = false;
var guiTime : float;
var seconds : int;
var startTime : float;
```

Ace Invaders – Part 2

Next, update the `Start()` function:

```
shield = gameObject.Find("shield");
shield.renderer.enabled = false;
startTime = Time.time;
```

Then the `Update()` function:

```
    if (shieldOn == true){
       activateShield();

    }else{
       deActivateShield();
    }

    guiTime = Time.time - startTime;
    seconds = guiTime % 60;
    print (seconds);
    if (seconds == 3){
       playerInvincible = false;
       shieldOn = false;
    }
```

Finally add two new functions:

```
function activateShield()
{
    shield.renderer.enabled = true;
}

function deActivateShield()
{
    shield.renderer.enabled = false;
}
```

The premise behind this code is to constantly have the shield attached to the **playerShip** object and turn it off and on using its renderer. So when the player is respawned the `shieldOn` variable is set to `true`, which activates the shield; we then start a timer which counts three seconds before turning off the shield. To make this happen, put the following code in the `RespawnPlayer()` function, after we instantiate the new ship:

```
startTime = Time.time;
var script1 = player1.transform.gameObject.GetComponent
    ("shipController");
script1.shieldOn = true;
```

We first reset the `startTime` to allow the shield timer to count to three in order to deactivate the shield. We then access the `shipController` script and set `shieldOn` to `true` to activate the shield. The variable `respawn` is then set to false to stop the function being called more than once.

To prevent the player receiving any damage while the shield is active we have to create a `playerInvincible` conditional statement. Now we have the variable declared from above, all that is left to do is navigate to the `OnTriggerEnter()` function in the **playerShip** script and put this `if` statement around the code inside there:

```
if (playerInvincible == false)
{
}
```

Set this variable in the `RespawnPlayer()` in the `shipController` like so:

```
script1.playerInvincible = true;
```

This ensures that the player can only be shot at when the shield is deactivated. Hit the play button now and see the results. Excellent, we are nearly at the finishing line. Next we will look at sprucing the game up a bit and adding in a GUI to track the player's score and number of lives.

On Screen!

As with all great 2D shoot'em ups, the GUI forms an important part of the gameplay. Specifically, the scoring system encourages the player to constantly strive for a better score, pushing hard and harder and playing for longer, which obviously is every game developer's wish.

A trend that has popped back up since the old coin op days is scoring on a very large scale, so rather than 1 point for destroying 1 enemy ship, it can be 10,000 upwards. Looking at a score in the millions is a heartening thing, the iPhone game **Solipskier** allows users to score into the hundreds of millions. I once proudly passed my iPhone around the table showing off my 6 million score in the game, only to have my very inebriated friend pull out his iPhone and trounce my score with a whopping 64 million! I resolved to beat his score and have been trying ever since!

Let's get cracking on our GUI, open up the **gameManager** script and declare these variables:

```
var playerLivesTxt : Texture2D;
var playerScore = 0;
var style : GUIStyle;
```

Put this in after the `Update()` function:

```
function OnGUI()
{
    GUI.Label (Rect (20, 660, 74, 85),playerLivesTxt, style);
```

Ace Invaders – Part 2

```
        GUI.Label (Rect (50, 660, 50, 50),playerLives.ToString(),
            style);
        GUI.Label (Rect (300,700, 200, 50),playerScore.ToString(),
            style);
}
```

Now head on over to the website and download this texture and font:

www.deeppixel.com/UnityBookPackages/Shooter/GUITexture.unitypackage

This texture is a nice little graphic of the ship that will sit next to the number of lives the player has left. Now navigate to the newly imported font and change the size to 24. Finally, go back to the **gameManager** inspector, apply the **PlayerLivesTxt** variable using the life texture you just imported. Then expand the style variable and make the following changes:

Chapter 5

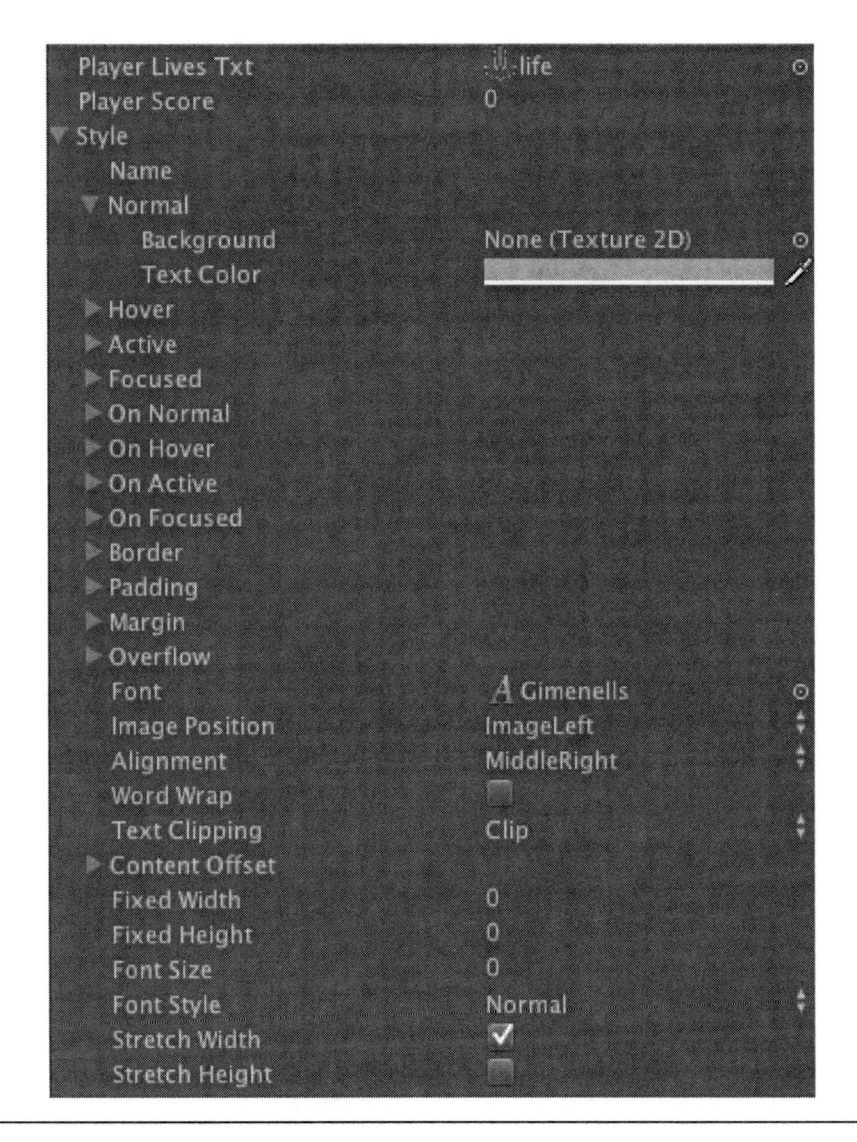

The text colour/color values: **R:** 255, **G:**123, **B:**0

We are ahead of the curve with regards to players' lives because, in the previous section, we put in a piece of code that takes away a life every time the player is destroyed. The only thing left is to tie in the scoring system. We are going to use the exact same piece of code that we used to access the game manager in the **shipController** script in the enemy's script. So open up the **normalEnemy** script and make these changes:

```
var gameMgObj : GameObject;
```

Ace Invaders – Part 2

```
function Start()
{
    shootSpwnT = this.transform.Find("shootSpwn");
    gameMgObj = gameObject.Find("gameManager");
}
function OnTriggerEnter(col : Collider)
{
    if (canBeHit == true)
    {
        if (col.tag == "laser")
        {
            canBeHit = false;
            renderer.enabled = false;
            deathAnim = Instantiate(enemyDeath,
                transform.position, transform.rotation)
                    as GameObject;
            deathAnim.animation["death"].speed = 2;
            var script1 = gameMgObj.transform.gameObject
                .GetComponent("gameManager");
            script1.playerScore +=10000;
        }
    }
}
```

Head back over to the editor and hit the play button to see the results. The values I gave you for the `OnGUI` function may not position the images correctly. The positions of images in the GUI depend on the dimensions of the game view screen. If they don't show up correctly, play about with the numbers until they do.

Summary

Over the last two chapters we have laid down the foundations of a very decent shooter game. We have looked at some nice techniques with a bit of path finding, parallax scrolling and object movement. Parallax scrolling is a hot topic just now in the games world with games like **Canabalt** and **SolipSkier** championing the game that only finishes when you do. This has resulted in top places in the iTunes app store and hundreds of thousands of sales.

This game we have made is by no means finished and the exciting thing for you should be the potential to expand on the game and make it your own. As we talked about in the previous sections, the design of these games makes and breaks their success. The challenge that you can provide the player with will go a long way towards creating a successful game that you would be proud of - firing up on the web for the general public to play. You could try implementing:

- A new wave system that allows you to quickly prototype different wave designs.
- Particle effects to go along with the destruction of the enemies.
- Power ups, and SFX.

Chapter 6

Temple Defense – Part 1

Temple Defense is… ahem… a Tower Defense game, and these have existed in the games industry since the early 1990s. The first of which - **Rampart** - was released by Atari Games in 1990. The concept of the game revolves around the strategic placement of towers along a path, upon which enemies (or in the case of Rampart: ships) march towards a goal, usually the player's base. Enemies come in "waves", and the goal of the game is to hold off as many waves of enemies as possible.

This is the perfect game to raise the bar, and provide us with our next challenge. A tower defense game uses many key techniques that you will be able to use in all manner of games. We will look at:

- Waypoints.
- Triggers.
- Quaternion rotations.
- Scripted Enemy Movement.
- Ballistic algorithms.

Basic setup

Let's dive straight in and create our new project and call it **towerDefense** and include the **Particles** package by selecting **Assets > Import Package > Particles** from the top menu. Set up your **Project View** in the same way as before with 3 folders:

1. _assets
2. _scenes
3. _scripts

In the **_assets** folder, add four additional folders called **Textures**, **Materials**, **Models** and **Prefabs**. With everything setup, save the project and save your scene into the **_scenes** folder calling it **game**.

Game Breakdown

Before we proceed any further, let's take a look at what makes up a Tower Defense game. Below is an early version that we fleshed out during the design stage of the process. The process generally involves a scrap piece of paper, a pen, and wherever we find ourselves at that time, on several occasions some fine brew dispensing establishments. These have often been the site of some of our best and most creative innovations.

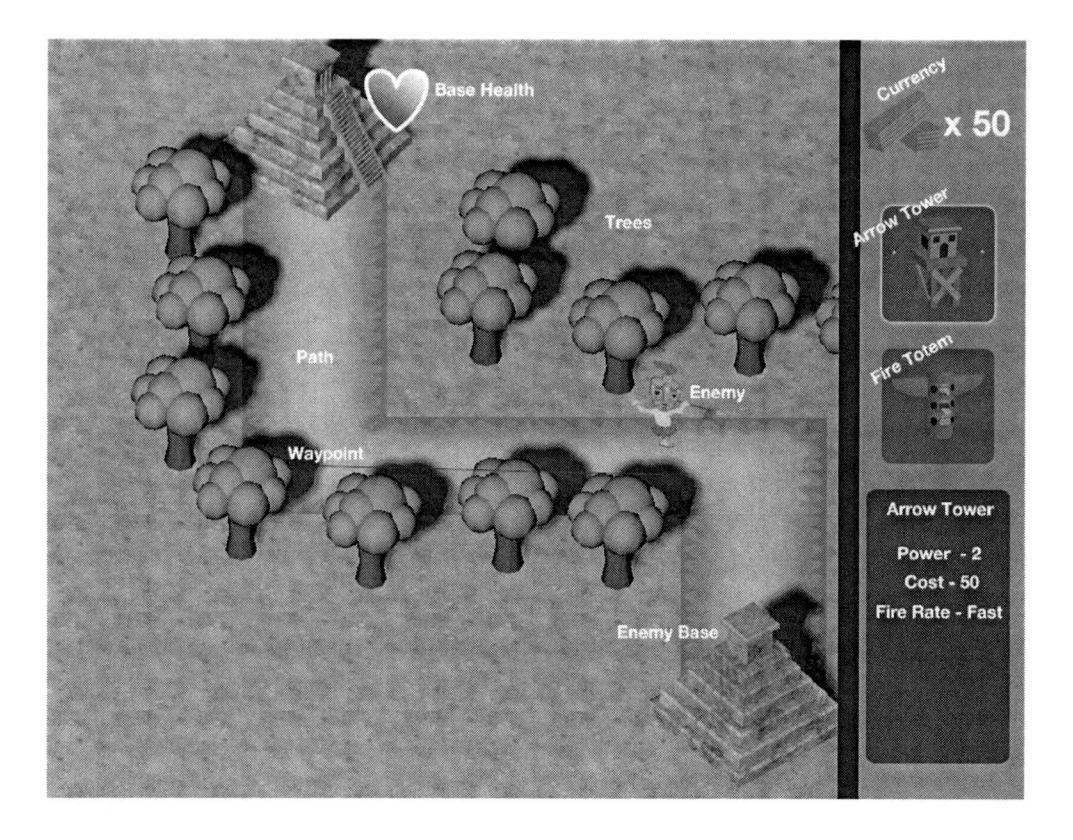

The **Tower** is the main attacking component that the player has at their disposal. Towers can be placed at certain strategic points in the level, and in the case of our design, they replace existing trees. Usually there are several different types of Tower, each with their own strengths and weaknesses. The player must utilize the Towers to destroy as many enemies as possible before they reach the base.

The **Enemies** are the targets that the player is trying to prevent from reaching their base. Similar to the towers, enemies come in different forms, with various skills and attributes. The enemies attack the player in **Waves**. With these waves comprising of many types of enemy, the player must employ different tactics depending on the formation of the wave.

The **Level** is made up of a **path**, which the enemies follow, **trees**, which the player replaces with Towers, and two **bases**. The **Enemy Base** is the origin of the enemies, and the **Player Base** belongs to the players. When an enemy reaches the player's base, a portion of health is lost; when all health is lost, the game is over.

The **Control Panel** is what the player uses to interact with the game. Here the player can monitor the game **currency** which is used to purchase towers. Typically in Tower Defense games, currency is gathered for each enemy destroyed, this allows the player to erect new towers or repair existing ones.

The Level

Now that we have a handle on the anatomy of our game, let's get straight into playing about with it. Download the level package using this url:

www.deeppixel.com/UnityBookPackages/towerdefense/level.unitypackage

Place the level object in the scene, ensuring that before you do so you set the **Scale Factor** to 1 and select **generate colliders** in the FBX component of the inspector.

Expand the node. This will reveal all the individual objects that make up the level, the ground, the temples, all the trees and also two objects called **arrowTower** and **Totem**. At the moment we don't need these last two objects so in the inspector next to the object names click the check box to **deactivate** them. We also have objects called **waypoint_01**, etc. that have been created using maya, we will get to these a little later...

Now, if you check the **Main Camera** in the scene you will see it at its default position. What we want is a more isometric 'top down' look for our game. Enter these values into the camera's inspector:

Temple Defense – Part 1

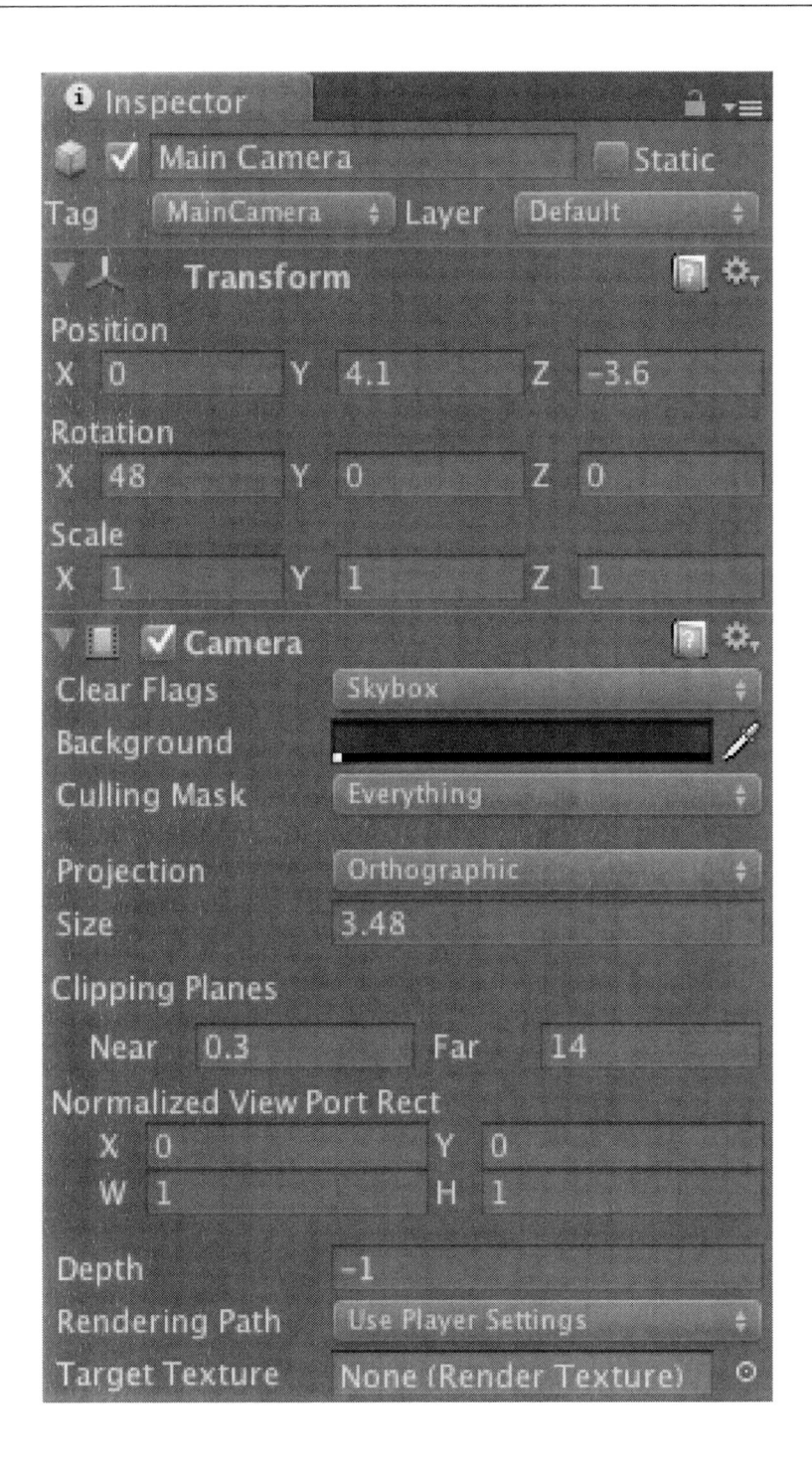

Inspector

☑ Main Camera ☐ Static
Tag: MainCamera   Layer: Default

Transform
Position X 0   Y 4.1   Z -3.6
Rotation X 48 Y 0   Z 0
Scale   X 1   Y 1   Z 1

Camera
Clear Flags: Skybox
Background:
Culling Mask: Everything
Projection: Orthographic
Size: 3.48
Clipping Planes
  Near 0.3   Far 14
Normalized View Port Rect
  X 0   Y 0
  W 1   H 1
Depth: -1
Rendering Path: Use Player Settings
Target Texture: None (Render Texture)

Chapter 6

We also need a bit of light to illuminate our scene, create a **directional light** with these values:

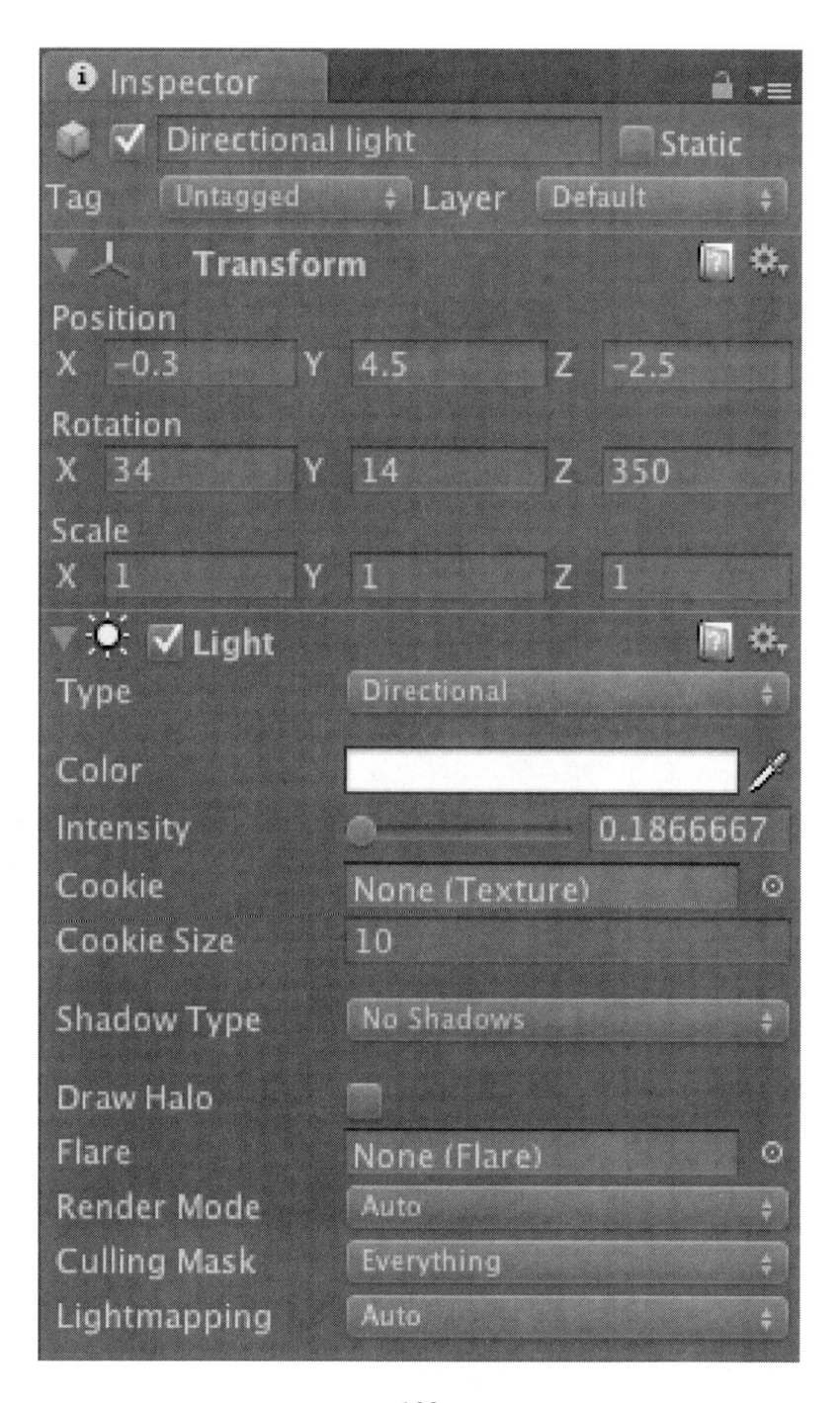

Temple Defense – Part 1

If your game view isn't set to **Standalone (1024x768)** set it now and move onto the game view to see your lovely level. Excellent work. Our scene is set up and we are ready to look into activating our waypoints and using them to move the enemies around the scene.

Waypoints

In game development, the ability for a NPC (Non-Player Character) to find its way through a level is generally called **Path Finding**. This technique involves the moving object navigating obstacles to find its way to a certain point in the level. The most commonly used technique in video games is called **A* PathFinding** or the **A* Search Algorithm**. The technique employs a *best-first* search practice to identify the best node order to go through in order to reach the goal.

For our purposes the A* algorithm would be slight overkill as our level isn't filled with obstacles and complex paths. To plot a navigation route through our level we will use a number of **waypoints**. Waypoints have been used in countless games to give the illusion that enemies are moving under their own volition, or to simulate a patrolling function. In the Xbox Live game **Alien Swarm**, waypoint graphs are used for enemy movement. Below is an image that shows the nodes and the paths between the nodes that will be traversed by enemies in our game.

The technique of using waypoints is a simple one. Basically a waypoint is a Game Object with a **transform** and a **collider** component attached, which as we know gives us the position of an object and allows us to identify collisions with the object.

110

If you select **waypoint_01** in the level parent object you will see in the inspector that it only has a transform component, which as we know holds the position, rotation and scale data of an object. Let's determine the functionality of the enemy and the waypoints:

- We want to know the transform of each waypoint.
- We can use these transforms as the positions that the enemies will move towards.
- Once the enemies reach a waypoint we then want them to move onto the next one, until they reach the final waypoint.

The final piece of functionality is the most interesting to us at the moment as we need to identify when an enemy has collided with a waypoint. This takes us into the world of **collisions** and **triggers**.

Collisions and triggers

Collisions are used in games to identify when the meshes of two objects have intersected. Generally upon detecting a collision the game identifies where it happened and performs a piece of code as a result of the collision. So, for example, when Mario is jumping about Bowser's castle getting into all kinds of trouble - every time Mario touches a platform or the ground, the collision between Mario and the object is registered; when this happens a little piece of Mario's code realizes he has hit a platform and stops him from falling through and allows him to move onto the next platform.

To identify a collision Unity utilizes **colliders**. You will remember in the **Match the Pairs** game how we used colliders to identify when a tile had been clicked. Unity offers a number of different collider components that can be attached to objects, and these can all be found under the **Component > Physics** drop down of the top menu.

At present our waypoints have only a transform component which (alone) will not allow us to catch collisions. Let's add a **Box Collider** from the **Component/Physics** menu.

> Each type of collider has its pros and cons. For example, a bounding sphere can be used for quick collision detection between itself and another sphere. A bounding box, like the one we have attached here is more accurate and generally used more in games.

The inspector should change to show this:

Temple Defense – Part 1

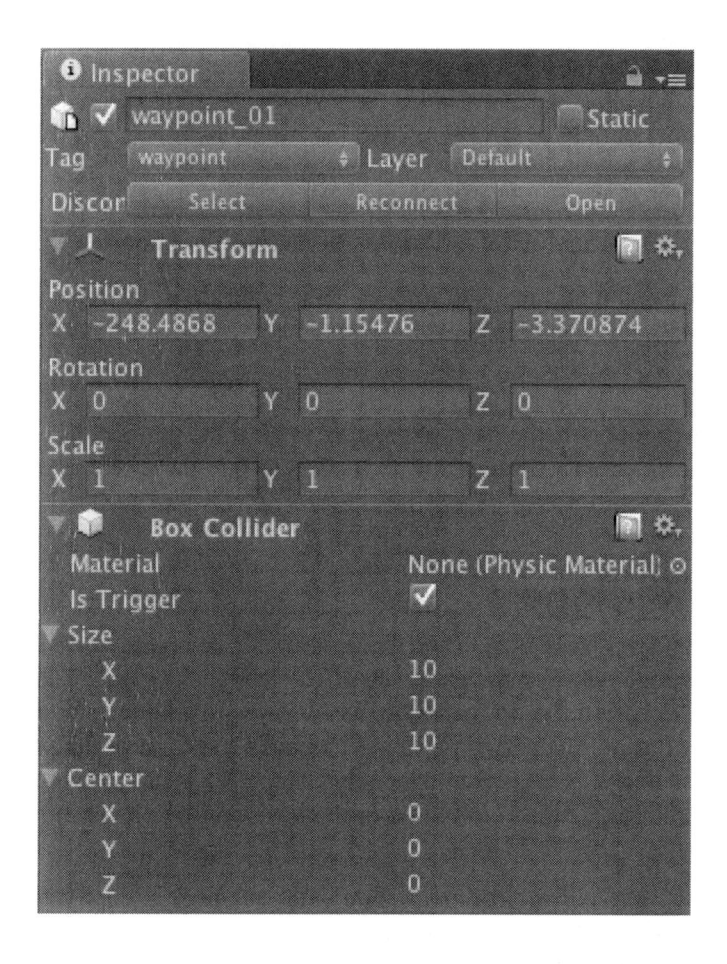

To make sure that we have an effective collider to collide with, change the X, Y and Z size values to 10 as shown above, and check the **Is Trigger** box. The value for the size of the box is an ideal value, it could be smaller, it could be bigger, but as you will see - 10 gives us a nice box that doesn't take up to much of a path and will allow the enemies to move around the path without cutting corners.

Finally we need to identify the waypoint objects, so let's create and assign a tag called **waypoint**. Repeat these steps for the rest of the waypoints in the level. Once you have altered each waypoint you will notice that the last waypoint is not near the last temple. We need our enemies to eventually reach the last temple as this is what we are trying to protect in the game. So duplicate **waypoint_08**, name the new one **waypoint_09** and move it to a position inside the last temple called **templeEnemy**.

Bingo. If you select each of the waypoints in the scene using the hierarchy view you should see them all laid out like so:

With our stage complete the next step is to call for our actor, in particular our rather evil marauding actor.

Enemy of the state

First we will create our enemy, so create a **cube Game Object**, make it half the size, call it **enemy** and activate its **isTrigger** value. Create a new script called **EnemyScript,** attach it to the enemy object and open it. Our **EnemyScript** will revolve around the manipulation of the waypoints we just created and our enemy object.

Let's declare some variables in our script:

```
private var state = 0;
var waypoints : Transform[];
private var activeWaypoint : Transform;
private var currentWaypoint = 0;

private var myPos : Transform;
private var currentSpeed = 0.0;
private var accel = 0.6;
private var rotationDamping = 6.0;
```

Temple Defense – Part 1

```
var wp1Obj : GameObject;
var wp2Obj : GameObject;
var wp3Obj : GameObject;
var wp4Obj : GameObject;
var wp5Obj : GameObject;
var wp6Obj : GameObject;
var wp7Obj : GameObject;
var wp8Obj : GameObject;
var wp9Obj : GameObject;
```

For the purposes of our **EnemyScript** we are going to be employing states; states that are similar to those in the previous Shooter chapters that were used to move the ship.

In this script we will use numbers to identify what state the enemy is in. The first variable we set is state to 0. This is our initial state for the enemy, basically 'walk'. The next variable creates a static array which will hold our waypoints. This is a public variable that we will use in the inspector to select the waypoints we want our enemy to go to, and in what order.

The `activeWaypoint` variable holds the transform data of the current waypoint that the enemy is moving to. The variable `currentWaypoint` is an incremental number that allows us to traverse the waypoint array to find out which waypoint our enemy should currently be moving towards. The final 4 variables are all set to give the enemy certain attributes such as speed, acceleration and rotation damping. The latter will ensure that our enemy turns in a nice smooth manner. The last variables are declared to hold each of the waypoint objects.

Let's begin by setting up our enemy. Put the following before the `Update()` function:

```
function Start ()
{
    state = 0;
    myPos = transform;
    wp1Obj = gameObject.Find("waypoint_01");
    wp2Obj = gameObject.Find("waypoint_02");
    wp3Obj = gameObject.Find("waypoint_03");
    wp4Obj = gameObject.Find("waypoint_04");
    wp5Obj = gameObject.Find("waypoint_05");
    wp6Obj = gameObject.Find("waypoint_06");
    wp7Obj = gameObject.Find("waypoint_07");
    wp8Obj = gameObject.Find("waypoint_08");
    wp9Obj = gameObject.Find("waypoint_09");

    waypoints[0] = wp1Obj.transform;
    waypoints[1] = wp2Obj.transform;
    waypoints[2] = wp3Obj.transform;
    waypoints[3] = wp4Obj.transform;
    waypoints[4] = wp5Obj.transform;
    waypoints[5] = wp6Obj.transform;
    waypoints[6] = wp7Obj.transform;
    waypoints[7] = wp8Obj.transform;
```

```
    waypoints[8] = wp9Obj.transform;
}
```

In the `Start()` function we set up our enemy, ensuring that the `state` is set to 0, and we put the enemy's current transform coordinates into the variable `myPos`. Finally each of the nine waypoints is found, and each element of the `waypoints` array stores the waypoint objects transform data.

Now let's take a look at what we want our enemy to do. We want him to:

- Find the current waypoint.
- Look at the waypoint.
- Walk to the waypoint.
- Upon reaching the waypoint, move to the next waypoint.
- If there are no other waypoints remove the enemy from the scene.

So first we want to know what the `activeWaypoint` is; put this code in the `Update()` function:

```
function Update () {

    activeWaypoint = waypoints[currentWaypoint];
    print (activeWaypoint.position);
    Debug.DrawLine (myPos.position, activeWaypoint.position,
        Color.red);
}
```

Here we set the transform variable `activeWaypoint` to be equal to the element that is in position 0 of the waypoints array. We then print out the position of the target waypoint and draw a debug line from the position of the enemy to the position of the waypoint. Debug lines are an incredibly useful tool for plotting a graphical line between two points, the ability to visually see the direction of an object is useful when moving objects between points (like we are doing).

Now before we press play, remember we *haven't* yet set up our waypoints array with any elements. So go back to the Unity editor, click on the **enemy object,** and in the inspector - navigate to the script component. Here you should see something like the following image. Change the size to 9.

Temple Defense – Part 1

If we hit the play button, we should see a red line connecting our enemy with the first waypoint in the scene view. We now have the information we need to make our enemy move to the correct coordinates. Next we need to ensure that when our enemy is in the initial state, it walks towards the currently active waypoint.

Before we move onto getting the enemy to move to the waypoint, we first have to add something that will help our enemy recognize when it has hit a waypoint. Click on the **enemy object** and add a **rigidbody**. Navigate to the inspector and in the **rigidbody** panel, disable the **Use Gravity** variable.

With our Game Object set up, delete the three lines in the `Update()` function, enter the following code and create two new functions:

```
function Update () {

    if (state == 0){
        walk();
        activeWaypoint = waypoints[currentWaypoint];
    }

    Debug.DrawLine (myPos.position, activeWaypoint.position,
        Color.red);
}

function walk()
{

}

function OnTriggerEnter (col : Collider)
{

}
```

In the `Update()` function we now have a condition that states that the enemy will only walk whenever the `state` of said enemy is at `0`. This will allow us (later on) to add other states such as when to destroy the enemy.

The next function is where we will add the movement code, and the final one will handle the time when the enemy collides with the waypoint. Let's take a look at the `walk()` function, the code is quite complex so we will take each line in turn:

```
function walk()
{
    var rotation = Quaternion.LookRotation(waypoints
        [currentWaypoint].position - transform.position);
```

```
        transform.rotation =Quaternion.Slerp(transform.rotation,
            rotation, Time.deltaTime * rotationDamping);

        var waypointDirection : Vector3 = waypoints
            [currentWaypoint].position - transform.position;

        var speedFactor = Vector3.Dot(
            waypointDirection.normalized, transform.forward);

        var speed = accel * speedFactor;

        transform.Translate (0,0,Time.deltaTime * speed);
}
```

Let's look at a **breakdown of the code above**, first we get the rotation value needed for the enemy to look at the current waypoint:

```
var rotation = Quaternion.LookRotation(waypoints
    [currentWaypoint].position - transform.position);
```

Here we use a **Quaternion** function called `LookRotation` to calculate the angle for the enemy to look straight at the waypoint. We use the position of the current waypoint and subtract it from the enemy's current position to give the rotational direction in which the enemy should look.

Set rotation value:

```
transform.rotation = Quaternion.Slerp(transform.rotation,
    rotation, Time.deltaTime * rotationDamping);
```

With our look at rotation calculated we can then use a **Slerp** function to interpolate the enemy's rotation between its own rotation (`transform.rotation`) to the current waypoint rotation (`rotation`).

Get waypoint direction:

```
var waypointDirection : Vector3 =waypoints
    [currentWaypoint].position - transform.position;
```

We now need to calculate the direction of the waypoint as a **Vector**. This is calculated in a similar fashion to the rotation.

Get speed using `Dot` product:

```
var speedFactor = Vector3.Dot(
    waypointDirection.normalized, transform.forward);
```

Temple Defense – Part 1

Here we use the direction of our waypoint and the forward vector of the enemy's transform to calculate the dot product. A dot product value is obtained by performing a mathematical operation on two vectors. The value we want is basically the vectorized angle between the two vectors (i.e. the vector of the waypoint and the vector of the enemy).

Set the speed of the enemy:

```
var speed = accel * speedFactor;
```

With the angle between the enemy and the waypoint worked out, we can then infer the speed of the object by multiplying our `accel` variable by our newly created `speedFactor`. The reason we do this is that as the enemy gets closer to the waypoint the angle between the two objects should shrink, thus the speed should dip slightly. We use this slight dip in speed to ensure that our enemy hits the waypoint and to prevent any unpredictable behaviours that come when dealing with objects colliding.

Perform translate to move enemy:

```
transform.Translate (0,0,Time.deltaTime * speed);
```

Finally with everything worked out we can use the object `translate` to move the enemy towards the waypoint at the indicated speed over `time.deltaTime`. Hit play and you should be confronted with the beautiful sight of your enemy moving towards the waypoint.

Our final port of call is to deal with the collision of the enemy with the waypoint. This function is activated when a rigid body enters the enemies' collider. Let's take a look at the code again:

```
function OnTriggerEnter (col : Collider)
{
}
```

When the function is fired, it collects collider information from whatever it collides with and places it into the variable `col`. Now since we collide with a Game Object we can assume that it will have the attributes of a Game Object, such as a name, a tag, a transform etc. Put this code in the trigger function:

```
function OnTriggerEnter ( col : Collider)
{
    if (col.tag == "waypoint"){
        currentWaypoint++;
    }
}
```

We check to see if the waypoint object's tag is called "waypoint" and if it is, we increment the `currentWaypoint` variable, which makes the `activeWaypoint` variable change to the next element in the `waypoints` array. Play the scene and the enemy should move along the waypoint

Chapter 6

path. Let's put in a final piece of code that will destroy our enemy once it reaches the final waypoint.

```
if (state==0){
    if (currentWaypoint != 9){
        walk();
        activeWaypoint = waypoints[currentWaypoint];
    }else{
        Destroy(this.gameObject);
    }
}
```

If the `currentWaypoint` value does not equal 9 then we continue walking, however if we reach the 9th waypoint we destroy the enemy. The `this` part of the code is used to directly relate to the object that the script is attached to.

Tribal Mania

At the moment our enemy is a bit of an eyesore. Aesthetically, a grey block is not really the nicest of game assets to use. But fear not we have got you covered with two rather kick-ass little tribal men.

Temple Defense – Part 1

Download and import their package from this URL:

www.deeppixel.com/UnityBookPackages/towerdefense/tribesmen.unitypackage

Let's take a look at our newly imported tribesmen in the inspector. As with all imported models we need to ensure that the **Scale Factor** is set to **1** and that **generate colliders** is checked. We also need to ensure that the animations that have been imported with these models are in working order. Check that each model's animation settings match the corresponding images below:

TribesManNormal

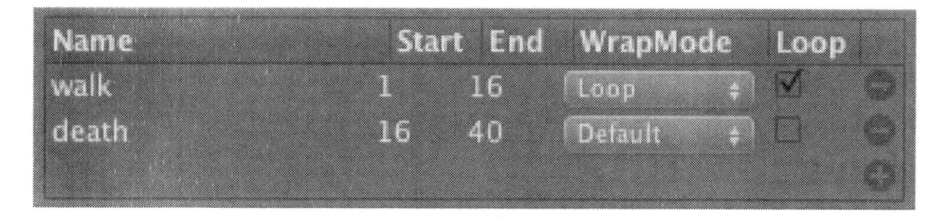

Name	Start	End	WrapMode	Loop
walk	1	16	Loop	✓
death	16	40	Default	

TribesManHeavy

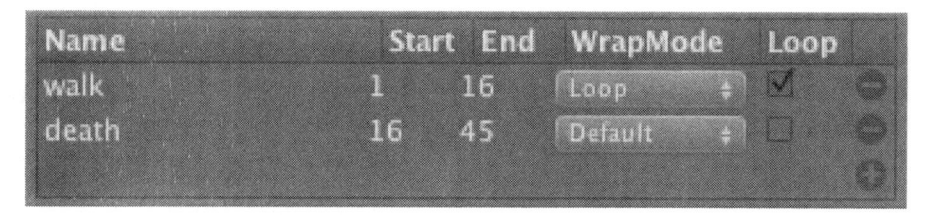

Name	Start	End	WrapMode	Loop
walk	1	16	Loop	✓
death	16	45	Default	

There are two main functions that the tribesmen have to adhere to, the first is moving between each waypoint, and the second is to always be looking at the camera. The reason for the second function is that the tribesmen models are made up from 2D planes, so to ensure that they are always correctly displayed - we have them face the main camera of the scene at all times. To achieve this we had to come up with a rig that would allow the tribesmen model to move, but to also rotate independently of the movement in order to look at the camera. The solution is a very simple one, shown in the following diagram:

Rotation Block →

Movement Block →

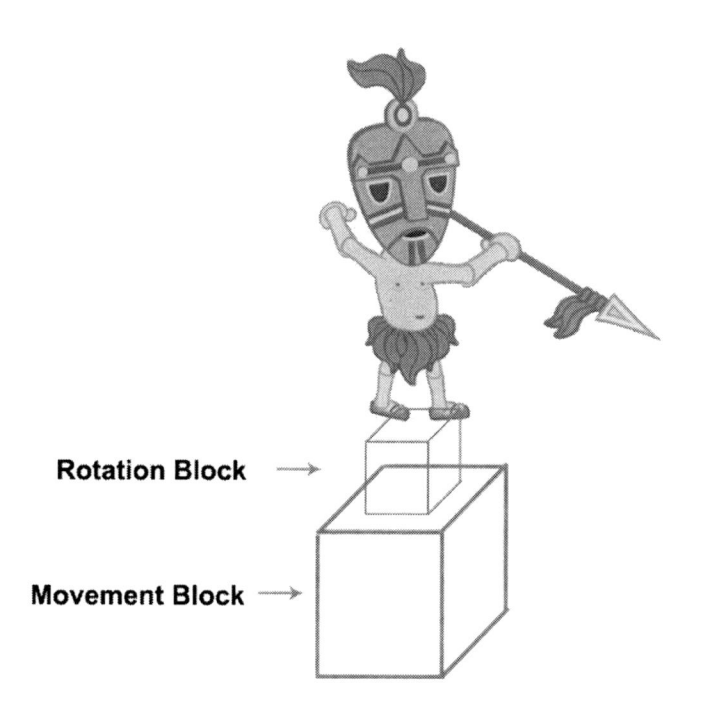

Two blocks are used. The first movement block is the parent of the rotation block which is in turn the parent of the tribesman model. This will allow the movement block to move all the parts of the model and the rotation block to only have an effect on the tribesman model itself. Let's start setting this up.

Drag the **tribesManNormal** model onto the hierarchy view to activate it. Check that the texture is displaying properly by navigating to the body child of the model and looking in the inspector. If the texture is not selected, activate it now using a **transparent/diffuse** shader setting.

The first component on our right is the **movement block**; create a new cube Game Object, change the scale to **0.3** in all axes, and name it **tribesManNormalMove**. Do the same again, only change the scale to **0.1** and the name to **tribesManNormalRotate**. Move the blocks to match the look below:

Temple Defense – Part 1

Now drag the rotate block onto the move block in the hierarchy to make it a child of the move block. Finally take the **tribesManNormal** model and parent it with the rotate block. So your tribesman hierarchy should look like this:

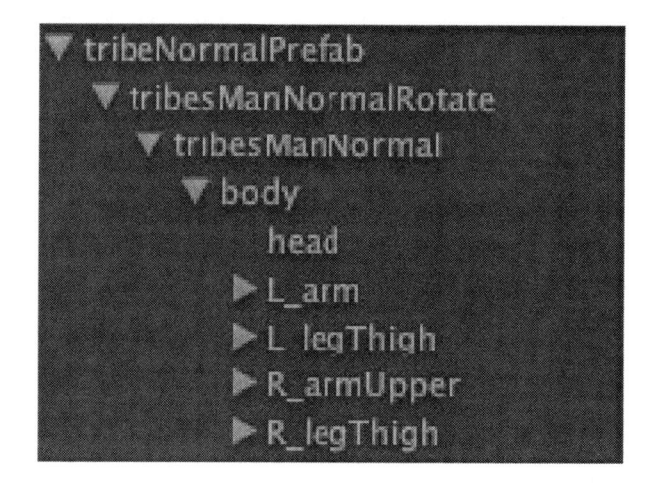

Now at this point you may or may not see this error:

122

Actor::updateMassFromShapes: Compute mesh inertia tensor failed for one of the actor's mesh shapes! Please change mesh geometry or supply a tensor manually!

> When setting up the models for the tribesmen I had tried to apply a **rigidbody** to all of the pieces that made them up. Strangely I was given the error above. A quick jaunt to the Unity forums and I found out that this is a result of the mesh of a plane having no depth and thus no mass! Therefore Unity cannot perform the necessary physics calculations on the model. By default Unity adds a Mesh Collider to any model it imports. The solution was to remove the mesh collider and replace it with a box collider giving it a small amount of depth.
>
> So starting with the **Body child** and working down, remove each mesh collider and replace it with a box collider with a Z size of 2, ensuring that `IsTrigger` is activated on each one.

Unity allows you to replace colliders by merely clicking on the object, choosing a new collider and hitting replace.

Movement

Let's take our **EnemyScript** and attach it to the movement block of our rig. Ensure that the waypoint array size is set to **9**, and hit play. It seems that we now have a tribesman that can dance; you should be confronted with the sight of a rotating tribesman around the first waypoint. This is due to the fact that we do not have a rigid body attached to the move block and rotate block, so let's add one to each now and uncheck the gravity option on each one.

Place the **tribesMan** at the first temple in a similar position to the old enemy (if the old enemy is still on the screen, deactivate it), hit play, and you should see your new tribesman moving between the waypoints.

Here's looking at you

Next we need a script that will make the rotation block move to look at the position of the main camera in our scene. We also need to ensure that the block only moves in the y axis. If our block was to rotate in the X, Y and Z axes then our enemy model would rotate constantly on all axes giving us a strange effect where the model always faces the camera. This is a technique known as **Billboarding**, which is used to create perspective in games.

Now we are in a 3D world so we don't really need Billboarding so the decision to use a flat model for the enemy was an aesthetic one. Create a script called **LookAtCamera**, attach it to the rotate block of each tribesman. Open the script and put in the following code:

Temple Defense – Part 1

```
var cameraToLookAt : Camera;

function Start()
{
    cameraToLookAt = Camera.main;
}

function Update()
{
    var v: Vector3 = cameraToLookAt.transform.position -
        transform.position;
v.x = v.z = 0.0;
transform.LookAt(cameraToLookAt.transform.position - v);
}
```

Here we identify the camera and place it in the `cameraToLookAt` variable. We then work out the position of the camera relative to the position of our rotation block. The x and y transforms of our newly worked out vector `v` are set to `0.0` to force the rotation around the y axis. Finally the `lookAt()` function is used, using the result of the position of the camera and the position of our object.

Tidying Up

Okay, we now have a cool little tribal guy that walks around our scene. Let's quickly do some tidying up before we move on. Firstly the blocks beneath the tribesman are a tad unsightly, let's make these invisible. Click on each block and in the inspector, underneath the mesh renderer, change the size variable to 0. This will remove the mesh from the object.

I know this is a heavy ask but it will be worth it in the end. Follow these instructions again for the **tribesManHeavy** model.

We also need to make our new tribesmen into prefabs, so create a folder called **Prefabs** under the **_assets** folder and create new prefabs in there called **tribesmanNormal** and **tribesmanHeavy**. Delete the old models from the scene.

Finally play about with the starting position of the tribesman and the height of the waypoints to make movement around the path nicer.

Forward March

The tribes people are gathering; they are hungry for the innocent townsfolk, it is time to unleash them. For this we need to create a script that will act as the glue for our game, allowing the player to interact with the game while also managing the enemies. Create a new empty Game Object and name it **gameManager**. Also, create a new script with the name **GameManager**. Attach the script to your newly created object and open it. Declare the following variables:

```
private var noOfEnemies = 0;
```

```
var tribeNormalPrefab : GameObject;
var tribeHeavyPrefab : GameObject;
private var startPos : Vector3;

private var spawnTime : float;
private var spawnTimeLeft : int;
private var spawnTimeSeconds = 2;
var i = 0;
var waveFormation = new Array();
```

As we talked about previously, tower defense games are all about the waves of enemies that the player has to stave off in order to survive. The creation of the wave is relatively simple, we need an array that details the order of the array, utilizing numbers as identifiers for the two types of enemy, and a timer to instantiate the objects one after another so that they don't all come out at the once. Let's start with the timer, put this code into the script:

```
function Awake()
{
    spawnTime = Time.time;
}

function Update ()
{
    spawnTimeLeft = Time.time - spawnTime;
    if(spawnTimeLeft >= spawnTimeSeconds)
    {
        print ("release enemy");
        spawnTime = Time.time;
        spawnTimeLeft = 0;
    }
}
```

Here we have a basic timer set up to **release** an enemy whenever the value in `SpawnTimeLeft` is greater than or equal to the number of seconds we set in the variable `spawnTimeSeconds`. Hit the play button and open the console, every two seconds the print statement should be shown.

Now after every two seconds have passed we want an enemy to appear and start walking along the path. Let's quickly set up the coordinates of where the enemy will appear:

```
function Start ()
{
    startPos = Vector3(-2.6,0,-3.1);
}
```

These coordinates should make the enemy appear from inside the first temple at the bottom left of the screen. If they don't, play around with the coordinates until they feel right. Next we need a

Temple Defense – Part 1

wave formation. For this we are going to use 1's and 0's, make these changes to the `waveFormation` variable:

```
var waveFormation = new Array(0,0,0,1,1,0,1,0);
```

Replace the 3 lines in the `if` statement in the `Update()` function with these:

```
if (i != waveFormation.length){
    if (waveFormation[i] == 0){
        Instantiate (tribeNormalPrefab, startPos,
            Quaternion.identity);
        spawnTime = Time.time;
        spawnTimeLeft = 0;
        i++;
    }else{
        Instantiate (tribeHeavyPrefab, startPos,
            Quaternion.identity);
        spawnTime = Time.time;
        spawnTimeLeft = 0;
        i++;
    }
}
```

In this piece of code, we check to see that we have not reached the end of our array by using a counter called i. We then use this counter to query the elements of the array, if the element is a 0 then a normal tribesman is instantiated, and if it's a 1 then a heavy tribesman is. We then reset the times and increment the counter by 1. Navigate to the **Game** script on the Game Object and attach the normal and heavy tribesman objects to the prefab variables. Hit the play button to see your first wave!!

You will notice that if you let the wave reach the next of the waypoints you get an Array index error since we no longer have any more waypoints for our tribesmen to move towards. To counter this you can make this quick change to the if statement in the Update() function of the **enemyScript**:

```
if (state == 0)
    if (currentWaypoint != 9){
        walk();
        activeWaypoint = waypoints[currentWaypoint];
    }
}
```

This will make the tribesmen stop walking upon reaching the last waypoint.

Summary

In this chapter we have laid down the foundations for the game. The fundamental functionality is now present with the enemy movement utilizing the waypoints that have been set out in the level. The waypoint system that we have developed is a very useful technique; almost all games with

Temple Defense – Part 1

NPC's or Non-Player-Characters require some form of Artificial Intelligence control that allows them to mimic certain behaviour, in this case walking along a pre-determined path.

We also saw how easy it is to set up a rig for models in Unity to allow them to move in a manner that may not have been intended by the artist. One of Unity's best features is its ability to let you create basic 3D models right in the editor. Remember to use that to your advantage when creating play experiences!

The next chapter will allow us to expand on the game, getting the Towers into the game and fleshing out more of the interactive features of the game.

Chapter 7

Temple Defense – Part 2

With our rather bad ass natives starting their march along their warpath, determined to cause damage, it seems only fair that we provide the player with an equalizer in the battle for middle earth... I mean temples. For this we shall provide them with those ever present, and most crucial elements of this game, the towers!

Towers are there to provide one function, and one function only - to stop the coming onslaught. For our game we have decided to stay traditional and not go for any fancy upgradeable towers. No what you see is what you get, and hopefully all the tribesmen will see - is a projectile to the face!

In this chapter we will look at:

- Towers of destruction – the player's ammunition in the game.
- Enemy health bars – these guys are strong, the player needs to know how strong.
- Death animations – just disappearing would be no good.
- The user interface – the glue that holds everything together.

All along your watchtowers

So we have the beautiful setting, our restless blood thirsty natives, now all we need are some kick ass towers. Two towers have been created for this game, an **Arrow Tower** and a **fire breathing Totem**. At the beginning of the chapter we turned off both of these models in the **level object**, so let's start by reactivating them and dragging them onto the top level in the inspector so they are no longer parented to the level object.

Temple Defense – Part 2

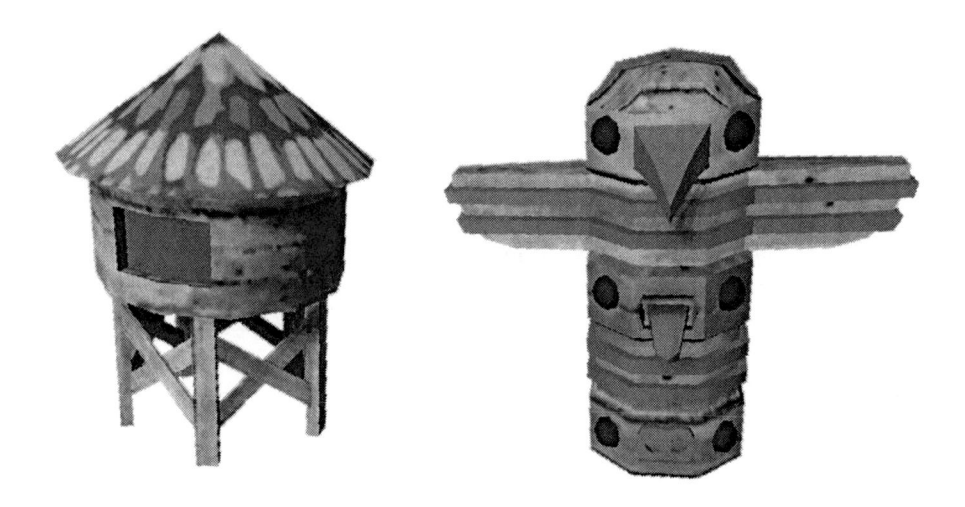

Arrow Tower

Let's begin with the Arrow Tower. Create a new script called **Tower**, attach it to the **arrowTower** object and open it. Let's take a quick look at the functionality we want the Arrow Tower to have:

- Identify the closest enemy.
- Check if enemy is in range.
- Fire arrow.
- Wait for reload time and fire again.
- When enemy moves out of range move to next enemy.

Identifying the closest enemy to the tower is the most important part of the tower's functionality so we will start there. Match your **Tower** script to this code:

```
private var ttag = "enemyAim";
private var target : Transform;

function Start()
{
    InvokeRepeating("getClosestEnemy", 0, 1.0);
}

function Update()
{
```

```
}
function getClosestEnemy() : Transform
{
    print ("get closestEnemy");
}
```

If you hit the play button and look at the console you will see that the `getClosestEnemy()` function is called every second. This is because of a cool little function called `InvokeRepeating()`. Let's take a look at the **script reference** for this one:

```
function InvokeRepeating (methodName : string, time : float,
    repeatRate : float) : void
```

The function takes 3 variables, the `methodName` as a string, the `time` as a float which indicates after how many seconds the first invocation is. Finally we have the `repeatRate` that takes a float to represent after how many seconds the function is continually called.

Our next step is to fill out the `getClosestEnemy()` function. We need to identify what an enemy is, in our scene, using the `ttag` variable. Check that the enemy is within range and set our `target` variable to hold the transform data of the enemy to be used in firing our projectile. Let's start with some new variables, add these to the Tower script:

```
var closestEnemy : Transform = null;
var dist : float;
```

Then put this code in the `getClosestEnemy()` function:

```
var taggedEnemys = GameObject.FindGameObjectsWithTag(ttag);
var closestDistSqr = Mathf.Infinity;
var closestEnemy : Transform = null;


for (taggedEnemy in taggedEnemys)
{
    var objectPos = taggedEnemy.transform.position;
    dist = (objectPos - transform.position).sqrMagnitude;

    if (dist < 3.0)
    {
        if (dist < closestDistSqr)
        {
            closestDistSqr = dist;
            closestEnemy = taggedEnemy.transform;
        }
    }
```

Temple Defense – Part 2

```
    }
target = closestEnemy;
```

The first line uses a function of the **GameObject** class to find all the Game Objects in the scene that have a certain tag. Now at the moment both our tribesmen are untagged. You would think that it would be a simple process of just creating a new tag and assigning it to the prefab. The only problem with this is that if we tag the entire **tribesman** object then we will get the transform data from the whole object which, as you will remember, includes both blocks that are beneath the tribesman model. This basically gives us a transform position that is at the feet of the tribesman. We ideally want the position to be at his body so that when we fire our projectile it will hit his body. Let's move on and fix this.

Click and drag the **tribesManNormal** prefab into the hierarchy view to activate it. Focus onto the object (⌘+F) and create a new cube object. What we want to do here is create a box that surrounds the body of the tribesman but *not* the bottom cubes. Like so:

Make the material equal to 0 and ensure that `IsTrigger` is activated. Next change the name of the cube to **tribesManAim** and make it a child of the **tribesManNormalRotate** object. While we are here, let's tag this object with the name **enemyAim**. Now do the same process for the **tribesManHeavy** prefab. Remember to always **Apply Changes To Prefab** after making alterations to your prefabs. If you forget, the changes that you made to the prefab won't be carried over to the game once it is run.

Back to our code. After finding all objects with our **enemyAim** tag, we declare a couple of variables to hold the closest distance squared, and the transform data of the closest enemy. A loop is used to go through each of the enemies that were found with the tag; for each of these enemies their position is ascertained, the distance from the tower to the enemy calculated, and an `if` is used when:

- the enemy comes into range (in this case `3.0` units).
- and the distance is less that the closest Distance squared.

Then we set the `closestDistSqr` to the distance of the enemy, and set the `closestEnemy` variable to be equal to the tagged enemy. The variable `target` is then set to equal the closest enemy. Basically, we take the position of the tower and all the positions of the enemies in the array and calculate the distance between them and the tower. When an enemy has a distance between itself and the tower that is smaller than the last closest distance squared variable, the variable `target` is set to the position of that enemy. Now, let's get some code in to see this in action. Put this in the `Update()` function:

```
if (target != null)
{
    Debug.DrawLine (transform.position, target.position,
    Color.yellow);
}
```

Position your tower somewhere near to where the enemies will march past, hit the play button, and move back to the scene view. When they get close you should see the debug line indicating that the tower has found the closest enemy and is locked on.

On my mark unleash hell...

The final piece of functionality to add to our tower is the ability to fire at the enemy. Time to declare some variables in the **Tower** script:

```
private var startTime : float;
private var shootTimeLeft : int;
private var shootTimeSeconds = 1.0;
var projPrefab : GameObject;
private var initialSpeed = 4.0;
var targetDir : Vector3;
```

Next we want to use a similar piece of code for our enemy wave generation by using a timer to determine when to fire our projectile, place this in the `Update()` function, inside the `if` statement:

```
targetDir = target.position - transform.position;
shootTimeLeft = Time.time - startTime;
if(shootTimeLeft >= shootTimeSeconds){
```

Temple Defense – Part 2

```
        Fire();
        print ("Fire");
        startTime = Time.time;
        shootTimeLeft = 0;
}
```

As you can see by the code above we need a `Fire()` function:

```
function Fire()
{
    var instantiatedProjectile : GameObject = Instantiate(
        projPrefab, transform.position, transform.rotation);

    instantiatedProjectile.rigidbody.velocity =
        transform.TransformDirection(targetDir*initialSpeed);
}
```

Before we look at this function, we need a physical object to fire at the enemy. Create a new sphere object, name it **arrow** and change its scale values to `0.1` and have its `IsTrigger` value on. We want to be able to manipulate the physics properties of this object so add a rigid body to it with no gravity. Finally, create a prefab called **arrow** using this object and delete the original from the scene.

In the `fire()` function we want to instantiate our new arrow Game Object using the `projPrefab` variable, so click on the **arrowTower** object and in the inspector set this variable to match our **arrow** prefab. The prefab is then instantiated at the position of the tower. Finally, we utilize the `velocity` of the arrow's rigid body to transform it in the direction of the enemy at a constant speed using the current direction of the closest target.

If you hit the play button at this point you will see that our projectiles behave rather strangely. They appear to be rising towards the camera. While the scene is playing, move back to the scene view and look closely at the tower; you will see that the projectiles are being instantiated at the bottom of the tower, not at the middle. To fix this we need to create a **Spawn Point** for our projectiles. Create a new sphere object and call it **spwnPnt**, make the scale values `0.1` and ensure that `IsTrigger` is on. Move close to the tower and position the **spwnPnt** object in the middle of the tower. Make the **spwnPnt** object a child of the **arrowTower**. Now remove the **Tower** script from the **arrowTower** object and place it on the **spwnPnt** object. Make sure that `projPrefab` is set in the inspector to the **arrow** object and hit the play button. The arrow projectile should now take a nice path towards the enemies.

He shoots he scores!

The last task to complete with our arrow projectile is to make it interact with the enemies. Create a new script called **ArrowScript**. Add the new script to the arrow prefab. Open the script and put in this code:

```
function OnTriggerEnter(enemy : Collider)
{
    if (enemy.tag == "enemyAim"){
        Destroy(this.gameObject);
    }else{
        yield WaitForSeconds (2);
        Destroy(this.gameObject);
    }
}
```

As before, the `OnTriggerEnter()` function is our friend. Here we check to see if the collider, that the arrow hits, is tagged with the name **enemyAim** then we destroy the arrow, otherwise we wait two seconds and destroy it. Hit play to see how the arrows disappear.

Totem Power

The totem tower is very similar to the arrow tower so we won't spend too long getting it up and running. We want our totem to be fire breathing so right click on the project view go to **Import Package > Particles** and add the **small flames** prefab to the scene (You will find it under the Legacy Particles folder).

Use the following settings to create the desired flame effect:

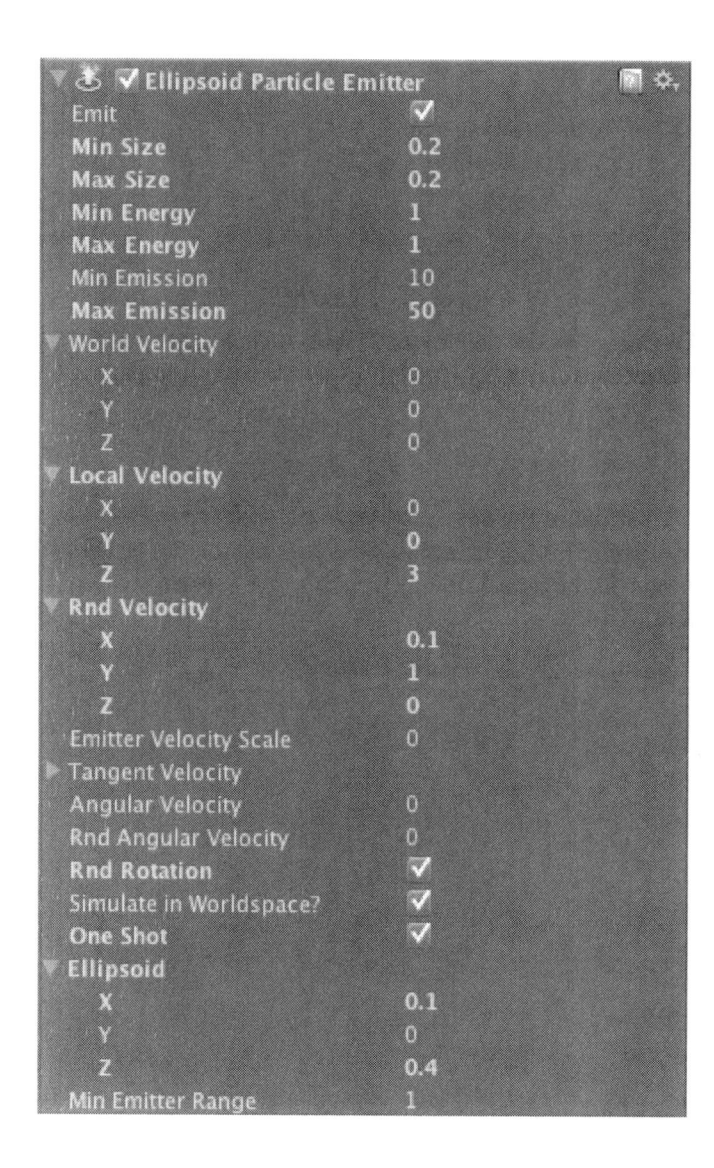

Ellipsoid Particle Emitter

☑ Ellipsoid Particle Emitter	
Emit	☑
Min Size	0.2
Max Size	0.2
Min Energy	1
Max Energy	1
Min Emission	10
Max Emission	50
▼ World Velocity	
X	0
Y	0
Z	0
▼ Local Velocity	
X	0
Y	0
Z	3
▼ Rnd Velocity	
X	0.1
Y	1
Z	0
Emitter Velocity Scale	0
▶ Tangent Velocity	
Angular Velocity	0
Rnd Angular Velocity	0
Rnd Rotation	☑
Simulate in Worldspace?	☑
One Shot	☑
▼ Ellipsoid	
X	0.1
Y	0
Z	0.4
Min Emitter Range	1

Particle Animator

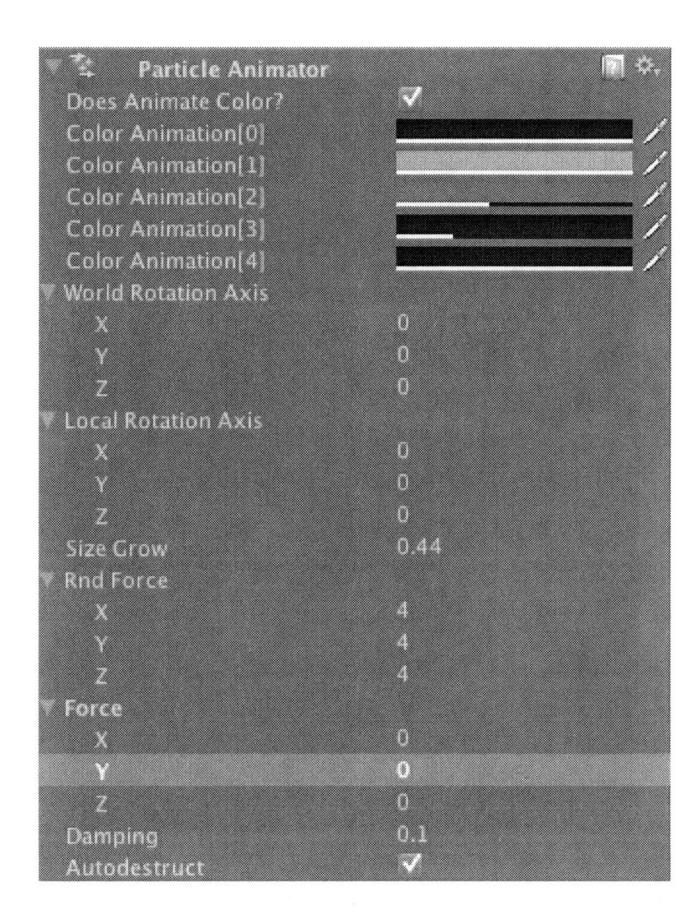

The colour/color animation values are as follows:
- Color Animations[0] = black
- Color Animations[1] = light grey
- Color Animations[2] = brown
- Color Animations[3] = black
- Color Animations[4] = black

Temple Defense – Part 2

Create a new prefab called **fireBreath** from this new particle system. We are going to use the same technique for firing the projectile for the particle system. Create a new sphere object called **particleSpwn**, set its overall size to `0.1` and position it just in front of the totem poles middle mouth as below (remember to set it as a `trigger` and material to 0):

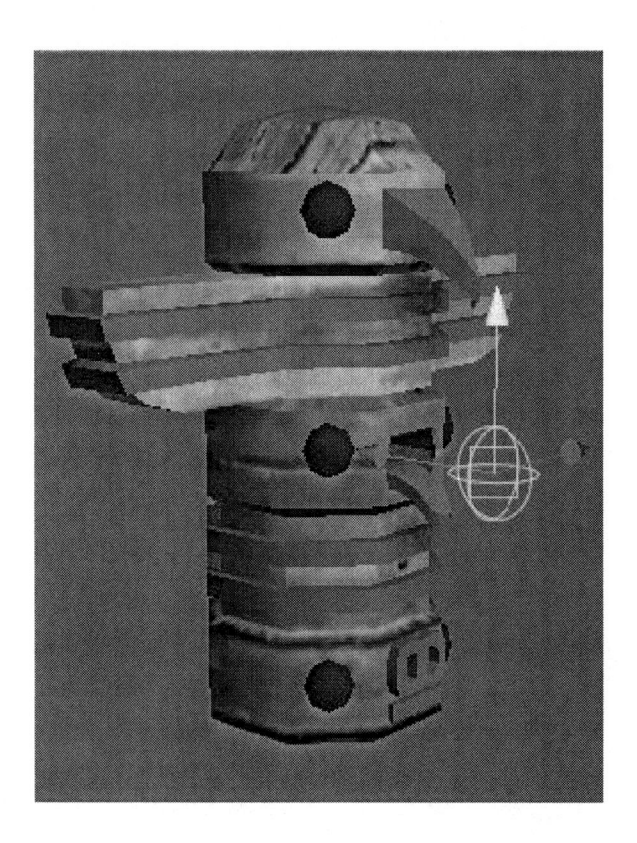

Make the **particleSpwn** object a child of the totem object. Create a new script called **Totem** and attach it to the **particleSpwn** object. Copy the code from the **Tower** script into the Totem script and make the following changes:

Delete this line from the `fire()` function:
```
instantiatedProjectile.rigidbody.velocity =
   transform.TransformDirection(targetDir*initialSpeed);
```

Update the `if` statement in the `Update()` function like so:
```
if (target != null)
   {
      Debug.DrawLine (transform.position, target.position,
         Color.yellow);
      targetDir = target.position - transform.position;
```

```
        transform.LookAt(Vector3(target.position.x,
            transform.position.y, target.position.z));
        shootTimeLeft = Time.time - startTime;
        if(shootTimeLeft >= shootTimeSeconds)
        {
            Fire();
            print ("Fire");
            startTime = Time.time;
            shootTimeLeft = 0;
        }
    }
```

These changes make the **particleSpwn** object look at the target it is aiming at, rather than staying static like the arrow spawn point. The `LookAt()` function takes a `Vector3` value and repositions the object to look at that point in space. To see the Totem in action go back to the editor and set the `projPrefab` variable in the inspector to match the **fireBreath** prefab. Position the totem pole near the path and hit play to see the result.

Excellent, we now have the tower set up and ready to do some damage to the marauding tribesmen. The next step is to give the tribesmen a health value which diminishes whenever they are hit by either of the towers. Let's crack on with that now.

A Clean Bill Of Health

Health bars are notoriously difficult to get right as there is a vast array of different techniques and methods that can be used to create them. Our tribesman is made up of planes, so it stands to reason that our health bar should follow suit. The tribesman also walks along the ground so having the positioning of the bar anywhere near his feet would be a mistake, the best bet is to have it above his head - clear and in plain sight for the player.

Let's start by making two Unity GUI textures. Choose **GameObject > Create Other > GUITexture** from the toolbar menu, name it **healthBarFront**.

We need some files for this exercise, so from the Deep Pixel website download the **healthbar** Unity package.

www.deeppixel.com/UnityBookPackages/towerdefense/healthbar.unitypackage

Import it into Unity and expand the Texture folder. Inside you will see two textures, **healthGreen** and **healthRed**. Click on your GUI texture and in the inspector set the texture variable to the healthGreen texture. Duplicate the same GUI texture and replace the duplicate's texture with healthRed, rename the object as **healthBarBack**.

Temple Defense – Part 2

We want these two objects to follow each other, so take the **healthBarBack** object and make it a child of the **HealthBarFront** object. Now, at the moment, the GUI textures don't look much like a health bar. Input the changes below into the inspector of each GUI texture:

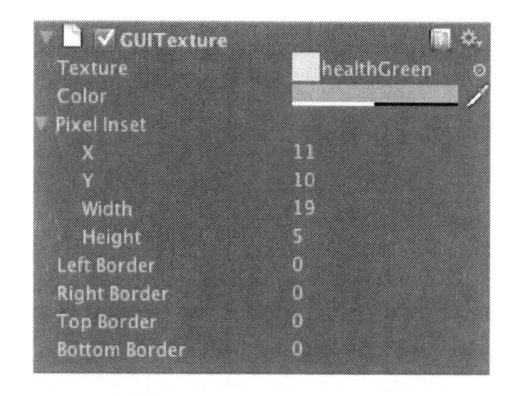

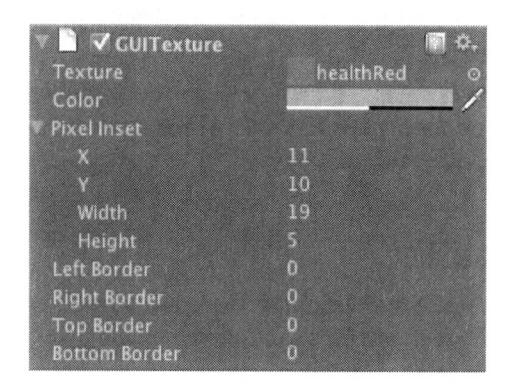

GUITexture	
Texture	healthGreen
Color	
Pixel Inset	
X	11
Y	10
Width	19
Height	5
Left Border	0
Right Border	0
Top Border	0
Bottom Border	0

GUITexture	
Texture	healthRed
Color	
Pixel Inset	
X	11
Y	10
Width	19
Height	5
Left Border	0
Right Border	0
Top Border	0
Bottom Border	0

Finally, create a prefab called `HealthBar` and use our new **healthBar** object to make it. Next we want to create a script that adds the functionality that makes our GUI textures behave like a health bar. Create and open a new script, call it **HealthBarScript**. Let's first declare some variables:

```
var healthBarPrefab : GameObject;
var healthBarObj : GameObject;
var currHealth : float;
var maxHealth : float;
var healthBarWidth : int;
```

First we declare two Game Objects. The first is used to hold the health bar prefab that we created, and the second to hold the instantiated object from the prefab. We then set two variables that identify the health parameters of the health bar. The first is the current health which updates whenever an enemy loses health, and the second is the maximum health which (as the name suggests) is the maximum health that the enemy can have. Finally we have an integer to hold the width of the health bar; this will be used when manipulating the bar. Let's create our `Start()` function:

```
function Start(){
    healthBarObj = Instantiate(healthBarPrefab,
        transform.position,transform.rotation);
}
```

When the script is run, we want to instantiate a new health bar object from our prefab; this is set to the transform and position of the object that the script is currently attached to (i.e. the position and rotation values of the object are used to position the newly instantiated object). With the health bar created we now want to align it to the object it is attached to:

```
function Update () {
    healthBarObj.transform.position =
        Camera.main.WorldToViewportPoint(transform.position);
    healthBarObj.transform.position.y +=0.13;
    var healthPercent : float = currHealth/maxHealth;
    if(healthPercent <0)
    {
        healthPercent=0;
    }
    healthBarWidth = healthPercent *20;
    healthBarObj.guiTexture.pixelInset =
        Rect(10,10,healthBarWidth,5);
}
```

The first line sets the object's position from world space into viewport space. The viewport space is normalized and is positioned relative to the main camera in the scene. The next line is an aesthetic fix to align the health bar with the top of the enemy's head. The next variable is a float value that is obtained by dividing the current health of the enemy with its maximum health. This gives us a percentage float value to work out the width of the health bar.

With the width of the health bar identified we can then set the GUI textures `pixelInset` to match the new width. The final step is to attach this script to the **tribesManNormal** and **tribesManHeavy** prefabs, and set these values:

Temple Defense – Part 2

Normal Tribesman

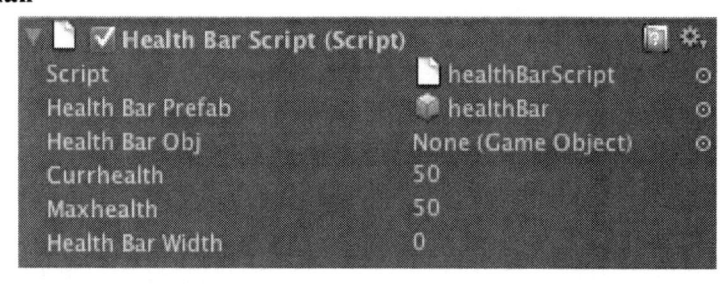

Health Bar Script (Script)	
Script	healthBarScript
Health Bar Prefab	healthBar
Health Bar Obj	None (Game Object)
Currhealth	50
Maxhealth	50
Health Bar Width	0

Heavy Tribesman

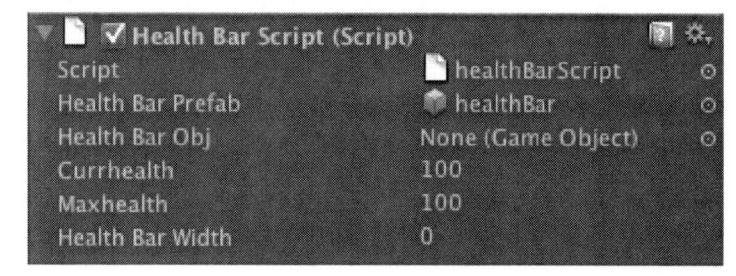

Health Bar Script (Script)	
Script	healthBarScript
Health Bar Prefab	healthBar
Health Bar Obj	None (Game Object)
Currhealth	100
Maxhealth	100
Health Bar Width	0

Click play and your tribesmen should have a nice health bar hanging above their heads, ready to be taken down by your towers.

Hurt Them!

With our enemies marching to battle, the towers in place, fire and arrows raining from the sky, the last thing we need is for the fire and arrows to do some damage. We now have a script called **HealthBarScript** on each enemy that directly links to their health bar. What we need to do is take health from the enemy every time they are hit. This is relatively simple. In fact, all you need is to open up the **ArrowScript** and put these lines before the object is destroyed, inside the `if`:

```
var script = enemy.transform.root.gameObject.
   GetComponent("HealthBarScript");
if (script.currHealth != 0)
{
   script.currHealth -= 15;
}
```

We get access to the script of the object we have hit using the `GetComponent()` method. Check if the enemy's health is not at zero. If it is not zero, take off 15 hit points from the `currhealth` variable. Hit the play button now and see the health bar go down.

For the totem pole we will need to do some fixes to the particles. Currently they have no mesh attached and therefore we cannot check the `OnTrigger` status of the particles. So let's go ahead and add a sphere collider. Check the `IsTrigger` property and make the size of the collider 0.1 on all three axes. Then create a new script called **FlameScript** and copy the code from the **ArrowScript** into there, attach this to the **fireBreath** prefab, and hit play to see the fire in action.

Till death do us part

Remember the first part of the chapter where we set up the tribesmen with their appropriate animations? Currently we are using the walk animation but we also have a death animation. Open up the **EnemyScript** and add the following:

To the variables:

```
var dead = false;
```

To the bottom of the `Update()` function:

```
var script = GetComponent("HealthBarScript");

if (dead != true)
{
   if (script.currHealth <=0)
   {
      playDeath();
      dead = true;
   }
}
```

Below the `Walk()` function:

```
function playDeath()
{
   state=1;
   var animation2 = GetComponentInChildren(typeof(Animation)) as
       Animation;
   animation2.animation.Play("death");
   yield WaitForSeconds (1);
   Destroy(this.gameObject);
   var script = GetComponent("HealthBarScript");
   Destroy(script.healthBarObj);
   Destroy(script);
}
```

Here we use a nifty little function called `GetComponentInChildren()` to get the animation component of our tribesman parent object. We then call the death animation on it and then destroy

Temple Defense – Part 2

the object and the scripts attached to it. Play the scene to see the results. Meet your doom tiny marauding tribes person!

We are in control

Our attention now turns to the player and how we get them to interact with the game. Before we move forward we need to do some housekeeping. Create two prefabs for the **arrowTower** and **totem** objects called **tower** and **totem**. Let's have a look at the functionality we want the user to have. We want the user to be able to:

1. Select the tower and totem to place in the level.
2. See the health of their temple.
3. Have a monetary system that allows for the purchase of towers.

We will start with the main piece of functionality which is placing the towers in the level. This works with the player selecting what tower they want to place, then selecting a tree in the level that will be replaced by the tower. Start by declaring a few variables in the **Game** script:

```
private var playersWood = 200;
private var towerCost = 50;
private var totemCost = 100;
private var objectToPlaceNm : String;
```

We require two buttons for selecting the towers so open up the **Game** script and put this code under the `Update()` function:

```
function OnGUI()
{
   if (GUI.Button (Rect (10,135,126,98), "tower"))
   {
      if (playersWood >= towerCost)
      {
         objectToPlaceNm = "tower";
      }
   }

   if (GUI.Button (Rect (10,225,126,98), "totem"))
   {
      if (playersWood >= totemCost)
      {
         objectToPlaceNm = "totem";
      }
   }
}
```

Here we create two buttons, one for the tower and one for the totem. Upon clicking either button a check is done to see if the player has enough wood (credit) to purchase their selected item. If they do the variable `objectToPlaceNm` is set to the name of the item.

The next action we want the player to perform is the selecting of the tree. Add in these variables to the **Game** script:

```
private var hit : RaycastHit;
private var placementPos : Vector3;
var towerObj : GameObject;
var totemObj : GameObject;
var inc = 0;
```

Quickly go back to the inspector and match the tower and totem prefabs to the **towerObj** and **totemObj** Game Object variables. Then add this code in the Update() function after the first `if`:

```
var ray = Camera.main.ScreenPointToRay (Input.mousePosition);

if (Input.GetMouseButtonDown (0))
{
    if (Physics.Raycast (ray, hit, Mathf.Infinity))
    {
        if (hit.collider.tag != "ground" && hit.collider.tag !=
            "enemyAim" && hit.collider.tag != "temple")
        {
            if (objectToPlaceNm == "tower")
            {
                playersWood = playersWood - towerCost;
                placementPos = hit.transform.position;
                var arrTwr : GameObject = Instantiate(
                    towerObj,placementPos,Quaternion.identity);
                arrTwr.name = inc.ToString();
                Destroy(hit.collider.gameObject);
                objectToPlaceNm = "";
            }
        }
    }
}
```

To make this code work we need three new tags that will ensure that the only objects in the level which the player can click on are the trees. So create tags called **enemy**, **ground**, and **temple**. In the hierarchy view expand the level object and apply the tags to the appropriate objects, finally tag the parent object of the two tribesmen with the enemy tag. Finally move to the **game** script in the inspector and assign the relevant prefabs. Hit the play button and click the **tower** button followed by a tree. The tree should be replaced with a temple.

To place a totem, put this code beneath the tower `if` statement in the **Game** script:

Temple Defense – Part 2

```
if (objectToPlaceNm == "totem"){
   playersWood = playersWood - totemCost;
   placementPos = hit.transform.position;
   var totem : GameObject = Instantiate (totemObj,
      placementPos, transform.rotation);
   totem.transform.Rotate(0,180,0);
   totem.name = inc.ToString();
   Destroy(hit.collider.gameObject);
   objectToPlaceNm = "";
}
```

GUI

It is really starting to come together now. All of the core functionality of the game is in place - the player can place towers and destroy the tribesmen. The last task is to create the GUI and present the user with all the information they are going to need throughout the game such as: the health of their temple and the amount of wood they have left. Let's start by downloading the GUI textures:

> www.deeppixel.com/UnityBookPackages/towerdefense/GUITextures.unitypackage

Start by swapping out Unity's *poor man's* buttons with our nice shiny new ones. We need two styles declared as variables at the top of the **Game** script:

```
var towerBtn : GUIStyle;
var totemBtn : GUIStyle;
```

Then apply these styles to our buttons like so:

```
if (GUI.Button (Rect (10,135,126,98), "", towerBtn))
{
    //print (playersWood);
    if (playersWood >= towerCost){
       objectToPlaceNm = "tower";
    }
}

if (GUI.Button (Rect (10,225,126,98), "", totemBtn))
{
    if (playersWood >= totemCost){
       objectToPlaceNm = "totem";
    }
}
```

Chapter 7

If we go back and look at the **Game** script in the inspector we should see the two styles:

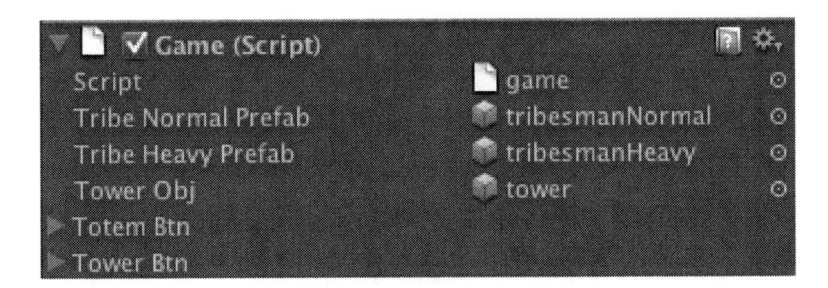

```
▼ ☑ Game (Script)
   Script                      game
   Tribe Normal Prefab         tribesmanNormal
   Tribe Heavy Prefab          tribesmanHeavy
   Tower Obj                   tower
   ▶ Totem Btn
   ▶ Tower Btn
```

Expand both of the button styles and make the following changes:

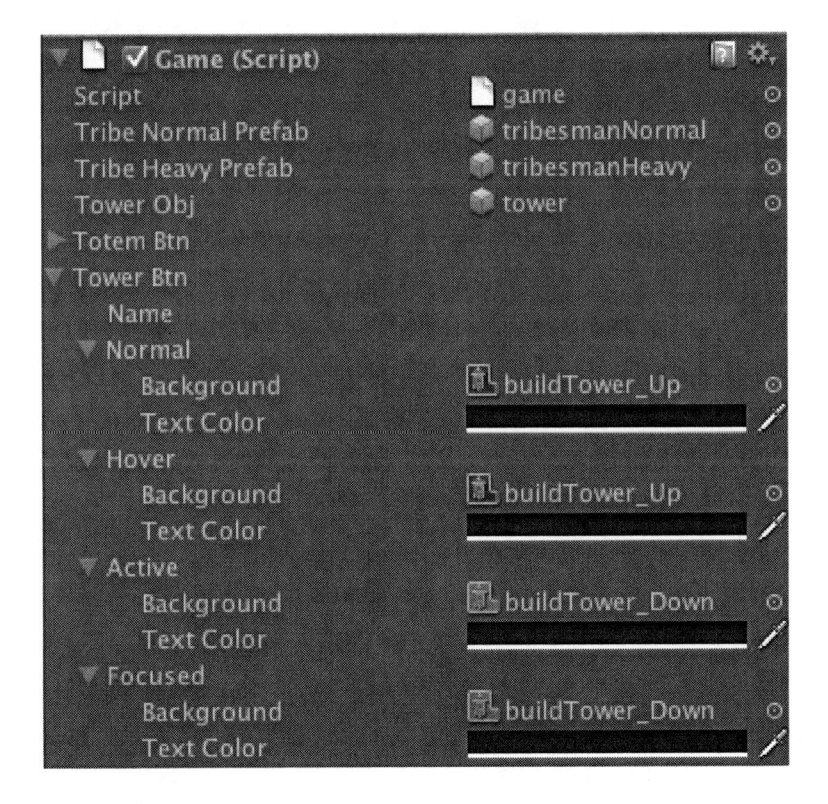

```
▼ ☑ Game (Script)
   Script                      game
   Tribe Normal Prefab         tribesmanNormal
   Tribe Heavy Prefab          tribesmanHeavy
   Tower Obj                   tower
   ▶ Totem Btn
   ▼ Tower Btn
      Name
      ▼ Normal
         Background            buildTower_Up
         Text Color
      ▼ Hover
         Background            buildTower_Up
         Text Color
      ▼ Active
         Background            buildTower_Down
         Text Color
      ▼ Focused
         Background            buildTower_Down
         Text Color
```

Temple Defense – Part 2

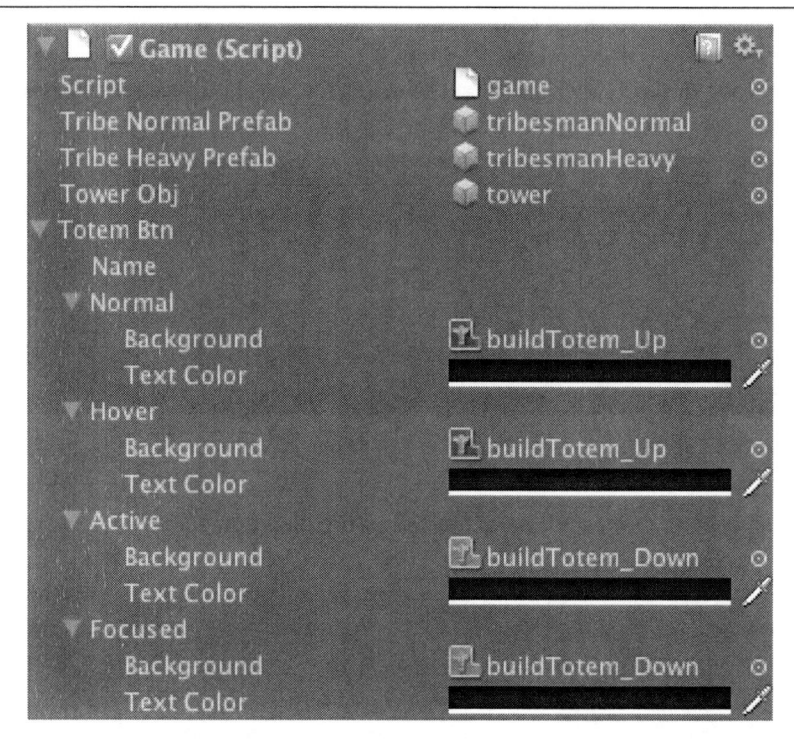

[Screenshot of Unity inspector showing Game (Script) component with fields: Script (game), Tribe Normal Prefab (tribesmanNormal), Tribe Heavy Prefab (tribesmanHeavy), Tower Obj (tower), Totem Btn with Name, Normal (Background: buildTotem_Up, Text Color), Hover (Background: buildTotem_Up, Text Color), Active (Background: buildTotem_Down, Text Color), Focused (Background: buildTotem_Down, Text Color)]

Hit the play button to see your lovely new buttons. If you examine the GUI textures we just imported you will see we have many more textures to use. Let's go ahead and declare these variables in the **Game** script:

```
var defenseWindow : Texture2D;
var scoreWindow : Texture2D;
var wood : Texture2D;
var health : Texture2D;
```

Move back to the inspector and change these to match the appropriate GUI textures. Now before we move on I came across something that wasn't in previous versions of Unity. When you import a texture it now comes with a **Texture Importer** component that is shown in the inspector like so:

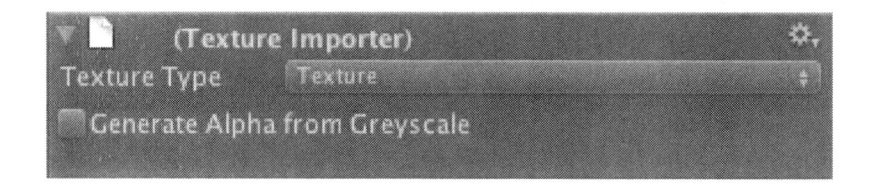

[Screenshot of Texture Importer showing Texture Type: Texture, Generate Alpha from Greyscale checkbox]

If we put our GUI textures in with the type set at **texture** we find that the scaling is off. To fix this all we need to do is select the **GUI** option from the drop down menu, this tells Unity that we our

148

texture is to be used as an *interface element* and the scale will not be affected. Change all the GUI textures we just imported to reflect the new GUI texture type.

We are missing a couple of variables from our code; put these at the top of the **Game** script:

```
private var baseHealth = 50;
private var playerScore = 0;
private var enemiesLeft : int;
```

With our texture sorted we can add these lines to the top of the OnGUI() function before the existing buttons:

```
GUI.Label (Rect (0,-3,103,317), defenseWindow);
GUI.Label (Rect (105,-3,328,64), scoreWindow);
GUI.Label (Rect (10, 23, 126, 98), wood);
GUI.Label (Rect (115, 0, 82, 68), health);
GUI.Label (Rect (85, 80, 100, 30), playersWood.ToString());
GUI.Label (Rect (160, 30, 100, 30), baseHealth.ToString());
GUI.Label (Rect (265, 33, 100, 30), playerScore.ToString());
```

The last piece of the GUI is to put the values of the totem and the tower on the buttons. Put these lines of code underneath the two buttons in the OnGUI() function:

```
GUI.Label (Rect (85, 190, 100, 30), "x50");
GUI.Label (Rect (85, 280, 100, 30), "x100");
```

Hit the play button and you will see your lovely shiny interface.

House Keeping

We are nearly there. The last couple of additions are both aesthetic and functional in nature. Let's start with the functional. Currently we display a score and the health of the player's temple but do not affect these values during the game in that we do not increase or decrease them depending on the state of the game.

A portion of temple health is taken from the player for every tribesman that manages to make it to the temple and sacrifice himself. Go back and open the **EnemyScript**, and make these changes:

Add this variable:

```
var gameObj : GameObject;
```

Add this line to the Start() function:

```
gameObj = gameObject.Find("Game");
```

Temple Defense – Part 2

Finally make these changes to the `Update()` function:

```
if (state == 0){
    if (currentWaypoint != 9){
        walk();
        activeWaypoint = waypoints[currentWaypoint];
    }else{
        var script1 =gameObj.transform.gameObject.GetComponent
            ("game");
        if (script1.baseHealth != 0)
        {
            script1.baseHealth -= 10;
            script1.enemiesLeft -= 1;
        }
        Destroy(this.gameObject);
    }
}
```

We again use the `GetComponent()` function to get access to the **Game** script that is attached to the Game Object and take off 10 points from the **baseHealth** variable. To check that health is indeed being taken off, play the scene now and allow the tribesmen to walk straight to the temple.

We also want to reward the player for stopping as many tribesmen as possible from getting to their temple. We have two values that we can use to reward the player with – wood and score. For every enemy hit the player will get 10 wood in return, and 1000 points will be added to their score. The reason I've made the score go up in thousands is an old game player adage of 'the bigger my score, the better I'm doing, the more fun I'm having'. Let's make the highlighted changes in the `Update()` function of the **EnemyScript**:

```
Debug.DrawLine (myPos.position, activeWaypoint.position,
    Color.red);
var script2 = GetComponent("HealthBarScript");
if (dead != true)
{
    if (script.currHealth <= 0)
    {
        var script2 = gameObj.transform.gameObject.GetComponent
            ("Game");
        script2.playersWood += 10;
        script2.playerScore += 1000;
        script2.enemiesLeft -= 1;
        playDeath();
        dead = true;
    }
}
```

Chapter 7

In both these changes we access the **enemiesLeft** variable, this allows us to track the number of enemies that are left in the game, and when the amount reaches zero we can stop the game. To make this work we need to add this piece of code to the Update() of the **Game** script:

```
if (enemiesLeft == 0)
{
    if (baseHealth == 0)
    {
        print ("Game Over - You lose");
    }else{
        print ("Game Over - You Win");
    }
}
```

Add this piece of code to the Start() function of the Game script to find out how many enemies are in the wave:

```
enemiesLeft = waveFormation.length;
```

Excellent, have a play about with the game and see the effects of the new code.

Particles are just the best

Rather than going through each particle, setting them up from now on, we will just provide you with a package to import the particle systems as prefabs. Download the particle systems from here:

www.deeppixel.com/UnityBookPackages/towerdefense/particles.unitypackage

We have 4 particles in this set. The **blueFlame** and the **redFlame** are for the tops of the temples. Take the **redFlame** and place it on top of the enemy temple, and the **blueFlame** on top of the player's temple. The **enemyHitParticle** is used to indicate to the player that the projectile from the **Tower** has hit an enemy. To get this working is very simple, open up the **ArrowScript**, declare the particle Game Object variable, and add the following line of code into the if:

```
var particleSystem : GameObject;

var ps : GameObject = Instantiate (particleSystem,
    this.transform.position, this.transform.rotation);
```

Make the **particleSystem** variable point to the **enemyHitParticle** prefab then hit play to see the new effect.

Temple Defense – Part 2

The final particle is our death smoke, for when a tribesman successfully reaches the temple and sacrifices himself. For this we need to open up the **EnemyScript** and:

Declare a new variable:

```
var deathParticle : GameObject;
```

Alter the `Update()` function:

```
if (state == 0)
{
   if (currentWaypoint != 9)
   {
      walk();
      activeWaypoint = waypoints[currentWaypoint];
   }else{
      var script1 = gameObj.transform.gameObject.GetComponent
         ("game");
      if (script1.baseHealth != 0)
      {
         script1.baseHealth -= 10;
         script1.enemiesLeft -= 1;
      }
      enemySacrafice();
      Destroy(this.gameObject);
   }
}
```

Create a new function:

```
function enemySacrafice()
{
   var deathSmoke = Instantiate (deathParticle,
   deathParticle.transform.position,
   deathParticle.transform.rotation);
   Destroy(this.gameObject);
}
```

Again go back to the inspector and make sure that in both tribesmen prefabs the **deathParticle** variable points to the **deathSmoke** prefab.

One final touch, click on the **Main Camera** in the hierarchy and change its background colour to a nice dark green (I know this is grayscale here and you can't really see it here, so have a look on the game itself):

Summary

Ah, I have to admit this is a nice looking game. You should be really happy with your progress; you have looked at numerous techniques that are going to provide you with a solid foundation for creating your games in the future.

Specifically, we have addressed how useful an object's transform data can be. Over the past two chapters we have used a Game Object's position and rotation to move enemies about the screen and fire projectiles. This data is crucial in performing calculations that allow us to create behaviours in our world.

The waypoint code that provides our walking behaviour will, in particular, be incredibly useful as the techniques used to create the script can be directly used in numerous gaming situations - from moving enemies to scripted movement of platforms.

Our next port of call is a game that has become very popular over the last 5 years with the release of the iPhone and iPad. We will be playing about with lots of cool physics and materials and utilizing some kick ass 3D content.

Chapter 8

Furry Hurry – Part 1

Furry Hurry is what we have called our "Marble Madness" game which brings us to our final game on our indie journey. Marble maze type games in themselves gained notoriety in the 1980s with the release of the Screwball Scramble (or Snafu) toy and Marble Madness arcade game. The premise of the toy version being to guide a small metal ball around an obstacle course, using various buttons and levers, with each of these controlling a specific part of the course. The goal was simply to complete the game as quickly as possible with most having a timer of 60 seconds to beat. In the case of the video game released by Atari Games in 1984, the ball was controlled by a "trackball", with players navigating the levels avoiding obstacles and enemies, again pressured by a countdown timer.

One of the most impressive marble madness type games to date was a game created in 2007 to demonstrate the capabilities of the AGEIA physics engine. **Switchball** had an ingenious mechanic where the player could change the ball into different types of balls that each had varying physical properties. The steel ball could be used to push heavier objects around, while the power ball could be used to perform a dash to reach previously inaccessible parts of the level.

We are going to take our inspiration from this game and create a game that utilizes Unity's physics engine to the fullest. In this chapter we will look at:

- General Physics.
- Moving Platforms.
- Physics Joints.

Basic setup

Create a new project and call it **marbleMadness** and include the **Particles** package. Set up your **Project View** in the same way as before with 3 folders:

- _assets
- _scenes
- _scripts

In the **_assets** folder, add four additional folders called **Textures**, **Materials**, **Models** and **Prefabs**. **Save** the project and save your scene into the **_scenes** folder calling it **game**.

Game Breakdown

We are going to design the game with two main types of components: puzzles and non-puzzles. The puzzle components will be designed to give the player a lateral thinking challenge on how to progress to the next part of the level. The non-puzzle components will be things like moving platforms and level dangers such as falling spikes. Over the course of the next two chapters we will look at 3 **physics based** puzzles and how to implement them in the game. Let's take a look at the first puzzle.

Puzzle the first

The puzzle itself is made up of the following interactive components:

- Moving Platform.
- Seesaw.
- Movement Block.
- Button.

The premise of the first puzzle is that the button to release the movement block from its unreachable platform cannot be pressed normally. The player will be able to scan the surrounding area and (hopefully!) see that there is a platform above the button that it is possible to fall from – in order to activate the button.

The player navigates to this platform, avoids falling off the moving platform, and falls off the correct platform - activating the button and releasing the movement block. The block can then be used and jammed underneath the seesaw to let the player pass over to the other platform without one end of the seesaw falling down. Simple!

One of Unity's best features is its ability to allow Indie developers to rapidly prototype ideas and mechanics without having to worry about building 3D components in an external program such as Maya or 3DS Max. It is with this in mind that we decided to get you to create the first puzzle from assets that can be made in Unity.

> This actually follows real life. During the development of this game, Simon had another job to complete so I was able to use Unity to prototype the whole of the game and later plug Simon's assets into the game. I say this often but Unity really is the nuts!

It may not be pretty...!

The first puzzle, as alluded to above, involves a seesaw, a button and a block. Let's take a look at what we are aiming to achieve so you can get a good image in your mind.

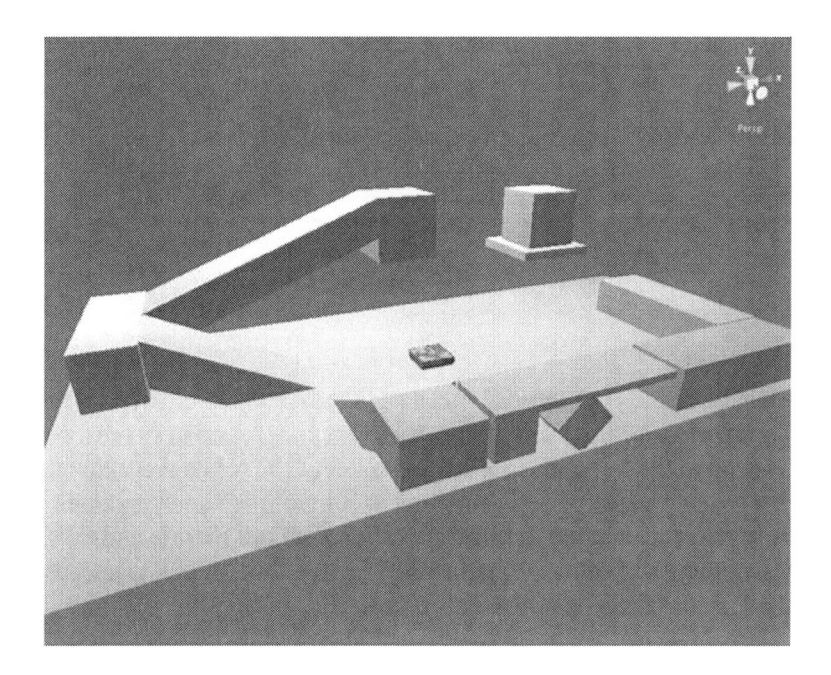

Hopefully you can make out all the different components from this image. The button has been given a texture to differentiate it from the rest of the components. Now the first thing we want to do is get the basics up and running. Create a **plane object** and give it the following scale values: X = 2, Z = 1. Make sure your models have their Z axis pointing backwards. To check this, click on an object and ensure that a blue line is coming out the back in the positive direction.

Then create a sphere object called **marble** and give it a **rigidbody** component, ensuring that **useGravity** is activated. Create a new directional light to illuminate the screen (you will probably have to move the light to get it to fully light the scene). Finally, position the sphere (or from now on the 'marble') high over the plane and hit the play button. The marble should drop onto the plane and not fall through.

We are in control!

The movement functionality is going to be relatively simple for this game, utilizing the standard arrow keys on a keyboard. The breakdown of the keys functionality looks like this:

- UP – Move positively into the Z axis.

- DOWN – Move negatively into the Z axis.
- LEFT – Move negatively into the X axis.
- RIGHT – Move positively into the X axis.

Create a script called **MarbleControl**, attach it to the marble and input this code:

```
var marbleSpeed : float = 15.0f;

function FixedUpdate ()
{
   var torque = Vector3(Input.GetAxis("Horizontal") *
      marbleSpeed, 0, Input.GetAxis("Vertical") *
         marbleSpeed);
   rigidbody.AddForce(torque, ForceMode.Force);
}
```

Here we set up a float that holds our desired speed of the marble, i.e. how fast it moves. Then in an `FixedUpdate()` function we use the `Input.GetAxis()` function to retrieve a value from the virtual axis that is set up to the left and right keyboard keys (Unity has these mapped automatically). This is a particularly useful function as it gives nice analog values in a range from -1 to 1. This allows us to create a softer application of force on our marble and thus gives us nice smooth control. Multiplying the values we get from `Input.GetAxis()` speeds up the movement of the ball, so the range is now from -6 to 6.

Another thing to note is the use of the `FixedUpdate()` function. By using this function we ensure that the performance of the computer (upon which the game is playing) never affects the movement of the marble, keeping it constant. As a little test, change `FixedUpdate()` to `Update()` in your script and hit play to see the difference in movement. Using `Update()` makes the physics application feel less realistic and loose when compared to using a fixed frame rate.

Where is Bob when you need him?

Now we come to the fun part. Building the first puzzle should be straightforward. Using the image below as a reference - try your best to recreate the puzzle using nothing but different sizes and shapes of standard game object cubes.

> We achieved the slanted surface effect by merely rotating a cube and allowing a portion of the mesh to go through the floor. You can also differentiate parts of the scene by using different coloured materials.

Now the seesaw requires a little more setup before it is ready to be used. Add a **rigidbody** to the seesaw plank and hit play. If you didn't see from the picture above - the side of the seesaw closest to the ramp has a small block underneath. When you hit play you are looking for the seesaw to move and rest on this block, so that if you move the sphere to the other side the seesaw will tilt and deny you access to the next platform.

When dealing with a physics based game there is always the chance that the physics may do something unexpected and effectively break the game. In this instance there is the possibility that if the player went too close to the edges of the seesaw it may tilt and fall off its stand.

To ensure this doesn't happen we will apply a component called a **Configurable Joint** to the top of the seesaw (Do this now – **Component > Physics > Configurable Joint**). A Configurable Joint performs two main functions: the restriction and the acceleration of the movement and rotation of an object. For our purposes we are interested in the latter of these two functions in that we want to restrict our seesaw to rotation in the Z axis only. That way we ensure that the player won't break the seesaw by moving too far to one of the sides and tip it over.

Move over to the inspector and match your joint settings to the ones below:

Furry Hurry – Part 1

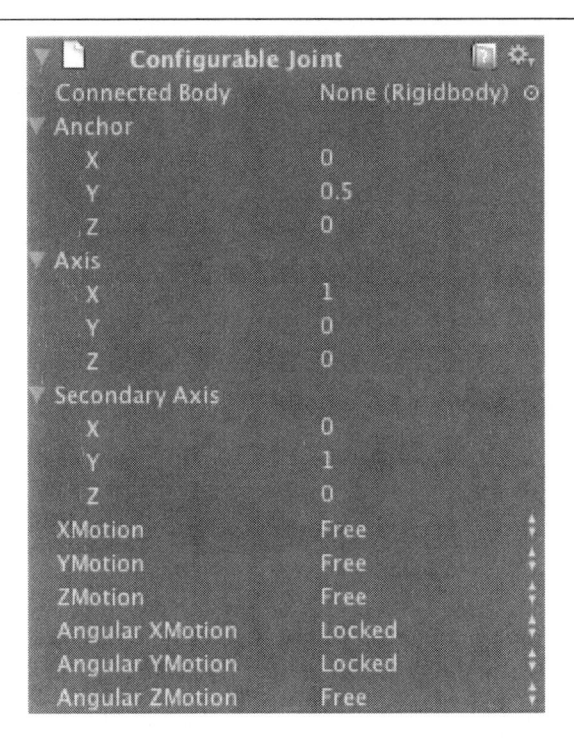

Configurable Joint	
Connected Body	None (Rigidbody)
Anchor	
X	0
Y	0.5
Z	0
Axis	
X	1
Y	0
Z	0
Secondary Axis	
X	0
Y	1
Z	0
XMotion	Free
YMotion	Free
ZMotion	Free
Angular XMotion	Locked
Angular YMotion	Locked
Angular ZMotion	Free

Notice how we have locked the X and Y angular motion of the object and kept the Z axis free. As we said above, this will ensure that there is no chance of the player breaking the seesaw; the only movement it will be able to make is around the Z axis.

Fire up the game and have a play with the seesaw. A configurable joint has a lot of properties that can be set, possibly too many to go through in detail here but check out the script reference and Unity's online resources to find out more.

Button, Button, Who's Got the Button?

The button that resides beneath our tall slanted platform makes up the main piece of functionality in our puzzle. It is the means to the player's goal, which is releasing the block and navigating across the seesaw. Before we look into any code let's do some set up in our level:

- Name the block on the platform in the air **movementBlock** and give it a **rigidbody** with gravity applied.

- Apply a configurable joint to the **movementBlock** and set all the Angular XYZ motions to **locked**.

- Name the platform holding up movementBlock – **blockGuard**.

- Name the button – **button1**.

Create a script called **Button1Script** and attach it to the **button1** object. For this script I decided to use an elegant solution that I found in the Unity forums. I had intended to use my own script but this one was so tight and clean that I thought it would be great to showcase the quality of the support that is out there in the Unity community. This particular submission was from a very active forum poster named **Eric5h5** on the excellent website **Unity Answers** (answers.unity3d.com). To find the original post, type **pressure pad** into the search and it should be the first result. Now, on to the code. Replace the `Update()` function with these lines of code:

```
static var canBePressed = false;
private var blockGuard : GameObject;

function Start()
{
   blockGuard = gameObject.Find("blockGuard");
}
```

We start by declaring two variables and finding the **blockGuard** object in our scene. This is in preparation for removing it to allow the block to drop once the button is pressed.

Next we declare a new function using `OnCollisionEnter()` to identify when our marble object collides with the button. We don't use `OnTriggerEnter()` since we want the button to be a physical part of the world. Put this collision code after the `Start()`:

```
function OnCollisionEnter(col : Collision)
{
   if (canBePressed == true)
   {
      MoveDown (transform, 0.2, 0.2);
      renderer.material.shader = Shader.Find (" Glossy");
      renderer.material.SetColor ("_SpecColor", Color.red);
      Destroy(blockGuard);
   }
}
```

Inside the function we create a conditional statement that only allows the button to be pressed when the `canBePressed` variable is true. This ensures that the player can't just roll over the button without having been to the higher platform beforehand. When the button has been pressed we call the `MoveDown()` function. Here we pass in the current transform of the button object along with `distance` and `speed` values. Put this code in the script:

```
function MoveDown (thisTransform : Transform, distance :    float,
speed : float) {
   var startPos = thisTransform.position.y;
   var endPos = startPos - distance;
   var rate = 1.0 / Mathf.Abs(startPos - endPos) * speed;
   var t = 0.0;
```

Furry Hurry – Part 1

```
    while (t < 1.0) {
        t += Time.deltaTime * rate;
        thisTransform.position.y = Mathf.Lerp(startPos,
            endPos, t);
        yield;
    }
}
```

The function takes in the distance and speed values and creates four variables. The `startPos` holds the current `y` value of the button's position. The `endPos` is calculated by subtracting the `startPos` with the `distance` value. The `rate` at which the button moves is calculated using the `Mathf.Abs` function that returns an absolute float value. Finally the `t` variable is created to hold the conditional value for the while loop.

When the `while` loop is initialized, `t` is set to `0.0`, this value is then increased in the loop incrementally using the values of `Time.deltaTime` and `rate`. We then use the `Mathf.Lerp` function to interpolate the `startPos` towards the `endPos` over a period of time. To see the script and the button in action move this line into the `Start()` function and hit play (remember to put it back afterwards!!!):

```
MoveDown (transform, 0.2, 0.2);
```

With the button in place, the next thing we need to look at is how to indicate to the game that the button can be pressed. So game-wise we want the button only to be pressed when the player reaches the peak of the ramp.

To do this, we need to create a **bounding box** at the top of the slope. Create a cube and name it **button1BB**, navigate to the inspector and make its materials **size** equal to 0 and ensure **Is Trigger** is activated. This gives us a nice bounding box. Move the box to the top of the slope similar to the image below:

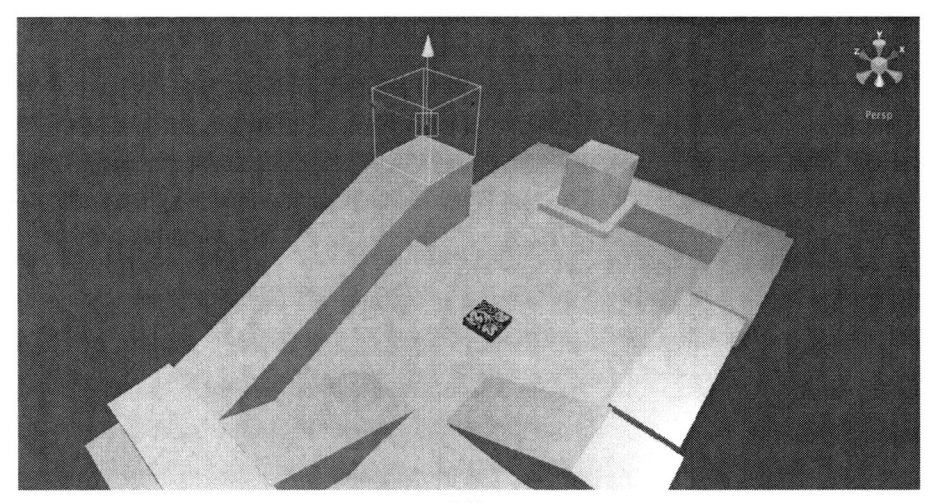

Create a new script called **Button1BBScript**, attach it to the **button1BB** object, and open it up. This is a very simple script:

```
var button1 : Button1Script;

function OnTriggerEnter(collision : Collider)
{
   button1.canBePressed = true;
}
```

At the top a variable called `button1` is declared and given a type of `Button1Script`. This allows us to directly access the script component that is attached to the **button1** object, a very neat trick that will be invaluable as you go through your Unity career.

Go back to the editor. In the inspector of the **button1BB** object, navigate to the script and **button1** variable. You will see that nothing is selected, click on the little circle icon to the right and it will open up a navigation window which will have the **Button1Script** object listed for you to select. This now gives us a reference to that object. We then use the standard `OnTriggerEnter()` function to catch our trigger collision and then use our new reference to access the `canBePressed` variable on the **button1** object's script and set it to `true`, thus making the button active!

Well done, you have made your first puzzle! Head on back to the editor and hit play, make your way up to the top and drop off onto the button to see it depress and the **movementBlock** released!! You can now move that block underneath the seesaw and safely move across to the other platform!

The final touch to add a little challenge to the puzzle comes in the form of a moving platform between the two slopes that gives the player access to press the button.

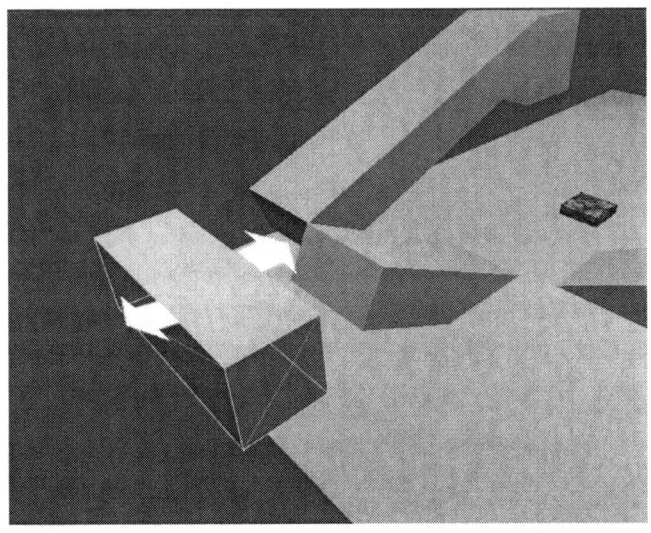

Like the image shows, we want the platform to move along the X axis to a point and then move back to its original position, repeating this process throughout. Click on this platform and call it **platform1**. Create a new script called **Platform1Script,** attach it to the object, open and copy the following code:

```
var speed : float = 1.0;
var startPosition:Vector3;
var moveDistance:float=3.0;

function Start()
{
   startPosition=transform.position;
}

function FixedUpdate () {
   transform.position =startPosition+ Vector3(Mathf.PingPong
      (Time.time*speed, moveDistance), 0.0, 0.0);
}
```

In the code above we use a `Mathf` function called `PingPong` which essentially ping pongs a value so that it is never larger than the declared length and never smaller than 0. If you compare this code to the sample in the docs you will see that we have altered it a bit by adding the `Vector3` value calculated using the `PingPong` function to the `startPosition` of our platform. When you hit play you will see that the platform doesn't perform as expected. What you need to do is move the moving platform so that its starting position is not touching the other platforms.

We can take a little breather now, the basics of the first puzzle are complete and we have created a nice little placeholder scene which we can use to insert our fancy new art.

> This section has highlighted essentially the beauty of Unity3d, you can quickly prototype a 3D scene to test out object placement and mechanics in no time and save lots of effort in having to redo game ready assets that have been created in Maya or 3DS Max.

Puzzle 1 is ready for its close-up

From here onwards we are going to use the final game art assets to complete the rest of the puzzles. It would be a bit of a longwinded two chapters if you had to create a placeholder scene first and then replace each asset(s) for every puzzle. Download the following art assets:

www.deeppixel.com/UnityBookPackages/marblemadness/models.unitypackage

In this package are all the assets needed to make the first puzzle without new (in game) assets. You will notice that a folder called **Materials** is created in the **Models** folder, leave this as it is, Unity sometimes is quite unpredictable when importing and exporting assets. Next download and import this package:

www.deeppixel.com/UnityBookPackages/marblemadness/puzzle1.unitypackage

This package has a prefab in it called **puzzle1**. Drag it onto the screen and you will see a similar sight to below:

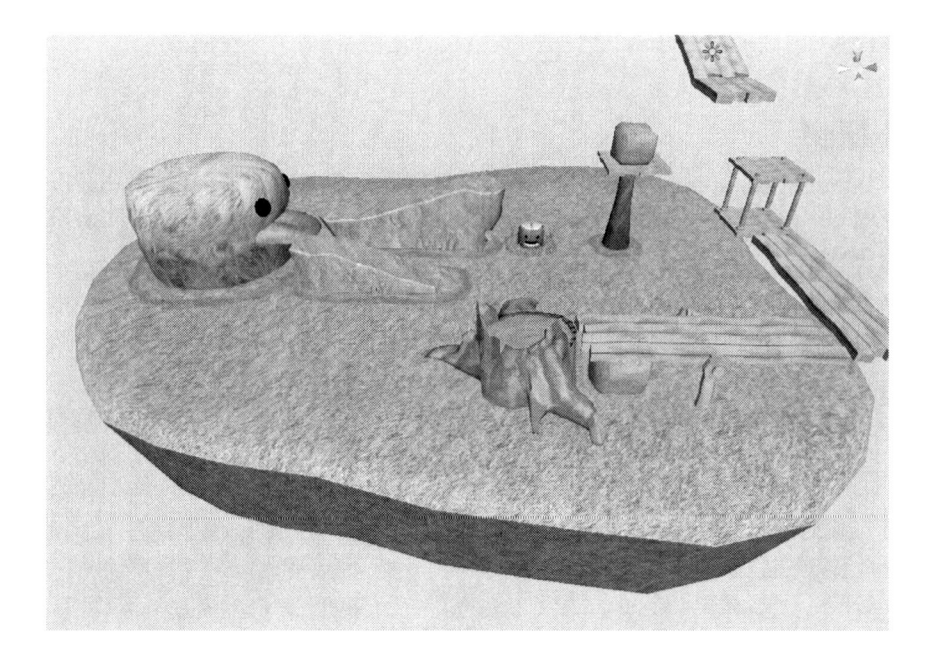

What you can do now is deactivate all your previous unity objects that made up the first puzzle to make room for the new assets. Before we move on to getting this level functioning, let's take a quick look at our character.

Fuzzy Red Guy

Select the **marble** model that you have just imported and drag it onto the scene on top of the grass platform. Add a **rigidbody** to the marble with gravity turned on. Then remove the **Mesh Collider** component and replace it with a **Sphere Collider**. Now, take the **MarbleControl** script and attach it to the prefab. Position him in the scene and hit play to test him out.

Furry Hurry – Part 1

> You will probably see that the scene is a bit dark, put in a directional light now to shed some light on the situation. The light will come in facing positively in the Z direction, we want our light and incidentally the camera facing positively in the X direction so rotate both the camera and the light 90 degrees in the Y axis.

We will also need to do a quick change to the **MarbleControl** script since our new models are facing in a different direction to our previous ones. This is a good place to highlight why you should always agree with the artist, specifically - what the axes are (which will be used to place objects). Simon's models face backwards positively in the X direction. Open the script now and change the current `torque` line to this:

```
var torque = Vector3(Input.GetAxis("Vertical") * marbleSpeed,  0,
Input.GetAxis("Horizontal") * -marbleSpeed);
```

Look At Me!

With our marble set up and ready to roll (horrid pun) our next step is to get it so that the Main Camera follows our fuzzy red hero around the scene. Create a new script called **MarbleCamera** and enter this code:

```
var target : Transform;
var xDist : float = 5.0f;
var dmpSpd : int = 2;
var height : float = 3.0f;
private var newPos : Vector3;

function Update () {
   if (target != null){
      newPos = target.position + Vector3(-xDist,
         height,0 );
      transform.position = Vector3.Lerp(transform.position,
         newPos, Time.deltaTime*dmpSpd);
   }
}
```

Attach it to the **MainCamera** object and set its `target` property to that of the **marble** object in our scene. Hit the play button and you should see the camera focusing in on your little marble. If it doesn't look quite right, play about with the values. Essentially what the code does is update a new Vector3 called `newPos` every frame, based on the target's position and a Vector3 that takes in a negative X distance, a relative height value in the Y and keeps the Z zeroed. We then use the resulting Vector3 in a `Lerp` function which moves the transform of the **MainCamera** to the new point in space, smoothly I might add.

Pink Button & Stone Block

Now to make this work we need a new **button1BB** object; create a cube, set the material size to 0 and position it on top of the second sloping platform. The premise with these models is that when you hit the little pink button not only does he hide in the ground but his tail which is next to him holding up the block also moves underground, allowing the player access to the block. The first order of business is to attend to the fuzzy pink head and make it act like our placeholder button, like so:

To start with, attach the **Button1Script** to the pink button object called **furryPinkHead** and open it up ready to make the following changes. Remove the following lines:

```
blockGuard = gameObject.Find("blockGuard");

Destroy(blockGuard);
renderer.material.shader = Shader.Find (" Glossy");
renderer.material.SetColor ("_SpecColor", Color.red);
```

Increase the speed of the object's movement:

```
MoveDown (transform, 0.2, 1.0);
```

Now hit the play button and test out the pink button. You'll notice that even if you miss the button when coming off the stone slope you can still go roll back and activate it from the ground. We want the player to do this properly so that if they miss the button they have to go back up to the top of the slope until they hit the button from a height. Create a new script called **GroundScript**, attach it to the **grassPlatform** object and put in this code:

```
var button1 : Button1Script;
```

Furry Hurry – Part 1

```
function OnCollisionEnter(col : Collision)
{
   if (col.gameObject.tag == "marble")
   {
      button1.canBePressed = false;
   }
}
```

So if the player (just the player) collides with the ground the variable `canBePressed` is accessed and set to `false`, disabling the pink button. Remember - to make this script functional - you will have to go back to the editor and in the inspector select the object for the variable `btnScript`, in this case **furryPinkHead**. You will also need to tag the marble with the appropriate name (Remember creating the tag doesn't automatically set it to the object).

Next we need the pink head's pink tail to move down to give the player access to the stone block. Move back to the **Button1Script** and make the following additions:

```
var tail : GameObject;

function Start()
{
   tail = gameObject.Find("furryPinkTale");
}
```

Underneath the `moveDown()` function call:

```
MoveTail (tail.transform, 2.4, 0.4);
```

Create a new function:

```
function MoveTail (thisTransform1 : Transform, distance1 : float,
speed1 : float)
{
   var startPos1 = thisTransform1.position.y;
   var endPos1 = startPos1 - distance1;
   var rate1 = 1.0 / Mathf.Abs(startPos1 - endPos1) * speed1;
   var t1 = 0.0;
   while (t1 < 1.0) {
      t1 += Time.deltaTime * rate1;
      thisTransform1.position.y = Mathf.Lerp(startPos1,
         endPos1, t1);
      yield;
   }
}
```

Hit save and move back to the editor and set the `tail` variable to the **furryPinkTail** object. Test out the scene by hitting the pink button. The tail should descend to where it is accessible by the player. Now, as you will see, the platform and rock don't descend with the tail. To make this happen, attach the platform to the tail as a child, therefore when the tail moves the platform moves. Finally we need to set up the rock as we had in our placeholder scene. Apply a **rigidbody** to the rock with gravity turned on, and remove its Mesh Collider and replace it with a Box Collider. We then need a Configurable Joint component with all its rotation values locked, so set the Angular Motion to **locked**.

Fuzzy Yellow's Tongue

To the left of the stone slopes you will see a fuzzy yellow guy sticking out of the ground, with his tongue protruding outwards. This will take the place of our moving platform in the placeholder scene. To get this tongue moving take the **Platform1Script** and attach it to the tongue, which should be a separate object from the head. We then want to change the code in this script, specifically the line in the `FixedUpdate()` to this:

```
transform.position =startPosition+ Vector3(0.0, 0.0,
    Mathf.PingPong(Time.time*speed, moveDistance));
```

Here we are manipulating the Z axis instead of the X axis as we did in our placeholder game. You will probably want to make the distance and speed properties smaller. I landed on `1.0` for distance and `0.5` for speed. You will also have to move the tongue about to get it sitting correctly in the yellow fuzzy's head.

I see your saw

As you will have noticed, the seesaw isn't working. Create a cube game object and place it underneath the seesaw (like below) to act as the pivot point. Remember to either deactivate the mesh renderer or change the material number to 0 to make it invisible to the player.

Next, replace the current Mesh Collider, on the seesaw plank of wood, with a Box Collider, and apply a **rigidbody** with gravity. When you hit play the seesaw might not move much, what you need to do is move the supports outwards a little bit as the box collider may be colliding with them a bit. Our final port of call is to attach a Configurable Joint and lock the angular movement in the Y and Z axes.

We have lift off

The final piece to this puzzle is the lift that gives the player access to the next area of the game. Essentially this is set up in exactly the same way as the fuzzy yellow guy's tongue. So let's start by duplicating the **platform1Script** and renaming it **lift1Script**. Attach the lift script to the lift object and open it and replace the line in the `FixedUpdate()` with this:

```
transform.position =startPosition+ Vector3(0.0,
    Mathf.PingPong(Time.time*speed, moveDistance),0.0 );
```

Similar to when we changed the platform script we now move along the Y axis to give our lift vertical movement instead of horizontal.

Summary

I have to say I really love the look of this game - big shout to Simon - excellent work my friend. With our first puzzle area complete I hope you can see the benefit of prototyping your scene before committing any time to real in game assets. Had I not made this placeholder scene first in Unity and play tested it before Simon started creating assets we could have had some real trouble guaranteeing that everything would work as it should, especially since we are using physics puzzles which by their very nature are unpredictable.

Our work on moving platforms (while short) will be a great foundation for you to start experimenting and creating your own mechanics for platform games. We have merely scratched the surface by moving an object between two points in a loop, and there is scope to expand and try to create new and exciting platforms that will challenge the player and also yourself.

We move on now to what is the final chapter in our journey together, we will look at some cool physics materials and implement the rest of our wacky fuzzy level.

Chapter 9

Furry Hurry – Part 2

We now find ourselves nearing the end of the road. This final part will tie off our Marble Madness game and our look through the development of 4 exciting game blueprints. The previous chapter highlighted the practicality of rapid prototyping using Unity and expanded on some nice mechanics that you will be able to keep in your Unity library to be used again on your own excellent game projects.

Unity is a unique beast in the game engine world. Not only have they, as a company, created a fantastic platform - they have helped nurture and grow the outstanding online **community** as well. Their new **Assets Store** is a testament to Unity's commitment to their users and with so much content available from other Unity users from one source the future can only be bright.

For our final chapter we are going to focus more on the quite lovely in-built features of Unity. We will take our first puzzle area and expand upon it creating two new challenges for the player to overcome. In detail we will look at:

- Physics Materials.
- More physics effects.

Puzzle (or challenge) the second

Our second puzzle is not so much of a puzzle as a challenge. The gist of the idea is to fire the marble character out of a cannon through a wall of ice cubes and onto a snowy platform without missing or sliding off. We have all of the necessary components already downloaded and in our project view so go ahead now and create a scene similar to the one below. (You will utilize, 4 x woodPlatformSmall, 6 x woodPlatform, 1 x furryBlue, 1 x furryPurple, 1 x iceCube, 1 x icePlatform, 1 x snowWall).

Furry Hurry – Part 2

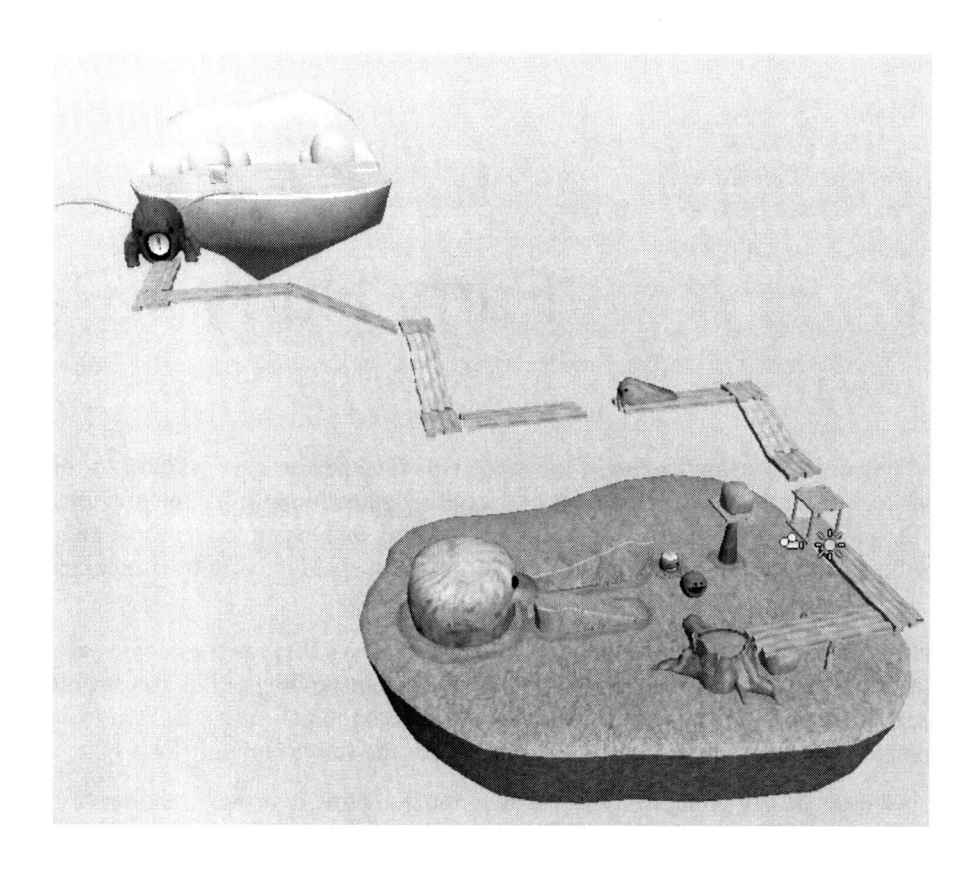

Just in case there is confusion about who the **furryPurple** (left) and **furryBlue** (right) guys are - here they are:

The final addition to our puzzle is to build a wall of **iceCubes** for our hero to smash through. To make sure the puzzle works properly, add a **rigidbody** and replace the Mesh Collider with a Box Collider. Then duplicate this cube to create your wall. I have made mine 7x5 but you can play about with the numbers and positions and see what feels right to you. To make your hierarchy view a bit tidier, place all these cubes in a parent object called **iceCubeWall**.

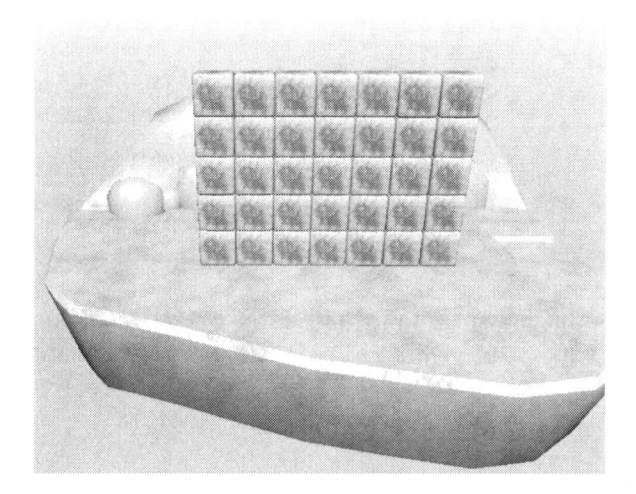

Excellent, now as you may have guessed, the **furryPurple** guy is our cannon, there to eat our little red friend and shoot him out towards the ice cubes. The functionality of the cannon is quite simple. When the character approaches the mouth of the cannon he gets removed from the scene (i.e. eaten). The cannon then rotates around towards the snow platform and starts to move from left to right; the view for the user will be first person so a camera will be attached to the front of the cannon.

The player then hits SPACE to fire which instantiates a new marble character and fires him towards the platform. Easy peasy. Let's get started.

Cannons at the ready

The cannon is set up very much like the furryPink button. We need a bounding box to indicate when the marble has reached the cannon's mouth. Create a new cube game object and name it **cannonCollider**, make its material size equal to 0 to make it invisible and make it a trigger. Now position the cube in a similar fashion to this:

Furry Hurry – Part 2

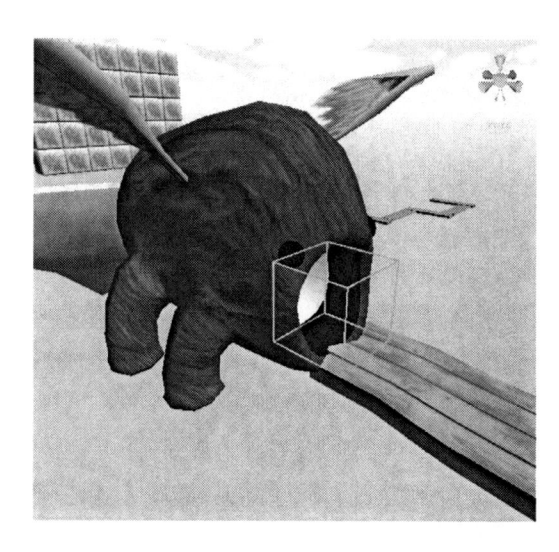

Create and attach a new script called **CannonColliderScript** and open it up. At this point all we want the collider to do is remove the character from the scene upon colliding with the box. Enter this code:

```
function OnTriggerEnter(col : Collider)
{
    Destroy(col.gameObject);
}
```

Save your new code, position the character on a platform near the cannon, hit play and test the collider by moving towards the bounding box; once it collides with the box it should be removed from the scene. With the marble removed from the scene the next port of call is to create a script for the cannon to move to the left and right.

Left, right, left right left

Duplicate the **Platform1Script** and call it **CannonControllerScript**. Attach it to the **furryPurple** cannon object. Open it up and in the line where we set the `transform.position` value change the "+" sign to a "-" sign. Change the `moveDistance` variable to around 8 in the inspector and hit play to see the **furryPurple** cannon guy move from left to right across the screen. (Your placement of certain objects may affect the size of the `moveDistance` variable)

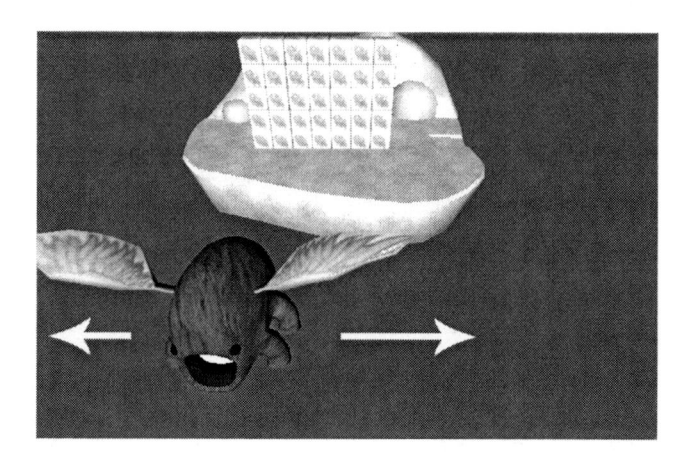

Rotation, rotation, rotation

The main (fun)ctionality for the cannon comes from the player being able to fire the character from the cannon into the wall of ice cubes. We will utilize a similar method to the shooting that we have done in previous chapters. The way we want the cannon to work is:

- Remove the character from the scene.
- Show a new view from a camera attached to the camera.
- Rotate the cannon to face the snowy platform.
- Move left and right.
- Allow the player to shoot using the keyboard.

We have removed the character and have the cannon moving left to right. Before we implement the shooting functionality we want to turn the cannon to face the platform. This should only be done when the character has been removed from the screen so we need to let the cannon know when the character is no longer in the scene. Open the **CannonColliderScript** and make the following changes:

```
var cannonController : cannonController;
function OnTriggerEnter(col : Collider)
{
    Destroy(col.gameObject);
}
```

Here we want to eventually access a new function that we will declare in the **CannonControllerScript** called `rotateCannon()`. So we create a variable called

Furry Hurry – Part 2

`cannonController` to get access to the function. Move to the **CannonControllerScript** and enter the following code:

```
private var rotating = false;

function rotateCannon (rotateAxis : Vector3, degrees : float)
{
   print ("rotate cannon");
   if (rotating) return;
   rotating = true;
   var rate = 100;
   for (i = 0.0; i < degrees; i += Time.deltaTime * rate)
   {
      yield;
      transform.RotateAround(transform.position, rotateAxis,
         Time.deltaTime * rate);
   }
   rotating = false;
}
```

This `rotateCannon()` function takes in 2 arguments. The first is the axis on which the object will rotate, the second is the number of degrees we want to rotate by. When the function is called, a check is done to see if the cannon is rotating. If it is rotating the code returns without running the code below the `if`. Otherwise the `rate` is set to `100` and we enter the `for` loop which controls the rotation of the object:

```
for (i = 0.0; i < degrees; i += Time.deltaTime * rate)
   {
      yield;
      transform.RotateAround(transform.position, rotateAxis,
         Time.deltaTime * rate);
   }
```

A `for` loop is used to call the `RotateAround()` function on the transform class where the exit condition is when `i` is no longer less than the number of `degrees` that was passed into the function. The `yield` line effectively tells the code to wait for one frame before moving on to the next line, this gives us a nice smooth rotation over a number of frames rather than an instantaneous move over 1 frame.

> If you were to comment out the `yield` statement now (don't - as it won't work) and run the code, on triggering the function the object would move over one frame to the desired number of degrees, giving an instantaneous rotation rather than having a nice smooth transition.

The final piece of the function sets the `rotating` boolean value back to `false` to ensure that the object stops rotating. Now to get this code working, move back to the **CannonColliderScript** and add in the function call after you destroy the marble guy:

```
cannonController.rotateCannon(Vector3.up, 180);
```

Here we pass two values to the `rotateCannon()` function, the first `Vector3.up` effectively tells the function that we will be using the Y-axis to rotate around, and the second is the number of degrees the object will turn. Before you test this code, move to the **CannonControllerScript** script and comment out the two lines of code in the `FixedUpdate()` function. Hit play and move your character into the cannon to see it rotate 180 degrees.

> Make sure you set the **cannonController** variable in the inspector on the **cannonCollider** object. Also remember to uncomment the lines before moving on.

All together now

We now have the cannon rotating to face the platform and moving, but it doesn't do this yet in one fluid motion. Now we don't want the cannon to move until it has rotated to the desired position, to do this we need a conditional statement.

Open the **CannonControllerScript** script and add the highlighted lines in the `FixedUpdate()`:

```
var startCannonMoving = false;

if (startCannonMoving == true){
    transform.position = startPosition - Vector3(0.0, 0.0,
        Mathf.PingPong(Time.time*speed, moveDistance));
}
```

This `if` checks to see if the cannon should start moving before executing the code inside. To make this condition `true` we need to go down to the `rotateCannon()` function and beneath the line where we set `rotating` to `false` enter this line :

```
startCannonMoving = true;
```

Hit play, upon colliding and starting the cannon moving you will see it moves abruptly to the right while rotating and then starts to move normally. **This is just no good!** Let's inspect the **CannonControllerScript** script and see if we can find the problem.

```
transform.position = startPosition - Vector3(0.0, 0.0,
    Mathf.PingPong(Time.time*speed, moveDistance));
```

Furry Hurry – Part 2

The highlighted text (above) is where we get our value that updates over every **fixed** frame, effectively starting from zero and (from thereon) providing a value that can be used to move the object. Now we don't know the exact time when the user will collide with the cannon, and since `Time.time` starts when the game starts it has become redundant in our code. Hmmmm, what if we were able to use the `Time.time` value to get a zero value and from there proceed as normal with the value increasing over time? Let's look at the solution. Add in the highlighted lines to the **CannonControllerScript**:

```
var startTime : float;
var timeleft : float;
var beginTime = false;

function FixedUpdate () {
   if (beginTime == true){
      startTime = Time.time;
      beginTime = false;
   }

   if (startCannonMoving == true){
      timeleft = Time.time - startTime;
      transform.position = startPosition - Vector3(0.0, 0.0,
         Mathf.PingPong(timeleft*speed, moveDistance));
   }
}
```

Three new variables are set up; the time variables are floats which will make sure that the movement of the object is kept smooth. We do a check - `if` the `beginTime` variable is set to `true`, we take the current time value from `Time.time`. When the `startCannonMoving` variable is set to `true` we enter the `if` and work out what the time is.

Now we want the movement of the cannon to start from its original position so `timeLeft` variable has to equal 0 at the start. If the `timeleft` was more than 0 then the cannon would start moving from a position further along. The `timeleft` variable is worked out by taking the current time at the frame and taking it away from our `startTime`. Then finally the code loops round while `startCannonMoving` is `true` and incrementally increases the `timeleft` variable as it goes, thus moving the cannon from side to side.

To get this working move down to the `rotateCannon()` function and put this line underneath where you set `startCannonMoving` to `true`:

```
beginTime = true;
```

Give it a try now! Next we want to give the player a nice perspective to see the cannon moving side to side from. To do this we will create a new camera.

I spy...

Let's create a new camera and call it **cannonCamera**. We want the camera to move with the cannon so make it a child of the **furryPurple** object, and position it similar to the image below:

We need a little script that will manage the cameras that are in the scene and turn them off and on when required. Create a new empty game object called **GameManager** and an attached script with the same name. Open it up and enter the following code:

```
var mainC : GameObject;
var cannonC : GameObject;

function Start()
{
    mainCameraOn();
}

function mainCameraOn()
{
    mainC.camera.enabled = true;
    cannonC.camera.enabled = false;
}

function cannonCameraOn()
{
    mainC.camera.enabled = false;
    cannonC.camera.enabled = true;
}
```

Furry Hurry – Part 2

The two functions here simply enable the **mainCamera** or the **cannonCamera**. If you move back to the inspector and select the two cameras for the variables in the **GameManager** script we will be all set up and ready to go. The only other thing to do is open the **CannonColliderScript** script and add this code. Add to the variables:

```
var gmMger : GameManager;
```

Add to the `OnTriggerEnter()` after the marble is destroyed:

```
gmMger.cannonCameraOn();
```

Move back to the inspector and select the game object with the **gameManager** script attached for the `gmMger` variable. Hit the play button and you should be able to activate the **cannonCamera** when loading the character into the cannon. *In the console you may see an indication that there are two audio listeners in the scene and there should only be one.* What you can do is select the **cannonCamera** and in the inspector turn off its audio listener component.

Eat, pray, fire!

We come now to the final aspect of the cannon, the all-important shooting functionality. To keep the shooting simple we will use the space bar as the trigger to shoot. Open up the **CannonControllerScript** and add the following:

Variables:

```
var cannonProjectile : GameObject;
var shootSpwn : GameObject;
var initialSpeed = 40.0f;
var canFire = false;
var mrblCam : MarbleCamera;
var gmMger : GameManager;
```

`Update()` function:

```
function Update () {
    if (Input.GetKey (KeyCode.Space)) {
      if (canFire == true){
          fire();
      }
    }
}
```

`fire()` function:

```
function fire()
```

```
{
    print ("fire");
    var cannon : GameObject = Instantiate(cannonProjectile,
        shootSpwn.transform.position,
            shootSpwn.transform.rotation) as GameObject;
    cannon.rigidbody.velocity =
        transform.TransformDirection(Vector3(-1,0,0)
            *initialSpeed);
    canFire = false;
    mrblCam.target = cannon.transform;
    gmMger.mainCameraOn();
}
```

You should be starting to recognize certain parts of code and begin being able to code them without having to search the documents. The code for shooting the cannon is very similar to that of the shooting functionality in the space shooter game in previous chapter(s). We have a condition in the `Update()` function that checks on every frame for the space bar key press, when this is `true` the `fire()` function is called, where it instantiates the object held in the **cannonProjectile** variable, at the position of the object held in the **shootSpwn** variable. The instantiated object's rigid body is accessed to apply a force to its velocity. When this happens and the character is sent through the air, the camera that followed the character around is turned back on with the target of the new instantiated object. Easy peasy :)!

What we need to do now is set up the scene and the variables for this code to use. First of all we need a point of origin for the character when it is instantiated. Create a new empty game object and call it **cannonShootSpwn**. Make it a child of the cannon object and position it in front of the cannon's mouth:

Furry Hurry – Part 2

With the spawn point selected, click on the button at the top of the editor next to the center button and change it to **local** if it is not set to that already. Ensure that the x axis (the red one) is pointing into the cannon's mouth; this is because we have the vector of the direction to fire in code as **(-1, 0, 0)** which is negative in the x axis. If you cast your eye back over the code you will see that our key press has a conditional statement that says that it will only fire if `canFire` is equal to `true`. Move down to `rotateCannon()` and put this line of code after the setting of the `beginTime` variable:

```
canFire = true;
```

We also have a piece of code that instantiates the marble. If we did this using the model prefab we could get horrid errors about not having a rigidbody attached to the object. So before we see this in action, create a new prefab called **marble** out of our nice marble hero in the scene. You can now move over to the inspector and under the **CannonControllerScript** assign the appropriate objects and scripts to the variables.

Physic Material Goodness

We are going to divert slightly from building our level and take a look at another of Unity's excellent in-built features, the physics material. The premise is simple, a physics material can be applied to objects that collide and affect the friction and bouncing effects that happen between them. Unity provides 5 pre-made materials that come with the **Standard Assets** package. Let's grab them now by right clicking on the project view and from the **Import Package** drop down menu click **Physic Materials**. Let's take a look at the basic variables in a physics material:

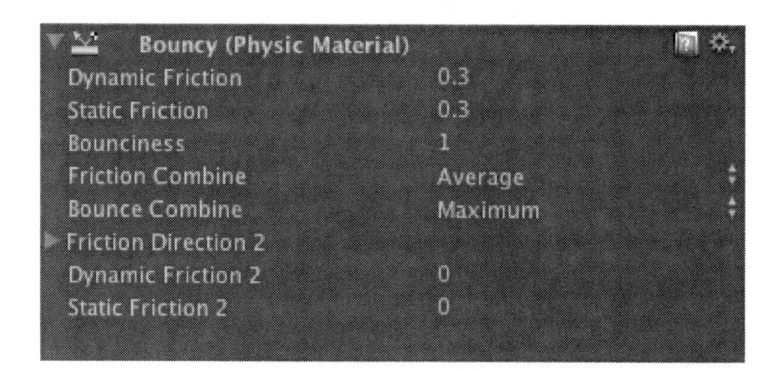

Bouncy (Physic Material)	
Dynamic Friction	0.3
Static Friction	0.3
Bounciness	1
Friction Combine	Average
Bounce Combine	Maximum
Friction Direction 2	
Dynamic Friction 2	0
Static Friction 2	0

Dynamic Friction allows you to play with the friction that is applied when an object is in motion. With 0 making the friction like ice and 1 making the object come to rest a lot quicker.

Static Friction is basically the same as Dynamic Friction but it is used when the object is motionless, effectively sliding at the lower end and sticking at the higher end.

Bounciness does exactly what it says on the tin; the higher the value the bouncier it is.

Friction Combine allows you to set what the friction will be between two objects when they collide.

Bounce Combine sets the bounciness of two colliding objects. As you can see above in the physics material, it is set to maximum to get a nice high bounce.

Let's move on now and get a physics material into our game, and get the rest of our in game assets into our level.

Platforms of Death

Select the **furryGreen** object and place three of them like so, just off the snowy platform:

Select the **Bouncy** material, duplicate it and call it **myBounce** and apply it to the furry green guys by clicking and dragging the material onto the objects. Now we want to make our material a little bouncier so change the dynamic and static friction values to **0.1**.

Our final physics material addition is to the icy platform. Hit the play button and have a play about with your new physics materials.

Ready, set, roll!

The next challenge to face the player is the dreaded dropping platforms of **DOOM**! Essentially when the character hits the platforms they start disintegrating underneath them, giving the player only a certain amount of time to safely pass across the platforms. Take the **woodBrokenPlatform** object and place it into the scene. Now we need to make some changes to this model. Expand the parent to reveal the children, each of these is an individual "shard" model that will fall away when the player is on the platform. Apply a **rigidbody** to each of these shards now. We will want the marble to interact with the **woodBrokenPlatform** object. Look at the parent object and you will see it doesn't have a collider. Add a Box Collider now and match these values:

Furry Hurry – Part 2

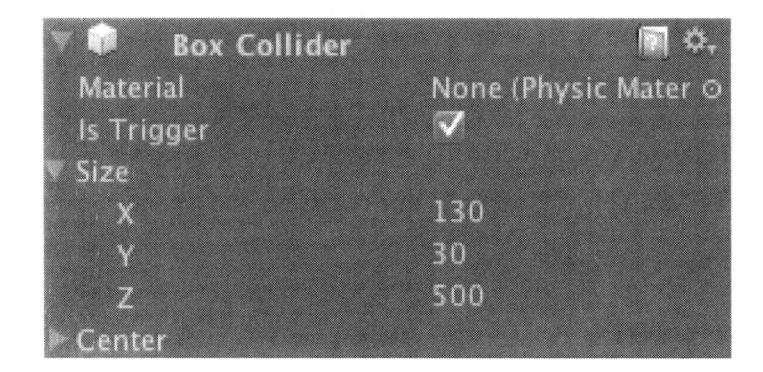

Box Collider	
Material	None (Physic Mater
Is Trigger	✓
Size	
X	130
Y	30
Z	500
Center	

This should give you a green collider box around the platform. If you hit play now you will see the shards uniformly fall away from the scene as their gravity is turned on. What we want to do is only affect the gravity when the marble guy is on the platform. But before we get to that, create and attach a script called **BrokenPlatformScript** then duplicate the **woodBrokenPlatform** object we have in the scene and make a path similar to the one below:

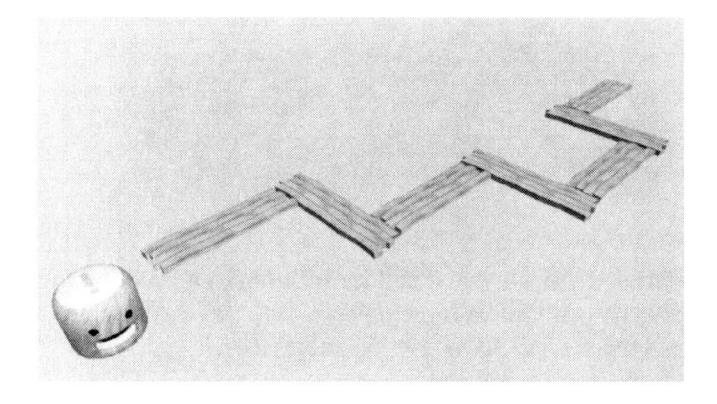

Open **BrokenPlatformScript**, and enter the following code:

```
var grav : Component[];

function Start()
{
    grav = GetComponentsInChildren(Rigidbody);
    for (var grv : Rigidbody in grav){
        grv.useGravity = false;
        grv.isKinematic = true;
    }
}
```

The code above is a nice piece of new code that we haven't encountered before. Here we create a static array called `grav` with the type `component`. When the `Start()` function is initialized we use the `GetComponentsInChildren` function to find all of the rigidbody components in the children of the object the script is attached to.

If you were to print out to the console the number of elements in `grav` it would equal 7, for 7 shards of wood. The `for` loop goes through each of the components in the array and turns the gravity off and **isKinematic** on; this stops the wood from falling away as soon as the game starts and stops the character from falling through the wood.

The final part of this script deals with when the player moves onto the wooden platform. Add this now:

```
function OnTriggerEnter(col : Collider)
{
    if (col.tag == "marble"){
        print ("Collided");
        yield WaitForSeconds(1);
        for (var grv : Rigidbody in grav){
            grv.useGravity = true;
            grv.isKinematic = false;
            yield WaitForSeconds(0.5);
        }
    }
}
```

When the character triggers this function by moving onto the platform the function waits for 1 second before beginning to add gravity back to each of the shards. When one shard's gravity has been turned back on the function waits for 0.5 of a second to ensure that the shards are removed in a manner that gives the player a chance to get across. Position the character on the snowy platform ready to move over and test the wooden platforms.

> I found my initial values for the wait times in the trigger function made it a little easy. Crank the times down and watch the mayhem unfold! :D

You have returned home!

Well we are nearly at the end my friends. As is our little red furry marble guy! Simon came up with this idea relatively late into the writing of this chapter, hence it being laid out here. Apparently your little red guy was lost, and he needed the help of all the other different coloured furries to get home to his mummy (a massive version of him!). So if you grab the **furryOrange**, **furryRed** and **nest** objects and fire them into the scene like so:

185

Furry Hurry – Part 2

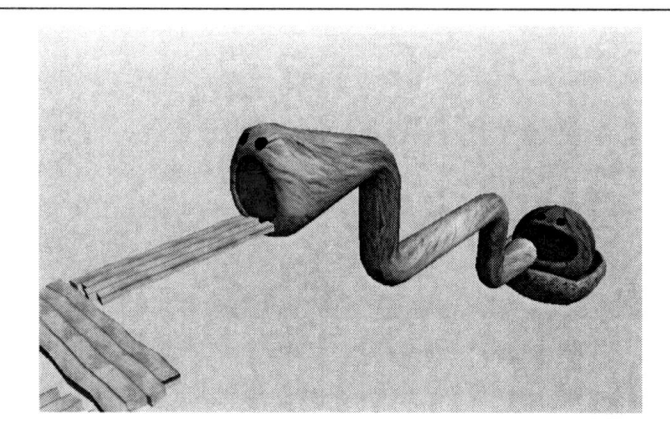

Arrange the objects in a similar fashion to below, hit play and give them a try out. You'll be surprised how smooth it is going through the orange snake's belly (I know I was, well done Simon!). Now we want something to indicate to the player that they have reached their goal so let's go ahead and create a new camera called **mommaCamera** (Be sure to take off the audio listener on the camera), and position it in a close position to the big momma, like this:

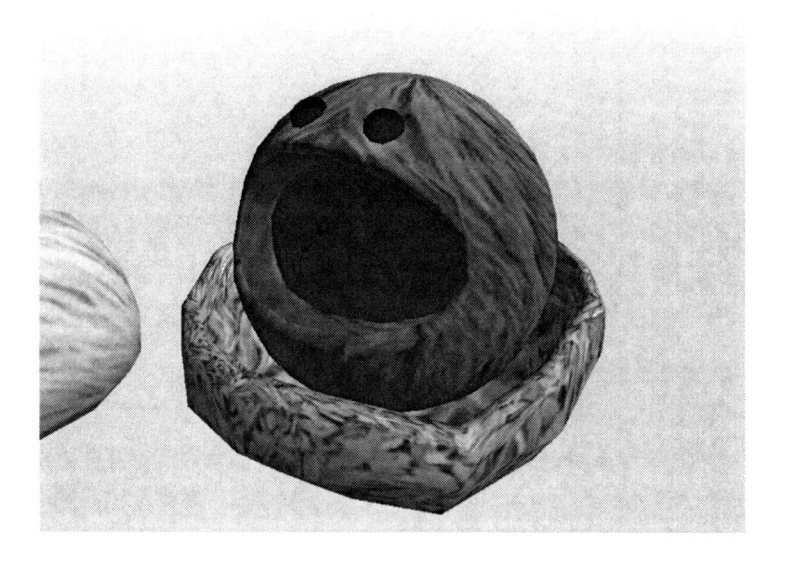

Next, create a new script called **FurryMomma** and put in this code:

```
var gmMger : GameManager;

function OnCollisionEnter(col : Collision)
{
```

```
    Destroy(col.gameObject);
    gmMger.mommaCameraOn();
}
```

Then in the **GameManager** script add in this variable:

```
var mommaC : GameObject;
```

And this function:

```
function mommaCameraOn()
{
   mainC.camera.enabled = false;
   mommaC.camera.enabled = true;
}
```

Be sure to add this line in the `mainCameraOn()` function:

```
mommaC.camera.enabled = false;
```

Go back to the inspector and select the **game** object for the `gmMger` variable and the **mommaCamera** for the `mommaC` variable. Hit the play button and jump into big momma's mouth to see the camera change.

Now I am going to leave this last little part with you as a test to make a really nice ending with what you have learned throughout this book. You may try to animate the big momma and make her dance around, or you may use some cool particle effects. Either way make it fun and make it snazzy. (Please send us pictures of your efforts.)

Little bit o' maintenance

Now the trouble with this type of game where you can fall off platforms etc. is that it can become really frustrating for the player if they have to go back to the start of the game every time. To solve this we will look to the tried and tested checkpoint method that has served so many games well in the past.

Create two cube game objects and call them **respawn1** and **respawn2**. Activate **isTrigger** on both cubes and place the first one just before the cannon like this:

Furry Hurry – Part 2

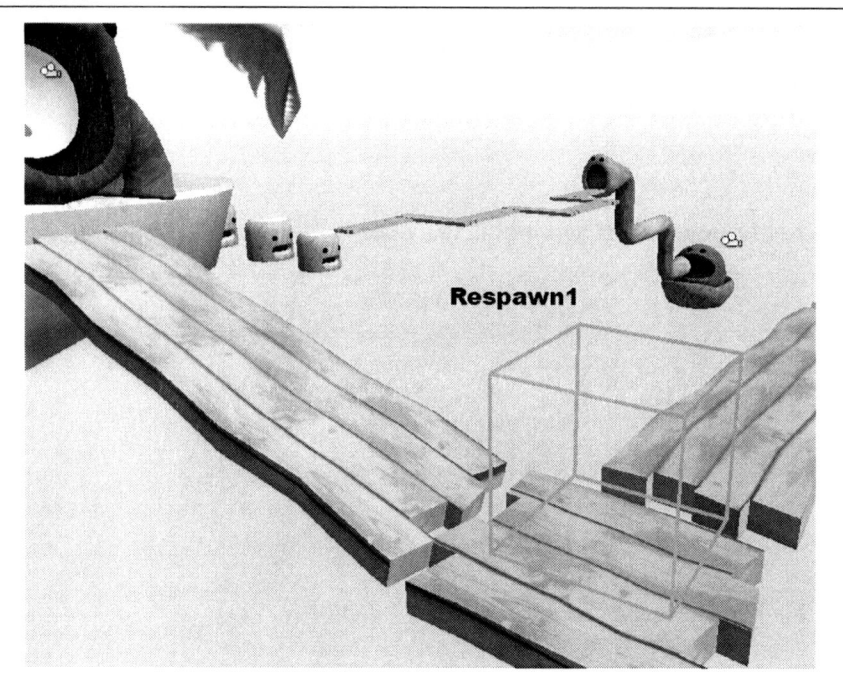

And the second before the lead to the green furry guys:

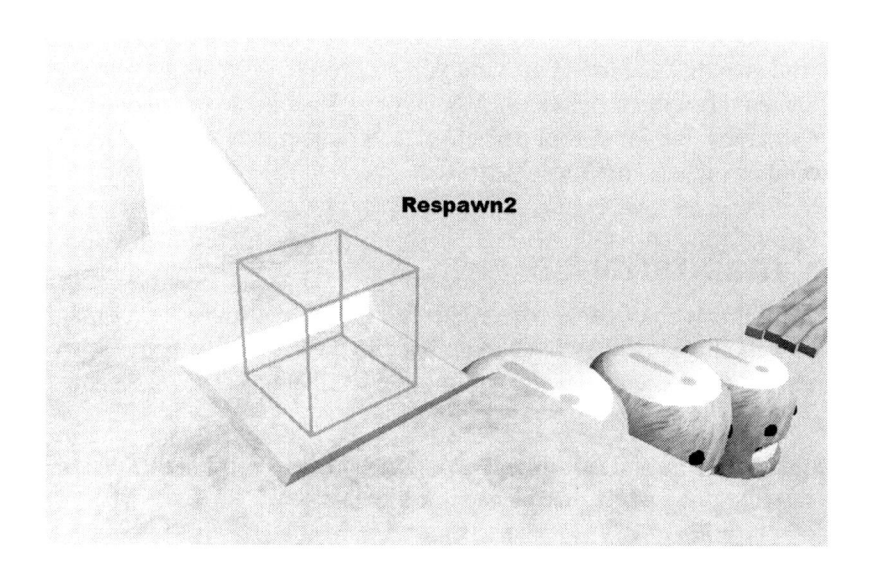

Create two new scripts called **Respawn1** and **Respawn2**. Put the following code in both scripts.
```
var gmMger : GameManager;
var cannonControl : CannonControllerScript;
```

```
function OnTriggerEnter(collision : Collider)
{
   if (collision.tag == "marble"){
      gmMger.respawn1active = true;
      gmMger.respawn2active = false;
      gmMger.respawnStart = false;
   }
}
```

In the **Respawn2** script, swap the `true` and `false` values of the two variables, making `respawn2active` equal to `true` and `respawn1active` equal to `false`. Attach the scripts to the two respawn objects and you are set up for them.

Move across to the **GameManager** script and add in the following variables:

```
var marble : GameObject;
var respawn1 : GameObject;
var respawn2 : GameObject;
var startPos : Transform;
static var respawnStart = true;
static var respawn1active = false;
static var respawn2active = false;
var mrblCam : MarbleCamera;
var cannonController : CannonControllerScript;
var woodBrknPlatforms : GameObject;
```

Change the `Start()` function:

```
function Start()
{
   Respawn();
   var wood1 : GameObject = Instantiate(woodBrknPlatforms,
      woodBrknPlatforms.transform.position,
         woodBrknPlatforms.transform.rotation) as GameObject;
   mainCameraOn();
}
```

Finally add the `Respawn()` function:

```
function Respawn()
{

if (respawnStart){
     var marble1 : GameObject = Instantiate(marble,
        startPos.transform.position,
           startPos.transform.rotation) as GameObject;
```

Furry Hurry – Part 2

```
            marble1.transform.position = startPos.transform
                .position;
            mrblCam.target = marble1.transform;
            cannonController.canFire = true;
        }

        if (respawn1active){
            var marble2 : GameObject = Instantiate(marble,
                respawn1.transform.position,
                    respawn1.transform.rotation) as GameObject;
            marble2.transform.position = respawn1.transform
                .position;
            mrblCam.target = marble2.transform;
            cannonController.canFire = true;
        }

        if (respawn2active){
            var marble3 : GameObject = Instantiate(marble,
                respawn2.transform.position,
                    respawn2.transform.rotation) as GameObject;
            marble3.transform.position = respawn2.transform
                .position;
            mrblCam.target = marble3.transform;
            cannonController.canFire = false;
            var brknWood = gameObject.Find
                ("woodBrokenPlatforms(Clone)");
            Destroy(brknWood);
            var wood : GameObject = Instantiate(woodBrknPlatforms,
                woodBrknPlatforms.transform.position,
                    woodBrknPlatforms.transform.rotation) as
                        GameObject;
        }
    }
```

Phew, that was a heavy piece of code! Before we move on to talk about the code, create a new empty game object called **startPos** and position it down on the first puzzle area, this will be where the player spawns at the start of the game. Also I came across a fault in my carefully laid plans to have nice simple respawns. What I realized was that if you fall off the broken platforms and respawn at position 2 you effectively spawn with no broken platforms to stand on. So for the purposes of the respawn code let's take the 7 platforms and parent them to an empty game object called **woodBrokenPlatforms** and make a prefab out of this parent object. Now that we have everything set up we can go back to the code.

The `start()` function effectively instantiates a new red furry character and places him on the `startPos` using the `Respawn()` function. Next we create a set of our broken platforms to wander over, and finally we turn the camera on as before.

The `respawn()` function handles when it is time to instantiate a new character at one of the spawn points. Spawning at the start and point 1 is self-explanatory, we create the new red character object, position him and make him the target of the camera. At point 2 we do things differently, as there is the possibility that the player only made it across the platforms half way and effectively the whole thing needs to be respawned with the character. To make sure that there is no conflict between two platforms we destroy the one that exists already, then instantiate a new one in the appropriate position. Simple!

You can head over to the inspector now and in the **GameManager** script assign all the appropriate object and scripts like so:

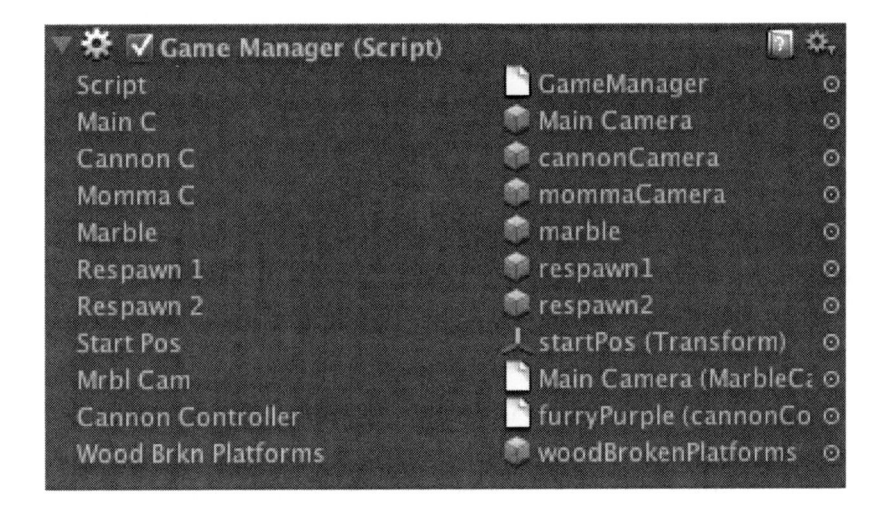

Script	GameManager
Main C	Main Camera
Cannon C	cannonCamera
Momma C	mommaCamera
Marble	marble
Respawn 1	respawn1
Respawn 2	respawn2
Start Pos	startPos (Transform)
Mrbl Cam	Main Camera (MarbleCa
Cannon Controller	furryPurple (cannonCo
Wood Brkn Platforms	woodBrokenPlatforms

Now we have our respawn points all set up and ready to go, we need to tell the game when to respawn the character. To do this create a cube game object called **deathFloor** and make it invisible by setting its materials to 0 and check the **isTrigger** property. Take the cube and make it as big as the level like so:

Furry Hurry – Part 2

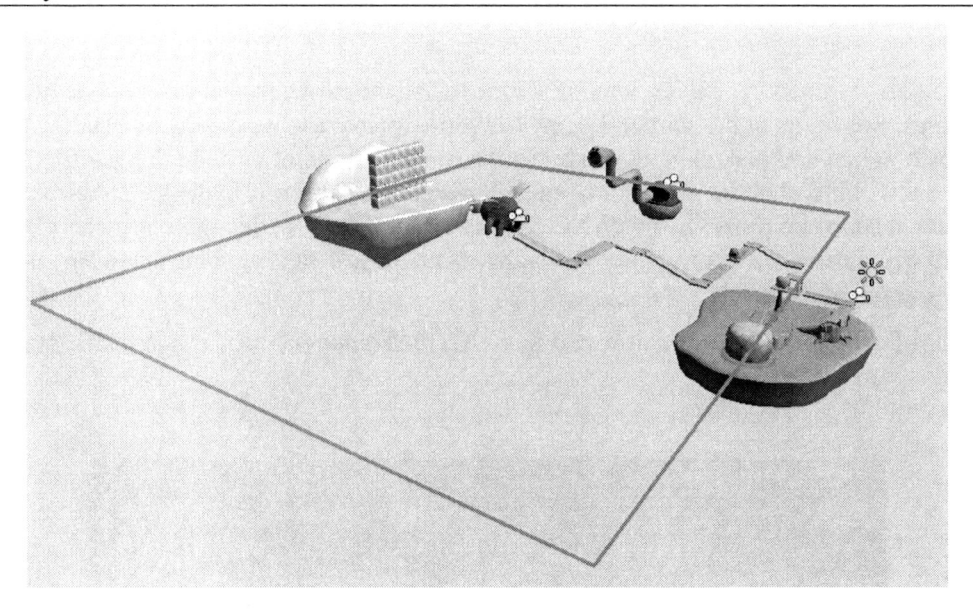

> Remember to make the height of the floor small, and make sure it resides below the lower puzzle platform. That way if someone falls off that platform the game will respawn them.

Create a new script called **DeathSpwn** and attach it to the **deathFloor** and put in this code:

```
var gmMger : GameManager;

function OnTriggerEnter(collision : Collider)
{
    if (collision.tag == "marble"){
        Destroy(collision.gameObject);
    gmMger.Respawn();
    }
}
```

Navigate back to the inspector and select the appropriate object for the **gmMger** property and that should be that.

Excellent, things should be cooking with gas now. Hit play and go through the whole level. Be sure to check each respawn point by falling off just afterwards to see if it respawns the character.

That was quite a heavy game, if you find that you have any errors be sure to download the whole game from the website along with the others and try to fix it alongside the working blueprint.

Summary

Many congratulations if you stuck this far and got to the end. You have another fine looking game that has been added to your Unity collection, and hopefully the whole book has given you the confidence to move onwards and create great Unity games.

We looked at a lot of neat Unity features over the course of this chapter. The physics materials in particular will be incredibly useful when you find yourself creating immersive worlds for your players.

Our work with physics joints has merely scratched the surface of this powerful tool. They can be used for a multitude of effects, including, if you are feeling particularly adventurous, rope physics.

We move on now to the last chapter, to take stock of where we have been and look ahead to where you can go, and what awaits you out there in indie game development!

Chapter 10

Go forth and create Unity

First off all let me congratulate you on completing your journey, we really hope this book has given you the inspiration and foundations to go on and continue creating games in Unity. The Unity platform has grown exponentially over the 5 years that I have been using it, I had the pleasure to be at one of the very first Unite conferences in Copenhagen a few years ago and when I met all the people involved with Unity from the CEO downwards I knew this was going to be something special.

Their mission of democratizing game development was always a heavy order. Achieving success in this industry is never guaranteed, but Unity have managed to not only become one of the top development platforms in the world right now, but they have (in my opinion) almost singlehandedly reignited the passion in the indie development scene.

Their excellent attention to their users and the community at large is nothing short of marvellous. The community is one of the best I have ever had the pleasure to be a part of and I'd like to take a moment to highlight it here.

All for one and one for all!

The Unity community has grown alongside the platform for a number of years now. I still remember my first experience with the Unity forums. I was looking into web service stuff for sending data back and forward to a database and for the life of me I couldn't understand why my code didn't work.

Until then I had never had much luck with community forums, usually my questions met with bland answers of "check the docs", and "this has been answered here" when it clearly hadn't. But on posting my code to the Unity forums I got a reply about 2 hours later, and not only had the person given me an explanation of where I was going wrong he had reposted my code with alterations.

Then a few more guys got in on the chat and we chatted about optimizing the code etc. In the end I got a really great piece of code from the community with none of the usual sarcastic coder chat that usually comes on other forums! All hail the Unity forumers!!

The community eventually shifted and grew adding new sites and ways to access the people in the know in Unity land. Let's take a look at some of the best:

- **Unity Answers** (http://answers.unity3d.com/) is an excellent forum for posting problems and generally researching solutions.
- **Unity Student** (http://www.unity3dstudent.com/) a fantastic place for beginners to start or intermediates looking to brush up on some of the fundamentals. The site is run by Will Goldstone the author of the first Unity book.
- **Unify Community** (http://www.unifycommunity.com/) Points you in the direction of all manner of material including the wiki.
- **Tornado Twins** (www.tornadotwins.com) Great resource for Unity videos!
- **Infinite Unity3d** (http://infiniteunity3d.com/) Full of tutorials and other goodies.

Regardless of what you are looking for - the community will have an answer and if they don't they will point you in the direction of someone who does. I greatly encourage you to get on there and become an active member.

Get out there!

Now that you are comfortable creating excellent games in Unity the next step is to get out there and share it with the world. Uploading your games to the web is a great thing to do not only for yourself but also your game.

In the long run you'll benefit from the exposure to players that are able to give you great feedback on your game. Their feedback will sometimes be brutal, and at times you might say to yourself "stuff this… what do they know?", but if there is anything I have learned in this industry it is **listen to your audience**!

The web offers some great places to show off your work, not just on the Unity forums. One of the best for Unity content is **Kongregate** (http://www.kongregate.com/). Kongregate is unique in that not only is it a portal for showing off your games but it is also a place to monetize them.

In addition to this there are some other great portals that you can take inspiration from:

- www.newgrounds.com
- www.blurst.com (great Unity dev guys!)
- www.wooglie.com
- www.shockwave.com
- www.shockwave.com
- www.zapak.com

Get it out there, get people talking about your games and you'll see your confidence grow along with your profile!

Moving forward

Like anything in life, once you have started something and built momentum you start to feel good and nothing can stop you. We hope we have given you this momentum and that you can move forward and start creating your own amazing game experiences.

We would like to share some tips and tricks to help you move forward on your path to greatness:

Performance

Being a 3D engine Unity is subject to some heavy processing when a game is being played. You must be constantly mindful of the ways that the performance of your game can be boosted. Here are a few tips:

- Monitor your **Texture Sizes**; often people make the mistake of using too high resolution textures for places that the player might not necessarily focus on. Only use high res for the parts of your game the player will definitely see. Also play about with reducing the size of the textures, often 256x256 can be just as good as 512x512.

- Again on the artist's side, **Polygon counts** are crucial in creating a high performance game. The lower the number of polygons the less the engine has to render during the game. Use textures to give your models a more detailed look.

- The way you **script** has a big bearing on the performance of your game. Unity has provided a nice breakdown of good scripting practices here (http://unity3d.com/support/documentation/ScriptReference/index.Performance_Optimization.html)

For Hire

A place I stumbled across recently was **Unity 3D Work** (http://unity3dwork.com/). This site documents freelance and contract work for Unity3d all around the world. If Unity is something you want to make a career out of - starting here couldn't hurt.

Deep Pixel

We are always looking to help the Unity community. If you think you have something that is worth shouting about send it to us at: **mygames@deeppixel.com**.

A word from the artist

Throughout the making of this book, I have endeavoured to keep the complexity of the art assets to a minimum in terms of polygon counts, shader layers, and effects. This was done for a number of reasons. Firstly, the book's main focus is on scripting the gameplay mechanics that make up the internal logic of a game's design, and I did not want to detract from that primary objective. Secondly, if you are an indie developer targeting a specific content delivery device (e.g. iPhone, Android, etc.) then there are certain restrictions that come with the hardware limitations of the intended platform.

I have tried to remain platform agnostic in this sense, but Unity is capable of a great number of advanced graphic effects which I urge you to experiment with once you are aware of your target hardware's specifications.

Just remember that multi-layered shaders and post-process effects can only enhance good art direction, they cannot replace it. Be mindful of both the core themes of your game and the tastes of its target audience when designing its aesthetics and you will reap the rewards. Good luck Indies!

Summary

Now much like the little red furry dude in the last game you must leave the nest and fly with your own wings, or in his case roll about on the ground!

Both Simon and myself and all the elves from behind the scenes bid you a most fond farewell, and wish you all the best in your future endeavours with Unity3d.

Index

A
A* Pathfinding	110
Access Parent	34
ActionShip() function	74
Add Curves	43
Add Keyframe	44
Alt Positive Button	32
Animation	42
Animation Component	43
Animation Mode Button	43
Animation View	41
Apply Changes To Prefab	44
Array	10,21,35
ArrowTower	130
Awake() function	48
Axes	32

B
Billboarding	123
Box Collider	9
Buttons	32

C
Camera Preview	22
Clamp Forever	46
Components	2
Configurable Joint	159
Console	32
Create New Clip	43
Custom Package	27

D
Destroy() function	38
Directional light	25

E
Enemy Waves	87
Enumerated Data Type	72
Eric5h5	161
Expect the worst	38

F
FBX – Calculate Normals	27
FBX – Generate Colliders	27
FBX – Materials	28
FBX – Scale Factor	27
FBX – Smoothing Angle	27
FBX – Split Tangents	27
FBX – Swap Uvs	27
FBX Importer	27
FixedUpdate() function	158
Flame Particle	54
Focus on object	132
Folders	16
For loop	11
Free Aspect	57
Functions	12

G
Game Loop	18
Game Object	2,18
Game View	9
GetButtonDown() function	31
Gizmos	5,6
Graphical User Interface	46
GUI Skins	56
GUI Styles	56
GUISkin Label	57

Index (cont)

H

Hand Tool	6
Health Bar	139
Hide Tile	44
Hierarchy View	5
Horizontal Scrolling	62

I

If statement	11
Ikargua	61
Import Package	27
Inherited Variable	23
Input Manager	32
Input.GetAxis() function	158
Input.GetKey	73
Inspector	8
Instantiate	21
isTrigger	76

J

JavaScript	3

K

KeyCode.Space	76
Keyframe	44

L

Lerp() function	166
LookAtCamera Script	124
LookRotation() function	117

M

Main Camera	22
Match the Pairs	15
Mathf.CeilToInt	49
Maximize on Play	57
Mesh Collider	28
Mesh inertia tensor failed	123
Mesh Renderer	29
Mouse Pointer	32

N

null	34

O

OnGUI() function	46

P

Parallax Scrolling	66
Particle Animator	53
Particle Animator – force property	53
Particle Emitter	52
Particle Renderer	53
Particle Systems	51
Particle Texture	53
Physics Materials	182
Play Automatically	45
Player Interaction	31
Point light	25
Prefab	3,17
Pressure Pad Script	161
Print Statement	32
Private	48
Project View	7
Project Wizard	16

Q
Quaternion.Slerp() function	117

R
Rate of Fire	77
Ray Casting	32
RaycastHit	33
Resolution and Presentation	64
Reveal Tile	43
revealCardOne() function	33
revealCardTwo() function	34
RigidBody	70
Rotate Tile	36
Rotate Tool	6

S
Scale Tool	6
Scene View	5
Scenes	2
Score	47
Scripting Reference	23
Scripts	3
Solipskier	101
Split() function	35
Spot light	25
Standard Assets Folder	54
Start() function	22
Static Array	30,114
Static Array – Size	30
Strict typed	3
String.Format function	49
Switch Statement	71

T
Tag	85
Temple Defense	105
Texture2D	58
Tile	17
Tile Generator	20
TileGenerator Script	18
tileObject	19
Time Line	44
Time.deltaTime	66
Time.time	49
Timer	48
ToString() function	48
Totem	135
Transform.Translate	66
Translate Function	66
Translate Tool	6
Transparent/Diffuse	68

U
Unity Answers	161
Unity Environment	4
Unity Scripting Reference	31
Update() function	12,31
Use Gravity	70
UV Animation	70
uvScrolling Script	70

V
Variables	10
Vector3	21,117
Vector3.dot () function	117
Vertical Scrolling	62

W
WaitForSeconds() function	38
Waypoints	110
Weakly typed	3
Web Player	64
Wrap Mode	46

Z
Z-Fighting	67